The Edge of God

The Edge of God

*New Liturgical Texts and
Contexts in Conversation*

Edited by
Stephen Burns,
Nicola Slee and
Michael N. Jagessar

✦ EPWORTH

Copyright © Stephen Burns, Nicola Slee and Michael N. Jagessar 2008

The Editors have asserted their right under the Copyright, Designs and
Patents Act, 1988, to be identified as the Editors of this Work

British Library Cataloguing in Publication data

A catalogue record for this book is available
from the British Library

978 0 7162 0641 5

First published in 2008
by Epworth
Methodist Church House
25 Marylebone Road
London NW1 5JR

Typeset by Regent Typesetting, London
Printed in the UK by
MPG Books Ltd, Bodmin, Cornwall

Contents

Part 3   Body Theology

Part 4   Gender and Sexuality

Editors' Acknowledgements

This book began to grow out of conversations between Stephen Burns and Nicola Slee,[1] who at one time co-taught a course on spiritual formation in the Christian tradition at the Queen's Foundation, Birmingham. Nicola also taught feminist theologies, among other things, while Stephen primarily taught liturgy. In conversation with each other and with students and colleagues at Queen's, we became keenly aware of a need to bring the matters often covered by liturgical studies into different kinds of conversations with other perspectives not always near the heart of the liturgical literature – black and Asian theologies, theologies about the significance of gender, queer theologies, theologies of disability and embodiment, and more. We were at the same time also conscious of the insight and resourcefulness of colleagues and students which we felt could help to address the lack we perceived, and so we decided to gather resources for a book. Soon Nicola and Stephen were joined by another colleague, Michael Jagessar, who brought to the editorial team an expertise not least in black theology.[2] Together we set about commissioning essays to begin some of the engagement we felt was needed.

The Edge of God is the result. It draws in colleagues and former colleagues from the Queen's Foundation, students and former students, others in the city of Birmingham with links to Queen's, some of whom are now scattered across the world. Like Queen's itself, this is an ecumenical collection: we are Anglican, Methodist, United Reformed Church, Baptist, Quaker; some are post-Christian – with their essays, in part, explaining why. We are happy to include them. And like the Church we long for, we are black and white, single and partnered, gay and straight, temporarily able bodied and disabled, young and old. Some preside in worship, others do not. Some are well known, others less so. Our commonality is that we bring different and related perspectives that together, we hope, enlarge liturgical studies for the good of the Church. We hope that these essays will help to nurture listening to perspectives that are not always evident in writing on worship or in gatherings in church buildings on Sunday mornings. Together we cover several broad trajectories, corresponding to the main sections of the book. Brief editorial commentary introduces each main section, and authors speak for themselves.

We are grateful to each person who has contributed to this collection, for their patience as it was produced; to those who hold the vision and contribute to community life at Queen's, enabling its sometimes vibrant expression of the inclusive Christian community we want strongly to affirm; and to Natalie Watson, formerly commissioning editor at Epworth Press, for her support of our project.

Notes

1 Our title, *The Edge of God*, is a conscious echo of chapter 10 in Nicola's earlier book *Praying Like A Woman*, London: SPCK, 2004.

2 See also Michael N. Jagessar and Stephen Burns, *Christian Worship: Postcolonial Perspectives*, London: Equinox, 2009.

Contributors

Alastair Barrett is a parish priest in Smethwick and Oldbury, in the West Midlands, and a jobbing liturgist and trainer in the Diocese of Birmingham. Al trained at Queen's, and occasionally returns there to do a bit of teaching.

Stephen Burns is Research Fellow in Public and Contextual Theology at United Theological College, Charles Sturt University, Sydney, Australia. He was formerly Tutor in Liturgy at the Queen's Foundation, Birmingham. He is a priest of the Church of England who currently holds authority to officiate in the Diocese of Canberra and Goulburn in the Anglican Church of Australia. His publications include *Worship in Context: Liturgical Theology, Children and the City* (2006); *Liturgy* (SCM Studyguide) (2006); *Exchanges of Grace: Essays in Honour of Ann Loades* (ed. with Natalie K. Watson, 2008) and *Renewing the Eucharist* (ed. five volumes, 2008–).

Clare Carson is an Anglican priest working as Hospital Chaplain at the Royal Free Hampstead, London. She trained at the Queen's Foundation from 2001 to 2003 where she started research into the theological, spiritual and pastoral needs of people with eating disorders.

Paul Collins is Reader in Theology at the University of Chichester, and a priest in the Church of England. He was formerly Tutor in Liturgy at the Queen's Foundation, Birmingham. He is also a member of the Faith and Order Advisory Group of the Church of England. His recent publications include *Christian Inculturation in India* (2007).

Pink Dandelion directs the work of the Centre for Postgraduate Quaker Studies, Woodbrooke and the University of Birmingham and is a Reader in Quaker Studies. He edits *Quaker Studies* and acts as Series Editor for the Edwin Mellen series in Quaker Studies. His books include *Introduction to Quakerism* (2007), *The Liturgies of Quakerism* (2005),

The Creation of Quaker Theory (2004), the co-authored *Towards Tragedy/Reclaiming Hope* (2004) and *The Sociological Analysis of the Theology of Quakers: The Silent Revolution* (1996). He is currently working on an Oxford University Press short introduction to the Quakers and an edited collection on the sociology of British Quakerism.

Deryn Guest teaches biblical hermeneutics at the University of Birmingham and is co-convenor of the Women and Religion seminar group that meets regularly at Queen's Foundation. She is the author of *When Deborah Met Jael: Lesbian Biblical Hermeneutics* (2005) and the co-editor of *The Queer Bible Commentary* (2006). She lives with her partner, Fiona, in the West Midlands.

Gary Hall served as a Methodist presbyter in Leeds and in Leicester, and is currently Tutor in Practical Theology at the Queen's Foundation. Until recently he was editor of *The Merton Journal*. Previous roles include those of school teacher, electronic engineer, farm labourer, factory worker and Taizé *permanent*.

John Hull is Honorary Professor of Practical Theology at the Queen's Foundation for Ecumenical Theological Education, Birmingham. He is Emeritus Professor of Religious Education in the University of Birmingham. His many publications include *Touching the Rock: An Experience of Blindness* (1991), *On Sight and Insight: A Journey into the World of Blindness* (1997), *In the Beginning there was Darkness* (2001) and *Mission-Shaped Church: A Theological Response* (2006).

Michael Jagessar lectures in ecumenical theology and interfaith studies at the Queen's Foundation for Ecumenical Theological Education, Birmingham, England, and is a minister of the United Reformed Church. He is author of *Full Life for All: The Life, Work and Theology of Philip Potter* (1997); co-editor (with Anthony G. Reddie) of *Black Theology in Britain: A Reader* (2007) and *Postcolonial Black British Theology: New Textures and Themes* (2007) and is reviews editor of *Black Theology: An International Journal*.

Rupert Jeffcoat is Director of Music at St John's Anglican cathedral, Brisbane, and a priest in the Anglican Church of Australia.

David Joy is a presbyter of the Church of South India and was a member of its synod Liturgical Commission. He is currently an associate professor in the Department of the New Testament and on the teaching faculty of the United Theological College, Bangalore, India. He is also the secretary of the Society for Biblical Studies in India and author of *Mark and Its Subalterns* (2008).

Lee Longden is a presbyter of the Church of England who previously enjoyed a career as a professional musician. He trained for ordination at the Queen's Foundation and is Vicar of Christ Church, Ashton-under-Lyne in the Diocese of Manchester. He is also a part-time postgraduate student at the Queen's Foundation, researching the training and deployment of curates in the Church of England.

Pam Lunn is a tutor at Woodbrooke, the Quaker study centre in Selly Oak, Birmingham, UK. She works principally in the areas of women's studies, spiritual journalling and auto/biography, and the spiritual dimension of climate change issues.

Andy Lyons is a probationer Methodist minister serving in the Bromsgrove Circuit. He is currently undertaking his PhD reflecting on change in Methodist worship practice over the last 50 years, with particular reference to the influence of the liturgical movement. Andy studied at the Queen's Foundation between 2002 and 2006.

Rachel Mann is an Anglican priest and poet based in South Manchester, UK. Her writing has appeared in magazines, journals, anthologies and newsprint. She likes wasting time and one day hopes to be sufficiently grown up to own a pet. She trained for ordained ministry at Queen's Foundation between 2003 and 2005.

Peter Privett is the UK Training co-ordinator for Godly Play, and author of *Living in a Fragile World: A Spiritual Exploration of Conservation and Citizenship Using the Methods of Godly Play* (2003).

Joshva Raja is the Tutor for World Christianity at the Selly Oak Centre for Mission Studies, the Queen's Foundation, Birmingham. His recent published books include *Introduction to Communication and Media Studies: A Text Book for Theological Students* (2006), *Did Jesus Feed Five Thousand People? Hermeneutical Secrets of the Fourth Gospel* (2007) and *Controversies in Theology and Media: A North/South Perspective* (2008).

Anthony Reddie is a research fellow and consultant in Black Theological Studies for the British Methodist Church and the Queen's Foundation for Ecumenical Theological Education in Birmingham. He is the author and editor of ten books. His more recent titles include *Dramatizing Theologies* (2006), *Black Theology in Transatlantic Dialogue* (2006), *Postcolonial Black British Theology* (co-edited with Michael Jagessar, 2007) and *Black Theology in Britain: A Reader* (co-edited with Michael N. Jagessar, 2007). He is the editor of *Black Theology: An International Journal*.

Alistair Ross is a tutor at the Institute for Pastoral Counselling, Nottingham, and a former tutor at the Queen's Foundation, Birmingham. He is a Baptist minister whose recent publications include *Counselling Skills for Church and Faith Community Workers* (2003).

Nicola Slee is Research Fellow at the Queen's Foundation for Ecumenical Theological Education, Birmingham, England. Her publications include *Faith and Feminism: An Introduction to Christian Feminist Theology* (2003), *Women's Faith Development: Patterns and Processes* (2004), *Praying Like A Woman* (2004), *Doing December Differently: An Alternative Christmas Handbook* (co-edited with Rosie Miles, 2006) and *The Book of Mary* (2007).

Susannah Synder is curate of St Mary's, Stoke Newington in the Diocese of London and a PhD candidate at the University of Birmingham.

Jane Wallman-Girdlestone is a research fellow in the Divinity School, Aberdeen University, and was formerly Tutor in Practical Theology at the Queen's Foundation.

Frances Young was for many years a governor of the Queen's College, and as Lecturer (1971–86) and then Edward Cadbury Professor of Theology (1986–2005) in the University of Birmingham, she taught many Queen's students over the years. In the early 1980s she was a student of the college in training for ordination as a Methodist minister (1984), while continuing her academic career. Her many publications include: *Sacrifice and the Death of Christ* (1975, 1983), *From Nicaea to Chalcedon* (1983), *Face to Face* (1985, 1990), *The Making of the Creeds* (1991), *Biblical Exegesis and the Formation of Christian Culture* (1997), *Cambridge History of Early Christian Literature* (ed. with others, 2004); *Cambridge History of Christianity: Origins to Constantine* (ed. with another, 2006), *Brokenness and Blessing* (2007).

Invitation

In *Fashion Me A People*,[1] Maria Harris speaks of liturgy as one of the fundamental forms of life in and through which God shapes the Christian community and calls it to be what it is. Called and gathered by God in the name of Jesus Christ, and inbreathed by the Spirit, the worship of the people of God is one of the most characteristic forms by which the Church realizes and expresses its identity. As 'the work of the people' of God, liturgy, to be authentic, must be rooted in the contexts and experiences out of which people live their lives, as well as being rooted in, and responding to, the sense of the divine emerging through the scriptures and traditions of the Judaeo-Christian heritage. The contexts out of which liturgy is born are always multiple, never singular. This has always been the case, but is perhaps now increasingly recognized to be so, amid postmodern sensibilities in which identities evolve fluidly in relation to a wide range of overlapping or competing communities, networks and discourses. Liturgy, as the work of the people of God, is always an 'encounter at the edges', in multiple senses: for example,

- At the edges between the diverse worlds we inhabit and the 'world' as received and understood through the testimony of Scripture and tradition.
- At the edges between 'church' and 'world' (even as we recognize the need to challenge the perceived edges of this interface).
- At the edges between our habitual, everyday environments and the sense of sacred time and space.
- At the edges where many lives from diverse contexts and understandings meet and mingle in sacramental celebration.
- At the edges where sound and silence meet, gesture and stillness, colour and darkness, movement and stability, text and spontaneity, languages of many different sorts gather and converge.

Without ignoring any of these 'edges' – indeed, seeking to explore and exploit them – the authors in *The Edge of God* focus in particular on a range of 'edges' which have been largely ignored in liturgical debate. So the notion of 'edges' suggests the kind of lenses through which we consider liturgy, each of which is marginal to the study of liturgy, and the insights of which are sometimes – indeed, often – entirely absent from the Church's authorized liturgical resources: feminist theologies, post-colonial theologies, queer theologies, theologies of disability, theologies of asylum and so on. The subtitle, '*new* liturgical texts and contexts in conversation', picks up this intention to bring fresh or marginalized discourses into conversation with Christian worship and liturgical studies.

The subtitle also indicates the dual foci of the book: liturgical *texts* and liturgical *contexts*; that is, we are concerned with both language (particularly expansive language which pushes beyond the conventional, the received and the habitual to open up fresh horizons), and with the non-verbal dimensions of worship that together constitute the ambience of liturgy. We are especially interested in exploring the *congruence* of text and context which optimizes liturgy's liberating significance. We hope that readers will find that each of the contributions separately, as well as cumulatively, engage this *conversational* element between text and context, though they may do so in diverse ways.

We describe the book as a series of 'conversations' also to indicate the provisional, exploratory nature of the enterprise in which we are engaged. Given that many of the 'edges' we seek to traverse in this book are ones which have previously not been much developed in liturgical studies, it is evident that a collection like *The Edge of God* cannot (nor would it want to) offer systematic or definitive treatments. Rather, we attempt in this text to identify and engage a wide range of conversation partners that need to be brought into dialogue with the public worship of the Christian community. Conversation itself is engaged in a wide variety of ways: in different settings, with fewer or more participants, in highly structured or more fluid ways, with different kinds of language and discourse, using story, poetry, silence and song as well as more theoretical constructions; and drawing on an eclectic – and, we think, exciting – range of resources. We have deliberately sought contributions in a wide range of styles and forms.

And so we invite the readers of this book to encounters on the edges we explore, and hope that this collection assists in the building up of robust and gracious Christian assemblies.

Note

1 Maria Harris, *Fashion Me A People*, Louisville: WJPK, 1989.

Part I

Mapping the Edges

Introduction

The three essays that form Chapters 1–3 of *The Edge of God* allow different points of access into some of our key concerns. Two of the authors are Methodist ministers, both of whom have some associations with the Queen's Foundation in Birmingham, and one is a priest in the Church of South India, who has recently arrived at Queen's as Tutor in World Christianity with the Selly Oak Mission Studies Centre. All write here in a 'personal' mode, akin to what James McClendon Jr teaches us to call 'biographical theology'.[1] They do so in different kinds of ways, however. Andrew Lyons shows how important liturgical questions *emerged* in his own experience; Donald Eadie suggests how important liturgical questions have *remained* with him 'for years'. And none of the narratives are simply 'personal', but related to questions of justice, truth and peace – most vividly in Joshva Raja's narrative.

In 'Participating in Public Worship', Andy shares something of his personal journey in which experience of worship came to be very important to him. In particular, he highlights the significance of his time at the Queen's Foundation, where he was a student. In telling his story, Andy links one particular Christian community's expression of and reflection on worship to larger contemporary debates, and outlines his own emerging convictions about tradition, power and change which different authors through the book negotiate in different and related ways. He also grounds his reflections quite explicitly in his own personal experience, as do many other contributions to the book, although perhaps more obliquely. Andy's essay brings to the surface the elements of human story which are integral to the rest. His primary purpose is to raise understanding – and expectation! – of how gracious and generous worship may reflect the beauty of encounter with a gracious and generous God.

Whereas Andy sets his years of worship at Queen's especially in the context of worship in his own Methodist tradition, Donald's 'More than Eucharistic Liturgies and Eucharistic Living' sketches out some particular liturgical 'fragments' that have lingered with him over time. He brings these into dialogue with sometimes acute experience of pain – his own and others' – as well as with his own and others' glimpses of the generous God whom Andy celebrates. Donald's fragments are profound reflections about how we might live what we might learn in the liturgy.

Joshva Raja shifts the focus from the UK to India, from an urban centre like Birmingham to a small tea estate, Manjolai. He draws from a concrete experience of a eucharistic service in Manjolai to demonstrate how the eucharistic table has the potential to become a space and place for a diverse group of people to gather and share not only bread and wine but also grievances, suffering and workplace problems. Raja makes a convincing case for the eucharistic table to become an alternative and reconstructed space for experiencing what it means to be a new creation in Christ in a concrete way.

Juxtaposed, the very different styles of these three introductory contributions to the *Edge of God* raise related concerns about worship evoking yearning for the divine, and about worship shaping the contours of the human condition, the human community and the relation of the human and the wider creation. Yet, the style of the essays pull against grandiosity: primarily, they ground reflection on worship in human life, personal experience and struggle for change for the better.

Note

1 James Wm McClendon Jr, *Biography as Theology: How Life Stories Can Remake Today's Theology*, Eugene, OR: Wipf & Stock, 2002.

Participating in Public Worship

ANDY LYONS

In this essay I offer a personal account of how I have come to see worship as a liberating experience and reflect on some aspects of what for me this involves in terms of practices. As a personal account, it is inevitably influenced by my own life-situations, and as one of the key things I have come to see is that my personal circumstances are not 'neutral', I acknowledge them at the opening of my essay: I am white; male; able-bodied; heterosexual; middle-aged; educated; and middle-class. I come from a Methodist family, attended Sunday School from earliest childhood and was educated in a Methodist boarding school. Such a life history should, one would suspect, shape me in a way that made me a 'mainstream' Methodist in every way. This would include my approach to liturgy – itself a word I might not expect to use. But, quite obviously, given that I am now writing in relation to liturgy, this is not the case.

I have recently entered the presbyteral ministry in the Methodist church. Prior to that, I had four years of theological education at the Queen's Foundation. In my reflections, I convey a series of emerging convictions related to my time at Queen's, and how that time 'fits' into the larger narrative of my life. I hope the reader may regard this chapter as one testimony to the process of being opened up to new possibilities of what worship has to offer us, reflected in my own personal journey.[1]

A personal narrative

Worship at Queen's often led me to encounter emotions that had never touched me before (at least not regularly) during corporate worship. We were encouraged to imbibe an ecumenical and intentionally eclectic repertoire of worship when Stephen Burns became the liturgy tutor and began to shape patterns and styles of worship that were unfamiliar to me.[2] While grounded in the norms of particular traditions, occasions of worship would highlight cross-denominational convergence in celebration and often include elements from a wide spectrum of sources. I had already been a Methodist local preacher for 20 years when I arrived at Queen's. On the whole, I think I had previously judged the quality of worship by the quality of the sermon and on the choice of hymns (a perhaps not unusual approach for a Methodist). Certainly when preparing worship I spent most time on writing the sermon and then trying to find hymns that met the theme. I primarily believed that the sermon had to be relevant to the modern world and people's everyday concerns. In consequence, I suspect I favoured sermons that were largely ethical in their content. I had been accused from time to time of being too political and too 'left-leaning' in my politics in my own sermon delivery. My choice of hymns would also reflect such concerns. I suspect I have chosen *Hymns & Psalms* 804 – 'The Church of Christ in Every Age' – more often than any other hymn in my own preaching life. In retrospect I think I could have been accused of understanding worship merely as a learning experience.

The reader may ask where the left-leaning theology comes from for this middle-class Methodist educated person. Such theology is an important strand of Methodism's history but I am not sure I learnt it in my home church or school chapel. Perhaps it was simply a by-product of my rebelliousness in adolescence. I only now recall that I understood Jesus primarily as the champion of the poor as I committed myself to God and to being a local preacher – and, of course, struggled with the political climate of my early twenties – in the Thatcher years. At this time, I entered into youth and community work and found myself at Southlands College, Wimbledon and through there in youth work in Balham, Clapham, Putney and Thornton Heath – and so became immersed in Britain's multi-ethnic urban life, working with African-Caribbean young people, many of whom were unemployed and in trouble with the law. In particular I worked at Parchmore Road Methodist Church, Youth and Community Centre, one of Methodism's pioneering social projects, where I spent four years as the full-time youth worker. As I reflect back on that time I recall how much I learnt about racism and its effects on real people.

In the late 1980s, I came to live in Birmingham to undertake a different kind of work – but still one engaged in the area of community relations. I was employed by the English Sports Council (now Sport England) to develop organizational links between service providers and community groups. Over the 15 years I worked for that body, I developed projects, policies and training programmes around the issue of race equality, gaining an MA in Race and Ethnic Studies from Warwick University in the early 1990s.

So when I came to Queen's, I was a local preacher who was shaped by a series of engagements in social and community affairs. I hope my preaching was more nuanced by then; but I had definitely not thought much, if at all, about how worship might, in its content and in its articulation, be an agent for liberation or oppression. The combination of being introduced to other approaches at Queen's and the personal response that engendered made me reflect on the practice of worship as I had never done before: in short, I came to see that worship might vividly depict the liberating God revealed in Jesus. And the practice of worship could itself be a liberating experience. So I want now to reflect on ways liturgy may liberate or oppress us.

An ecumenical and eclectic approach to worship

The three editors of this book have each shaped worship at Queen's. Nicola's own feminist approach leads her to emphasize the use of inclusive language and a style that is warm, embracing and deeply spiritual. Michael has a unique and engaging style that is highly poetic and in which he employs the dynamics of contrapuntal reading found in postcolonial criticism. Stephen, who was then the lecturer primarily responsible for liturgical studies at Queen's, is committed to developing worship that is deeply structured by ancient tradition, yet committed to being participative and inclusive, encouraging an approach that is gracious and hospitable to both the Christian inheritance and contemporary experience.[3]

In the Introduction – 'Invitation' – to this book the editors refer to Maria Harris's idea that Christian communities are shaped by liturgy. The liturgy that was offered at Queen's was worship shaped by the ecumenical Liturgical Movement's insight that worship can be structured in a fourfold way – Gathering, Word, Response, Dismissal[4] – but that this shape can be populated with a wide variety of texts and rites and actions that can make substantial differences to the actual services experienced. The liturgy then was shaped by some rules or at least guidelines – often all recognized by the three main denominations at Queen's in their own liturgical texts. This meant that where denominational and theological leanings differed, we were always held together by a common shape for our worship, with spaces for differences in terms of what constituted particular worship experiences. I think this meant that we had opportunity to gather before God in such a way that opened up the possibility of shaping the community to recognize and appreciate diversity. In worship, and beyond it, people could be tolerant and accommodating of others – and this, I believe, is a truly liberating experience.

Still, I do not mean that at Queen's there was, perhaps, no discussion and dispute over worship. There is, perhaps even more than in many local churches, an enormous range of preference for specific types of liturgy. However, my own experience, like that of others, has been that as I grasped more of the dynamics inherent in the liturgy, and the more I was encouraged to embrace diversity of expression in its content, the more I have been able to accept and enjoy variety in worship. This has encouraged me to come to two significant convictions: first, no judgement should be made on the liturgical life of the community from any one specific act of worship or specific rite in worship. It should be taken as given, and graciously accepted, that in shared experience of worship over time some acts will be more appealing to self than others. Second, every single act of worship must to some degree reflect something of the diversity represented by the congregation as a whole – perhaps in terms of age, ethnicity, gender, sexuality, apart from theology – and consequently, every act of worship must have a measure of eclecticism. Perhaps the fundamental thing necessary for these convictions to live is recognition of the ways in which both those who lead and those who participate in worship need to be willing to be gracious and generous to each other. This, I believe, is a theological challenge, because it concerns our capacity to embody and enact conviction about graciousness and generosity as attributes of God's own self.

In what follows, I want to reflect on my growing sense of the kind of practices in worship that affirm conviction in God's generosity.

Worship over time

It seems to me crucial that participants in worshipping communities are encouraged to grasp and welcome the fact that experience of worship shapes them over a period of time. We need to know that, over time, worship will change us – for better or worse. So a longer-term view of the potential of worship to transform a community needs to be built into a congregation's vision for its life together. Longer-term views of the liturgy – not judgements based on a single exposure to a worship event – allow for the generosity of God to be encountered in unfolding liturgical life. So we can hope on the basis of a longer-term view, with Elaine Ramshaw, that the 'very purpose' of liturgy:

> is to transform us to be agents of change ourselves – and to be agents of change we will need to be human beings that have had our own needs met, that have grown in Christian maturity and discipleship, that have begun to learn what it means to be human and who wish to enable others to live more human lives.[5]

Long-term experience of worship needs to embrace diversity, and what I have called eclecticism, as means of embracing God's wide love.

Issues of power

Yet issues about power skirt around questions of eclecticism in worship.

It is easier to see how a non-eclectic approach can concentrate power with the few who control how worship is conducted. Those few are often men like me – white, middle-class, heterosexual, educated. But there is also a need to interrogate other approaches that may at first look more egalitarian: what kinds of principles might be applied to invite diversity, balance power and keep in touch with the tradition, not least in its contemporary ecumenical manifestations?

Anyone who has encountered equality training will be sensitive to the dynamics of power in social ordering. My own learning in equality training has been to realize, first, that understanding of the language I (and others) speak is determined not only by what I think I mean but by what is heard by the recipient. Second, language is not the only important determinant in what includes or excludes people in any particular activity or community. Embodied practices are also important. It is possible to learn from equality training that questions need always to be asked about who determines, and why they determine, particular practices and processes, and how these might encourage or discourage access to things. So it must be with liturgy and worship.

At Queen's, Stephen often directed us towards the reforms initiated in liturgy and worship through the Second Vatican Council in the mid 1960s – and, specifically, to the idea of full, conscious and active participation: 'Mother Church earnestly desires that all the faithful should be led to that full, conscious and active participation in liturgical celebrations which is demanded by the very nature of the liturgy.'[6] This 'desire' expressed at the Second Vatican Council has been enormously important in ecumenical liturgical renewal – echoed not least in my own Methodist tradition at the opening of the *Methodist Worship Book*: 'The congregation is not an audience'.[7] Yet rather than itself setting a new precedent, the Council was drawing to a particularly vivid focus an understanding that was emerging in many denominations through several years, sometimes several decades, previously. Certainly, in my own denomination a strong sentiment about participation in worship had been expressed through the Conference Committee on Public Worship in 1960.[8]

Such ideas of participation are of course predicated on the long and widely held view that liturgy is 'the work of the people'. Yet while 'full, conscious and active participation' is a familiar 'strap-line' among liturgists, a sentence less often quoted but of equal significance follows in the succeeding paragraph of the Vatican documents: 'Therefore, in all their apostolic activity, pastors of souls should energetically set about achieving it [that is full, conscious and active participation] through requisite pedagogy.' As Michael Jagessar would say: 'This is risky business!' Why? Because when people are educated in what they are doing and envisioned with other ways of doing it they may well ask questions that lead to change in local situations. In light of what I have learned from equality training, I hold that if worship is to be full and active and participative then the type of education offered by pastors will need to explore what worship means in the perception and reception of participants. A quotation about inculturation that I have found extremely helpful (from the Roman Catholic writer Kevin Irwin) suggests how the liturgy can open up a space for creativity and adaptation that assists in the process of persons articulating their faith for themselves:

> Because the liturgy offers so many areas for creativity and adaptation, a contemporary method for liturgical theology requires this variety and flexibility to be taken into account. Yet this also raises the question of how normatively one ought to regard the revised liturgy . . . Yet even in this [postconciliar] period the liturgy is still normative in the sense that it shapes the way varied communities pray in terms of basic ritual to be observed. Normativity here does not mean precise imitation of rubrics. It means that familiar ritual structures are used to articulate the present faith vision of the liturgical rites.[9]

This speaks to me of the liturgy as a vehicle through which to meet a liberating God: creativity and adaptation can reflect God's generosity and graciousness, divine responsiveness to our diverse needs. Yet so might norms of some kind, in so far as at their best they can resist the tyranny of some over others – not least pastors called to 'instruct' their congregations – and enable a certain equality of access. Non-tyrannical norms are needed. In search of these, it can, I find, be helpful to refer to debate in liturgical theology around what Irwin calls the normative and Gordon Lathrop calls *Ordo*,[10] by which Lathrop means the way content is put together in a specific order for one thing to lead to another and give purpose and meaning to each other.[11] Gathering, Word, Response and Dismissal is the normative shape of the liturgy in many mainstream denominations, including the Roman and Lutheran traditions to which Irwin and Lathrop respectively belong, as well as the Anglican, Methodist and United Reformed traditions represented at Queen's. The fourfold shape of gathering, word, response and sending seems increasingly to me to be a ritual shape that serves as a sound container for the expression of local and contextual diversity and yet resists one person or group's preferences gaining sway.

Practising public worship

I believe that God is gracious and generous to us. Public worship celebrates this affirmation when it is practised by people who are learning to express graciousness and generosity to one another, by embracing diversity in and beyond their midst, and by honouring God's love for all and not least those on the margins of power. And the fourfold shape of worship we inherit from the deep tradition as a gift of contemporary ecumenical liturgical renewal might yet offer protection against the tyranny of presiders' individual peccadilloes and interest groups' quirks, but hold us open over time to encounter with the Holy One and the edges where the Holy One is quite at home.

Notes

1 Readers familiar with, for example, Brian Wren's *What Language Shall I Borrow? God-Talk in Worship: A Male Response to Feminist Theology*, London: SCM Press, 1989 will be able to recognize self-confession and identification as important contributions to locating the writer in his/her context.

2 I came to discover that Methodism, at least officially, had already sanctioned such appropriation of the ecumenical Liturgical Movement's insights through the publication of the *Methodist Worship Book*, Peterborough: Methodist Publishing House, 1999. However, I had not really studied the book and had therefore missed what it has to offer.

3 To understand more of Stephen's approach, see his book *SCM Studyguide: Liturgy*, London: SCM Press, 2006.

4 This shape has been recovered from Justin Martyr, in *First Apology*, describing worship in Rome around the year AD 150 and is now used by nearly all the mainstream churches as the official shape to their denominations' worship.

5 Elaine Ramshaw, *Ritual and Pastoral Care*, Philadelphia: Fortress Press, 1987, p. 27.

6 'Sacrosanctum concilium, 14', Austin Flannery, ed., *Vatican Council II: The Conciliar and Post-Conciliar Documents*, New York: Costello Publishing Co., 1977.

7 *Methodist Worship Book*, Peterborough: Methodist Publishing House, 1999, p. 5.

8 Methodist Church, Conference Minutes, Representative Session, 1960. *Conference Committee on Christian Worship*.

9 Kevin W. Irwin, *Liturgical Theology: A Primer*, Collegeville: Liturgical Press, 1990, pp. 69–70.

10 Among his many writings see primarily for an understanding of *Ordo*, Gordon Lathrop, *Holy Things: A Liturgical Theology*, Minneapolis: Fortress Press, 1993.

11 'The Sunday meeting of Christians, no matter what the denominational tradition, has focused around certain things: primarily a book, a water pool, bread and wine on a table; and secondarily, fire, oil, clothing, a chair, images, musical instruments. These things are not static, but take on meaning in action as they are used, especially as they are intentionally juxtaposed', Lathrop, *Holy Things*, p. 10.

2

More than Eucharistic Liturgies and Eucharistic Living

DONALD EADIE

I recall as a teenager going with my school cricket team to play the Roman Catholic School, Downside. After the match I wandered alone into the abbey and there encountered a deep silence, a mysterious sense of presence that has remained with me ever since. There have been similar resonances and in a variety of less obvious contexts. They have spoken of the mystery of transformation within the heart of the life of the world and within our human story. I have never understood transubstantiation with my head, but the transformation of the people of the highways and byways into becoming the body of Christ within the life of the world is a mystery that we may trust and enter.

What I offer is a gathering of fragments that resonate with eucharistic echoes; disconnected, random, held together, permitted to interact in the hope that the process will lead to something richer, deeper, fuller though inevitably still only a partial understanding. What I am attempting emerges from an increasing awareness that the mystery of the Eucharist is larger than eucharistic liturgies and eucharistic living, though both are more fundamental than I first thought. The Eucharist is the central act of Christian worship. What I reach after has to do with what I will call 'Mass at the heart both of creation and of humanity'. This is how things are. And our altars, liturgies and our living provide glimpses and draw us into this pervading and transforming mystery.

I have lived with a serious spinal condition since 1993 and during these years have experienced three periods of hospitalization, each followed by long periods of convalescence. My relationship to and perception of the Church's eucharistic practice was changed. I experienced what I will call 'eucharistic deprivation' and this paradoxically deepened the longing, encouraged exploration and enabled connections to be made that I had not discovered before.

I have found rest and solace in the Cistercian Monastery of Mount St

Bernard's Abbey for 40 years. The daily Mass in that religious house has a simplicity, brevity, beauty and a sense of mystery within which I feel strangely at home even though I have never been permitted to receive the bread and wine. The reserved sacrament in the tabernacle above the altar is for many a continuing sign of real presence. The abbey has become for me a place of prayer. The encounter is with the mystery of transforming presence within all creation, all humanity.

Graham Greene, in his novel *The Power and the Glory*, places the mass in a very different context. The priest is fat and wretched, growing to look like a beggar and hunted like a hare on the run during an anti-clerical purge in South Mexico. There were rumours of police a mile off coming through the forest.

> It was dark: no sign as yet of dawn. Perhaps two dozen people sat on the earth floor of the largest hut while he preached to them . . . He was talking about heaven, standing between them and the candles in the ragged peon trousers and the torn shirt. They grunted and moved rest-lessly: he knew that they were longing for the Mass to be over: . . . He cried out stubbornly in a voice of authority '. . . heaven is here: this is part of heaven just as much as pain is part of pleasure'.[1]

Greene's priest was on the edge, detached from church structures and conventional morality and celebrated the Mass within the context of human messiness, ugliness and fear.

So what of the eucharistic nudgings?

Eucharistic living

Michael Wilson was both a doctor and a priest. He was also nephew of Edward Wilson who went with Scott to the Antarctic. In the concluding period of Michael's life, he asked that I be his 'eucharistic person'. He suffered with a huge cancerous tumour on his neck. I assumed there would be discussion of choice of liturgy and practical procedures. I quickly learned that I was being drawn into much more than a pre-arranged devotional slot on a Thursday afternoon.

Michael was more interested in eucharistic living than eucharistic liturgies. 'Eucharistic living,' he said, 'is about being open, open to receive the gifts of God through dark and light, the creative and the destructive, through our essential otherness, our differences within world faith communities, sexual orientation and cultures. It is an open-ness that lays itself wide open to the possibility of transformation.' Eucharistic living is about expressing gratitude. And about sharing. 'The unshared remains unredeemed.' Eucharist is about being caught up in the essential 'we-ness of God', being held within the interrelatedness of all things, the interconnectedness of past, present and future. And prayer? Prayer is a way of engagement, of being alive, alive to God who is present in all things. And companionship? Companions are those, as the root of the word shows, who share with us the bread of life.

Michael spoke of Hans-Ruedi Weber and of his book *Experiments with Bible Study* where he searches for the original meaning of the 'This' in the 'This is my body, this is my blood.' Weber suggests that 'this' refers back to the whole sequence of gestures connected with the bread and wine. In making the gestures of 'receiving, thanking and sharing,' Jesus explains, 'This is me, this is my life'.[2] And on those weekly visits we naturally settled into that pattern of receiving, thanking and sharing. We asked, as we can ask, what has been received in the last few days that has been a source of relish, wonder and thanksgiving? We realized that the mystery into which we enter is not only one of remembering but also one of incarnation, the incarnation of mystery.

Bread making

For a number of years I have been in regular email correspondence with Barbara Glasson, a Methodist minister working in the centre of Liverpool. Barbara has been set free by her denomination to wander and to wonder among the inhabitants of those streets interpreting what the Spirit is saying to the Church and the world.

On the second floor of a shop in Bold Street, Barbara and others bake and share bread. They live their vocation among people who don't trust the institution of the Church enough to enter a conventional church building. They explore the mystery of yeast in the kneading and the rising of bread, within their own life story and also in the stories of their communities. On Tuesdays and Thursdays, people spend the day making bread and within the day they celebrate a Eucharist. The bread that they make is not for selling but for sharing, giving away in the city centre. Bread for the seller of the *Big Issue*, for Jack dying of cancer at home, for a peace vigil held for the people of East Timor, and for a Catholic priest to take home to the presbytery. Bread for friends. Bread for Eucharists.[3] After I had shared some of Michael Wilson's thinking with Barbara, she wrote: 'So, it seems Eucharist is not about the death of Jesus but rather about incarnation. When he said, "Do this to remember me" it wasn't a means of saying: "This is a way of bringing me back to mind after death" but rather, "it is in this way I will give you new life".' So we have a paradigm of being nourished, literally and metaphorically, in this life – not just in some world after death.

More than re-membering

I am learning that the mystery of the Eucharist is not, as is often the case in my Methodist tradition, hidden under a fair linen cloth on a communion table approached only by the ordained. The bread and wine are signs of a reality which is always and everywhere present, present in all things, present in and for all people. In the Eucharist we say: God is for us. God gives God's very self within the ordinary things. This is the nature of God.

Gerard W. Hughes wrote in a letter: 'Creation is the sacrament, the Eucharist, the self-giving of God. Our sacraments are, in Ivan Illich's words, "celebrations of our awareness of God at work in all things, in all people. Creation is not God, but a sacrament of God".' In an article in *The Tablet*, Hughes wrote: 'The Eucharist is a sign signifying a reality, in which creation lives and loves and has its being. Jesus, image of the unseen God, took a piece of bread, broke it and said, "This is my Body, given for you. Do this in memory of me".' He continues:

> Whenever the Eucharist is celebrated we are not creating something, producing something which does not exist before; we are remembering a once for all happening, a once for all sign of a continuous reality. We celebrate our awareness of the reality that the love of God informs, sustains, gives life and being to everything, a love without limit, which does not discriminate even between the good and the wicked.

And he concludes: 'If in the sacrament of the Eucharist we are celebrating the limitless and continuous love of God in Christ for all creation, how can we dare to exclude anyone who approaches to receive the Eucharist in good faith, without implying that we can control and put limits on God's love.'[4]

Meals

On arrival in our neighbourhood in 1996, we were warmly welcomed but also warned 'we don't go into each other's homes'. Nevertheless our neighbours have become significant for both Kerstin, my wife, and for me. When I venture out for short daily walks, I make a point of pausing, chatting at the end of drives and over hedges. It is surprising what can be shared in a few minutes at the end of a garden path. These short conversations have led to invitations to share in coffee or tea. We also found courage to follow our intuition: we asked certain neighbours if they would like to bring food, drink and share a meal. And over those meals we talked in a way that we had not done before. And something for our common good is happening through sharing our lives in our road. On another occasion, we shared in a meal and this time around tables pushed together in a Balti restaurant in Balsall Heath. There were 16 of us; we scarcely knew each other; we struggled with language and culture. And during the meal four of the largest naan breads I have ever seen were placed among us, and broken as neighbour became aware of the needs of neighbour – and we laughed. And we were watched over by the smiling Muslim proprietor. The experience of sharing food and drink with friends or strangers, of open hospitality, carries within it the possibilities of eucharistic resonances.

Rarely are we in the West exposed to learn from the insights of the poor themselves in relation to the Eucharist. Israel Selvanayagam writes:

I grew up in the midst of grinding poverty. It was every time a challenge for my mother to work out a fair share among the hungry children and her husband. After eating my share, as the youngest in the family, I always waited to have a little from my mother's hand. It was very little and because she mixed the rice with the sticking bits of the fish curry mud-pan, sometimes with deep sighs, it was so special and so tasty. It was for me no less sacred than sharing a tiny piece of bread and a few drops of wine in a Communion.

Whenever I see babies suckling from the breast of their mothers I in my mind travel back to the upper room where Jesus and his disciples met for their last supper. Here there is a feeding with feet-washing, stroking, cuddling and at times shedding tears![5]

Bread for the world

There was another meal, glimpsed on TV, as aid workers drove large lorries full of bread into refugee camps during the Kosovo crisis, throwing bread into the outstretched hands of girls and boys, women and men. I wonder what has to happen for us to link the bread we break at the altar with the bread we throw to the desperately hungry?

Father Tissa Balasuriya, a Sri Lankan Catholic priest giving the first Dietrich Bonhoeffer lecture at the Queen's Foundation in Birmingham, said,

> A billion Eucharists take place where we share bread – but we still refuse to share our bread with the world. We share eucharistic bread but not the bread that the world needs. Perhaps there is a need to call a moratorium on Eucharists until we come to share our bread with the world's hungry and thirsty. Who controls the world's food and water – and how does this affect the way we share Eucharist? How could our Eucharists become a real sign of sharing in the world?[6]

Gerard W. Hughes expresses the same sentiment writing in *The Tablet*: 'In all our Christian denominations we have nurtured a cultic solution – disconnected with the world around us – so we don't see the contradiction between celebrating the Eucharist – and tolerating international debt which starves so many to death.'[7]

In every version of the miracle of the feeding of the 5,000 or 4,000 there are eucharistic overtones. Why, I wonder, does it never seem to appear in the texts of the Church's eucharistic liturgies?

Mass at the heart of creation and of humanity

I began by saying that the process of pondering and connecting was recent. But that is only partially true. I recall years ago trying to understand the writing of Teilhard de Chardin and being drawn to the Pensées in the back of his book *Hymn of the Universe*.[8] Later I was helped by the biography written by Robert Speaight.[9] He wrote of the man, Jesuit priest and also lecturer in geology and palaeontology in Paris, who spent long periods alone doing research in some of the remotest parts of the world. Teilhard found himself a long way from any Catholic Church or chapel. On expedition, just as he would daily go off alone to meditate and to pray the Divine Office in his breviary, so too he would disappear for a short time in order to celebrate his own 'Mass' without altar, without bread or wine. The Eucharist had central place in his life. He did not see it as cut off from everyday life and separate from the world. On the contrary, he recognized the Eucharist as central to reality. Here is part of his 'offering prayer':

> Since once again Lord, I have neither bread nor wine nor altar, I will raise myself beyond these symbols, up to the pure majesty of the real itself; I your priest, will make the whole earth my altar and on it will offer you all the labours and sufferings of the world.
>
> Over there, on the horizon, the sun has just touched with light the outermost fringe of the eastern sky. Once again, beneath this moving sheet of fire, the living surface of the earth wakes and trembles, and once again begins its fearful travail. I will place on my paten, O God, the harvest to be won by this renewal of the labour. Into my chalice I shall pour all the sap which is pressed out this day from the earth's fruits.[10]

Robert Speaight quotes what he believes to be the heart of Teilhard's inspiration:

> It seems to me that in a sense the true substance to be consecrated each day is the world's development during the day, the bread symbolising appropriately what creation succeeds in producing, the wine (blood) what creation causes to be lost in exhaustion and suffering in the course of its efforts.[11]

If bread sharing in a hungry and thirsty world belongs to our eucharistic journey so also does the care of the world's environment. Teilhard's offering prayer embraces creation as sacred.

Well springs and manna

It was during my years in Notting Hill that I became more aware of the significance of the biblical images of well springs and of 'manna' in the wilderness. 'But Reverend,' Inez from Barbados said, 'we know what "manna" is. We are in the wilderness place.' She loved the story of the raven bringing bread and meat to Elijah by the stream (1 Kings 17.4). I wonder about the Eucharist as a sign of the mystery of God's providing in unexpected ways and places. This also belongs to the nature of God.

As a teenager I was taught in confirmation class before receiving bread and wine, 'Open your hands, closed hands receive nothing'. To pray 'give us to-day our daily bread' assumes that we remain open to receive what is being offered. So I wonder at times if there is a deep flaw in our Church culture, our spirituality. Much worthy activity, much worthy giving, but a slowness, a reluctance in our willingness to receive. Perhaps the saying, 'It is more blessed to give than to receive' has much to answer for?

The story of Jesus stooping to wash the feet of his disciples draws us into an interweaving paradox of humility and harshness. The issue is not just humble service to each other, there is something harsher: unless you are prepared to expose yourself to encounters where you are open to receive what you have not expected from God, to receive and not just to give, then you can be no follower of mine. Is this what Jesus is saying?

Who are the priests and where in this world are the altars?

A friend, an Anglican lay person who was my tutor at the William Temple College in the 1960s, after reading my book *Grain in Winter*[12] wrote showing links in the writing that I had not then seen. The links were around priest, altar and Eucharist. He was the one who formulated the question that has remained with me, 'Who are the priests and where in this world are the altars?' He linked the following passage with one later on in the book on transformation, the mystery of evil transformed into good within the life of the world:

'Oliver Tambo was a devout Christian and always wanted to be a priest,' said Archbishop Trevor Huddleston. Who was Oliver Tambo? For many years he was the exiled President of the African National Congress. With others he worked for the transformation of South Africa, he struggled to keep the process humane and non-violent. He died, frail, in his eighties, after spending two days watching over the funeral rituals of Chris Hanni, the murdered Communist leader. He died within months of the first genuine democratic elections in South Africa.

He always wanted to be a priest . . .[13]

For years, I have lived with these interpretations of priest and altar and not known how and where to engage with them. Another friend wrote: 'What you and others must constantly remind us is that the

Christ sacrifice is still offered "outside the camp". Our human calling is to reflect and say Amen to ongoing creation and redemption. And to be deeply thankful at being part of it.'[14]

And a eucharistic party under a motorway

We met on a chill, windy street corner in North Kensington and recognized each other. The young Moroccan said, 'There is a party at four this afternoon under the motorway. Come, and bring a bottle and some food. And pass the word around!' It was a spontaneous party for Sister Cecille, one of the Sisters of the Assumption living in a convent situated in Notting Hill. Cecille was a community nurse shortly to return to the mother house in Paris and from there she was to be directed on to a health clinic in Tunisia. She was the old nun reputed in anger and pity to have tucked up her habit, mounted her bike and gone off to the Imam in the magnificent mosque in Regents Park, demanding local provision, a mosque, a place to pray, for 7,000 Moroccan Muslims. And the people came to the party carrying with them bottles and biscuits, crisps and cakes, fruit and presents. And they sat, their carved faces watching: Portuguese and Moroccans, Spanish and Afro-Caribbean, social workers, community workers, teachers and a policeman, people who trade in Portobello Market and people who wander in the back streets. In the middle of them all Sister Cecille sat, pale and drawn, tired and stooping, looking even older, her eyes full of love and tears. It was a party with all the marks of a gospel feast. A Eucharist under a motorway.[15]

Notes

1 Graham Greene, *The Power and the Glory*, Harmondsworth: Penguin Books, 1940, p. 69.

2 Hans-Ruedi Weber, *Experiments with Bible Study*, Geneva: World Council of Churches, 1981, Study 15, pp. 180ff.

3 Barbara Glasson has explored what these things can mean in two recent books, *Mixed up Blessing: A New Encounter with Being Church*, Peterborough: Inspire, 2006 and *I Am Somewhere Else: Gospel Reflections from an Emerging Church*, London: Darton, Longman and Todd, 2006.

4 Gerard W. Hughes, 'Listen to the Music', *The Tablet*, 22 January 2000.

5 Personal communication. Israel Selvanayagam is from Tamil Nadu in the Church of South India and was formerly Principal of the United College of the Ascension in Selly Oak, Birmingham. He now serves as interfaith consultant for the Birmingham District of the Methodist Church.

6 Taken from notes of Fr Balasuriya's lecture.

7 Hughes, 'Listen to the Music'.

8 Teilhard de Chardin, *Hymn of the Universe*, London: Collins/Fontana, 1970.

9 Robert Speaight, *Teilhard de Chardin: A Biography*, London: Collins, 1967.

10 de Chardin, *Hymn of the Universe*, p. 19.

11 Speaight, *Teilhard de Chardin*, p. 127.

12 Donald Eadie, *Grain in Winter: Reflections for Saturday People*, Peterborough: Epworth Press, 1999.

13 Eadie, *Grain in Winter*, p. 96.

14 Personal Correspondence.

15 Eadie, *Grain in Winter*, p. 144.

3

Eucharist as an Alternative Space to the Globalization of Media

JOSHVA RAJA

A story of a Eucharist

Manjolai is a small tea estate, owned by a group of shareholders under the name of Bombay Burma Trading Corporation.[1] It has seven estates with more than 2,000 full-time workers. The majority of the labourers are from Dalit communities. I worked in this place as a priest in 1994 and 1995. During my ministry there I experimented in a project for the Church of South India (CSI) synod named a 'Labourer's awareness project'. Interestingly the church became the centre of the community and the priest was seen as a labour union representative. As I ran this project, I could mediate between the company managers and labourers. Very often during and after the Holy Communion service the congregation shared their problems and issues among themselves. This provided space for the members and even for non-Christians to express their voices. The church invited the managers to many of our project initiatives and so had a reasonably good relationship with the executives in the company.

Our project co-ordinator raised many of their problems with the managers and thereby they attempted to address a few of them. At times managers and executives themselves were present in our post Communion discussions. When I left for studies, the priests who followed me also had good relationships with people and the company. But unfortunately in 1998, the CSI priest and a new political group joined together and encouraged the labourers to agitate against the company. This led to the closure of the company and the murder of a number of people by the political groups and by the police. My bishop, the company's former executives and I attempted to mediate but the local political group known as Pudhiya Tamilagam (New Tamil Nadu), which has become a well-known Dalit party in Tamil Nadu,[2] did not allow any immediate solution to this problem. After my research degree in Edinburgh, I returned to the church in March 2001. My bishop in Tirunelveli asked me to go to Manjolai to celebrate Holy Communion services among the seven CSI churches, as no other priest was allowed in either by the police or the company.

As I conducted the communion service in each church, most of the members were crying and trying to stop the service. The first Eucharist was held at Manjolai CSI church. Nearly half of the congregation members were in favour of compromising with the company, as they needed monthly salaries to manage their lives,[3] whereas the other half were against any settlement and committed to achieving their full rights, backed by the Pudhiya Tamilagam party. The community was divided and the factions were suspicious of each other in every area of life, and a number of those who were trying to work out a compromise formula had been murdered. The total number of deaths during these years was more than 30 people, mainly labourers.[4] In such a context, I was managing myself to come to the point of sharing of the communion elements. I stopped and asked people to forgive each other. It was a tense moment as no one wanted to do so. I then called on the community to greet each other with the sign of peace. No one turned to the other group, but within their own groups they shared peace. I challenged them not to come and receive if they had not shared peace with those outside their own group. It was at this point I was told by a group of members to go ahead and share the bread and wine with the people as a priest. They had not had regular communion for two years since 1999.

I challenged them to share peace among their own brothers and sisters even if they belonged to the opposite groups. It was a tense moment, and they took a long time to recognize and share peace with each other. I knew many of them by name and they knew me. Many of them cried aloud as they were challenged and peace was finally shared. They realized that the pastor would not share the communion elements unless they gave peace to each other. This service lasted for four hours on Easter Day. After this service I continued with services in the other six churches and returned to my home. This was a very symbolic and moving experience for me as my own awareness programme started with a gathering around the communion table. I found people standing around the communion table as an alternative space where they can be challenged to recognize each other's dignity and to belong together as the body of Christ. This provided the tea estate labourers with an alternative space where they expressed their views among themselves and also found a way to express their grievances even with the company authorities. Thus, after division among themselves the eucharistic table provided a space for reconciliation and renewal in their lives.

People in Manjolai are still wrestling with the company and trying to get their wages regularly through the court. Since then the company and the people have been working with the CSI church and have accepted the priest and the local bishop to be mediators at times. The court cases are still going on with occasional political intervention. This is in the context of a globalization process in which labour laws are flouted in favour of liberalization. The companies are no longer owned by a single owner, but rather by shareholders. The media often side with the rich and the executives rather than with the labourers and poor people. The local mass media often provided a negative picture of the labourers' issues. The global media was not aware of the problem until many people were deprived of their living. There was no space where the estate labourers found themselves able to communicate their problems until such a space was created in the church.

The communion service provided a space for the people to come and participate not only in sharing the body and blood of Jesus Christ but also in sharing their suffering and their problems among themselves in the presence of the priest. Other religious workers usually waited outside the church until the Eucharist was over. In the context of global media, can the communion table become a model for an alternative form of communication in providing a space for the people whose voices are silenced by power, structure, money and culture? An ideology of neo-liberalism cannot be countered by another political ideology that can also harm the very people whom it seeks to liberate. But the space created around the Holy Communion table provides a reconstructed space where labourers and managers can meet and address their issues through critical and tough negotiation. This scenario offers a background for me to deconstruct the globalization of the communication systems and thus provide a direction for reconstruction of alternative spaces within the churches. Let me begin with a historical critique of the globalization of communication.

Eucharist as alternative space?

It is essential for a theologian to reflect upon such situations as described and provide a reconstructed alternative space for the people to reaffirm the importance of life and of faith – both individuals and communities who can interact among themselves. One cannot reconstruct an alternative without deconstructing the ideologies and concepts that tend to monopolize and promote false consciousness among the people. Can churches provide an alternative space where the voices that are not heard through the mass media can be heard? Can the practice of Eucharist in which human dignity and life are affirmed provide a counter and alternative space to a global media dominated public space? These are a few questions with which I struggle in this essay.

In this chapter, I give a historical background of the New World Order which sets the basis for globalization of the neo-liberal values particularly in the media markets. Then I point out the need for alternative media to counter such values and the process of globalization that are promoted through the mass media.[5] In conclusion, I argue that churches can redefine the rituals of Eucharist as community space to counter the values and ideologies that are promoted by the process of globalization. Secular initiatives on alternative models have often failed as they cannot bring people on to a platform that binds them through a particular faith or worldview.

For me, globalization[6] refers to the inevitable interconnectedness of cultures, economies, communities, societies, nations and races at international level. Thus globalization of the media means internationalization of the process of information and communication through huge media corporations and cultural industries in every part of the world. Before we analyse the effect of globalization we need to look at the background of the globalization of media. Globalization is an escalating reality of global interdependence. If globalization is one of interdependence, we need to address the issue of internationalization, universality of values, emerging multi-polar values and meanings, intercultural communication and so on. The globalization of media has particularly eliminated all other small, alternative and counter voices and spaces by using power, money and neo-liberal ideology. The voices of people who have lost their dignity, power, values of life and resources have been silenced by the global communication system.

To counter globalization one needs to create alternative spaces where the human dignity of all can be recognized and respected. In this space, life is not commodified, but rather celebrated as part of the community. The Eucharist provides an alternative space within the concept of the body of Christ where not only is life affirmed and resources shared but the human dignity of all the participants is accepted and respected. The Eucharist can be an alternative space where not only dignity is shared but communicated, reiterated and voiced. It is the place where all can hear the voice of the silenced. First one has to highlight the rise of globalization as a process. In the following section, I will highlight how the global public space was taken over by those who supported the New World Order and thus commodified the public space where even life is identified as a commodity. Before identifying and recognizing the Eucharist as an alternative communicative space, it is essential to highlight how the global space enhanced and further marginalized the poor, victims, differently abled people, minorities and people living with HIV/AIDS. The global network of communication has reinforced local exploitation through a neo-liberal ideology. Thus the process of communication eliminated all the other voices even from the local community space by providing an entirely negative image of such voices.

Background of globalization of communication

In 1973, the fourth summit of the Non-Aligned Movement (NAM) in Algiers called for more co-operation in the field of mass media among developing countries.[7] The member countries established the Non-Aligned New Agencies Pool (NANAP), regional news agencies and the Broadcasting Organization of Non-Aligned Countries (BONAC). NAM wanted such co-operative efforts to operate at the international level through the United Nations. The New International Information and Communication Order (NIIO) was accepted by NAM countries and was brought to UNESCO in 1976 in Nairobi and was accepted as the New World Information and Communication Order (NWICO) resolution. A commission was set up in 1977 under Sean MacBride. The MacBride Report was accepted in 1978 at the twentieth General Conference of UNESCO. In 1978, the UN General Assembly adopted this resolution. It was in 1981 that the Reagan Administration began to interpret NWICO as a threat to press freedom and asked UNESCO to eliminate NWICO from UNESCO. This was one of the reasons for the withdrawal of the US and UK from UNESCO in 1987. From this time onwards NWICO lost its momentum. The US President Ronald Reagan and UK Prime Minister Margaret Thatcher came up with new ideas for a New World Order in which intellectual property rights and patent issues were brought up. Thus new world bodies such as the International Monetary Fund (IMF), World Bank (WB), World Trade Organization (WTO) and G-6/8 nations have been introduced to bring about this New World Order.

The NWICO movement highlighted a number of problems with the old international information order, including: the big gap in the worldwide distribution of the means of communication; the imbalance in the worldwide information flow; the one-sided and distorted coverage of the developing world by the dominating Western mass media.[8] Against the above problems the NWICO emphasized five major objectives in communication development: first, there should be equity and autonomy within global communication. It emphasizes a vision of national self-reliance in communication and reaffirms national cultural identity within an expanding system of international news agencies and other transnational cultural industries. Second, there is a need for establishing national communication policies that will support the developing countries' communication systems. Third, a more participatory communication institution within every nation needs to be promoted. Fourth, there is a need to stimulate indigenous cultural expression and local culture industries in the midst of transnational marketing of the media. And fifth, major non-governmental and autonomous institutions should be encouraged to provide free expressions and raise the voice of the voiceless people within and outside the nation.[9]

These are the five major objectives of the NWICO movement in bringing about changes in communication and media systems around the world. It aims at eliminating the imbalances and inequalities of information and communication, eliminating the negative effects of certain monopolies, public or private, removal of internal and external obstacles to a free flow and wider and better balanced dissemination of information and ideas, plurality of sources and channels of information, freedom of the press and of information, the freedom of journalists and all professionals in the media. Respect of each people's cultural identity, respect for the right of all peoples to participate in international exchanges of information on the basis of equality, justice and mutual benefit, respect for right of the public to have access to information sources and to participate actively in the communication process.[10] If these are the aims and objectives then it is unfortunate that a few powerful countries with the clear intention to dominate and control the process of communication stopped the NWICO movement.

Global public space and 'no people'

Globalization as a process has created an international public space where many people are identified as 'no people', because they do not have money for buying advertised goods, do not have power to manipulate and are not meeting the qualities of a consumer. If people do not have money to buy the goods that are advertised they are not counted as part of the audience. They are neglected as 'no people'. This is why I argue that in this internationalized space many people are recognized as 'no people'. The New World Order has created a large number of 'no people' who cannot be counted as people or audience for the markets. This has been enhanced by four kinds of impact of the globalization process. There is no space that exists for the people – or the public – to share or express their concerns unless a counter means is established. It becomes very difficult to survive in the world of the media market and competition. In this way, the media are often used as weapons of mass distraction (WMD) to divert people's interest towards a desire for material goods and possessions, thus creating artificial needs. This often leads to misrepresentation of other people in the media, thus polluting the information itself.

A few elite individuals who are primarily motivated by profit-based or political interests control the international communication systems. Media technology, content, messages, professionals are all controlled by a few multinational corporations (star agencies/Microsoft industries) or owners such as Rupert Murdoch and Bill Gates. Thus the globalization process has created new global media giants who can influence and change the political, social and cultural lives of the masses with their media industries (Time Warner, Walt Disney Co., Sony).[11] Information, like other indices of wealth, tends to cluster around the already rich and powerful. It is far from being a common resource available to all on an equal basis. The heavy influence of commodities and communications, with advertising seeking aggressively to forge in consumers ever stronger links of product-related desire and purchase, leads many to fear that cultural diversity will be lost.[12]

Thus the diversity of voices is eliminated, and the people who are poor and live at the margins of the society are not recognized by such communication as 'people' at all. If information is a commodity, and thus communication is sold, then it is available only to those who buy it. Most of the international organizations have used this to their advantage and thus continue to dominate the weaker and peripheral nations, through a process sometimes referred to as 'Westoxification' – that is, converting people to adopt non-indigenous forms of behaviour that could result in a certain schizophrenic paralysis of creative power.[13] People who cannot access these international communication systems are not consumers and cannot be counted as audience even if they have free access to them. They are considered as 'no people' because they are not worthy of being reported or gaining access to any content of this international communication. Only if they exist in huge numbers (either in death or protest) are they reported or communicated in the public media, but often more negatively than positively.

'Silencing people's voices rationally'

Within the New World Order the concept of intellectual property rights and neo-liberal values are embedded and promoted around the world.[14] The mass media plays a major role in promoting neo-liberal values of the markets, as the global media moguls have bought many of them. It is about free flow of goods, resources and enterprises across the borders of the world. There is competition between enterprises that make goods available at cheap prices and with high quality. The five basic tenets of neo-liberalism are: first, there should be greater openness for the international trade and market, thus allowing the rule of the market; second, the government should cut the public expenditure on, for example, education and social security; third, the government should reduce the regulations on the social conditions of the people, such as the working environment of labourers; fourth, state-owned companies should be privatized; and finally the concept of public good or existence of community is eliminated by replacing it with individual responsibility. These are the core values of neo-liberalism. In simple terms, for a company or business institution to survive one has to compete with the other and thus provide quality goods to succeed in the market at cheap price.

Neo-liberal values have found an easy way into the media market, thus eliminating all other voices that would not bring in money to the owners of the media industry. Only those things that can be sold can be shown or broadcast. This has led to degradation of the quality of programmes and a focus mainly on making profit for the media industry. If anything good is done by the churches or by the community at large it cannot be a newsworthy issue; rather the exploits of a mass murderer or a rapist fill the front page. The more negative the news is, the more it becomes worthy of being published. Industrialists and rich owners have bought the shares of the media industries and thus eliminated the concept of public service from such cultural industries. Thus the media industries survive today merely as entertainment agencies or private means to sell goods via media. They not only do not show any interest in public service but also tend to highlight only the problems and mistakes of those institutions that are trying to serve the public. Of course there are still a few public broadcasting institutions that serve the people with the help of the support from the government.

The mass mediated public space is bought and sold for huge sums of money, and only those who can convert religious values into a package that can be sold like soap can find room in such a space. Otherwise religious, social service organizations and particularly those whose voices are never heard in public are silenced, rejected and negated. It is therefore essential for the churches and other socially motivated organizations to use the existing space or create new spaces among communities where they can enable the voices of poor, differently abled people and HIV/AIDs infected and other marginalized communities. Many of these people's voices are sidelined or silenced either by not providing a space for them or by creating negative stereotypical images about them. For example the mass media often present mass protests by people against any government policies in a negative way.

In order to counter the neo-liberal ideology that degrades human life into a commodity, it is necessary to affirm human life at the centre of one's faith and to respect the dignity of all human beings. The basic values of many religious communities are questioned due to the commercialization of human life in the public sphere. Communities find it hard to express alternative views among themselves in many contexts and so become dragged into a passive acceptance of neo-liberal views. Here, religious institutions and also social service organizations can play a major role by creating an alternative community sphere where people can communicate to themselves. This is not to return to old values without being critical of them and not to maintain the status quo of the structure of the society where some people's dignity is not respected. But it is an attempt to develop an alternative space where human life is not commodified and where human dignity is affirmed regardless of gender, caste, colour and class.

Let my people speak – Eucharist as alternative space!

Though the New World Information and Communication Order was not given importance by UNESCO under the pressure of a few rich countries, the concepts have remained in the mind of many communication scholars and practitioners who were committed to the cause of the poor and marginal communities. This enabled many to identify alternatives to the New World Order and the Global Media that work in favour of such order. Alternatives were developed in many ways including concepts, perspectives and practices. But alternative types of communication already existed in some South American countries.[15]

The concept of alternative media is often explained in binary opposition to the mainstream media – horizontal/vertical; communication/information; democratic/authoritarian; dialogic/monologic.[16] The alternative media are those media that play an alternative role in a community, often as alternatives to the mass media, as means for social change, as agents of harmony and peace, as voice of the voiceless, as liberating agents and as counter, participatory and democratic methods. The alternative media are accessible, affordable and easily available to the people. An alternative medium does not necessarily meet all the aspects of the definition stated above, but can be called alternative if it meets a few of the characteristics.

Our question here is this: can the Eucharist be an alternative model for Christians and non-Christians? Can it provide an alternative space for people to think, imagine and communicate in dignified and life-affirming ways? This is not possible either through mass communication or through any other communication that divides people and communities. More often than not the Eucharist is seen by the churches as a sharing of the bread and wine among their own denominational members, thus affirming their affiliations and confessions. It becomes an exclusive denominational ritual act that does not involve anyone who is outside the particular denomination and community. But the Eucharist can be an inclusive and open community that not only invites people but also demands that participants recognize each other's dignity and become part of the alternative community of love. For the Eucharist is not merely a ritual sharing of the body and blood of Jesus Christ; it is the community gathering around the table of the Lord in the Church. If it is the community of Christ, it invites all and includes anyone who wishes to join in this fellowship and recognize each other's dignity and share their resources.

The Eucharist is a celebration of the life in Christ. It is also an act of affirming our being part of the body of Christ. In Christ there is no male and no female and there is no Jew and Greek (Galatians 3.28). This does not eliminate all differences and does not make all into one race or colour. Rather it invites us to accept each other's dignity and accept each other as we are. Of course the denominationalism and religious narrowness of many Christian traditions tend to eliminate or reject others from being part of this wider body of Christ. But in its real sense the Eucharist provides a space for all people to come together and share the body and blood of Jesus Christ. There is a unity among the participants, not uniformity; there is also demand for oneness but not sameness (1 Corinthians 12.11–27). Those who affirm life and who accept others' dignity are to be invited to be part of this celebration of life in God (John 6.56–57). This is in continuity with what Christ did and so the body of Christ becomes inclusive of all those who affirm life in God and respect others' dignity (1 Corinthians 10). If this is the case, then the Eucharist can be a counter space where dialogue can happen between people who affirm human life and the dignity of all.

In effect, the Eucharist becomes an alternative space that: is dialogic, intercultural, local and interpreting universal/global; promotes values; entertains but is not only about entertainment; is secular, democratized and development-oriented; promotes the dignity of people; highlights justice and ecological concerns; remains cheap; is both top-down and down-top; is culturally rooted; is non-profit but not at loss; promotes a culture of peace, reconciliation and harmony; involves people's participation; identifies and highlights alternative issues; not merely accepts the public opinions but challenges them; highlights public concerns as well as minorities' concerns; is simple and not professionally communicated; represents the voice of the voiceless; accepts people as they are; and engages in people's search for meaning (Ephesians 4.11–16; Romans 12.3–8; 1 Corinthians 12). (See Figure 1.)

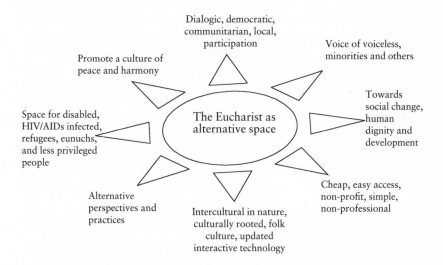

Figure 1. Eucharist as communicative space for people at the margins

One may rightly ask the question 'Why should Eucharist provide alternative communicative space?' Isn't this a Christian ritual celebration of the body and blood of Jesus Christ which is given only to those who belong to a particular denomination and also to those who are confirmed through a certain process of education? The Eucharist was originally a celebration of life in God and being the body of Christ. It was intended as a space for inviting people to join and experience the body of Christ which is the Church. Having made it into an exclusive gathering such an act of open celebration led Christians not only to separate themselves from others; it also led to conflicts within the Christian community. Yet, the Eucharist offers us a model for widening the reign of God to include all. The eucharistic communication should also take into account the concerns of ecology, refugees, disabled people and women (as Figure 1 suggests). It needs to become the means of connecting and relating people at the margins and people at the centre.

Eucharistic space can be used as an alternative method of communication where human dignity is assured and all are considered to be part of the body of Christ. In my example I have pointed out that the ideologies have failed in their attempt to bring about radical changes among these communities. Such concepts divide people and lead to violence among, within and between communities. It is the community's gathering before, during and after the Eucharist that brings about radical changes and enables them to think of an alternative community where people's dignity is restored and where everyone is invited to share this dignity and share their resources as well. I argue that without such a faith-centred approach a critical engagement alone will not bring about social change among communities. The Eucharist provides a space for communities to share their issues and facilitate discussion on the issues of globalization. Thus it becomes a reconstructed alternative space where not only is faith expressed and experienced but also where experience and social realities are communicated and discussed among the communities. Such communication cannot happen elsewhere in the public or community sphere through the mass media or any other mediated public communication.

The churches' mission is to provide an alternative space where values affirming human lives are discussed together with other religious communities. The churches can use their communication methods and practices to create, sustain and develop such spaces where globalization is critically discussed and alternatives are developed locally and globally. In this chapter, I have suggested the Eucharist as an alternative space. In order to create an alternative community space, the churches have to widen the present practices of communication which only serve the Christian community. The churches need to use the available methods and means of communication for this purpose or invest in new media to create such space for critical engagement of the community with the process of globalization. Without theologically sustaining such alternative communication the churches may find it difficult to provide an alternative space for communities at large. It is only through the Eucharist that a new community is created and reconstructed. In this new community there is a demand from the participants not only to recognize and accept human dignity but also to facilitate each other and thus make it a participatory, dialogic dynamic and an alternative to the dominant voices. It also provides a space for those voices that are never heard and that are sidelined. In this way, the Eucharist becomes an alternative and reconstructed space for leading people into new creation in Christ. (See Figure 2.)

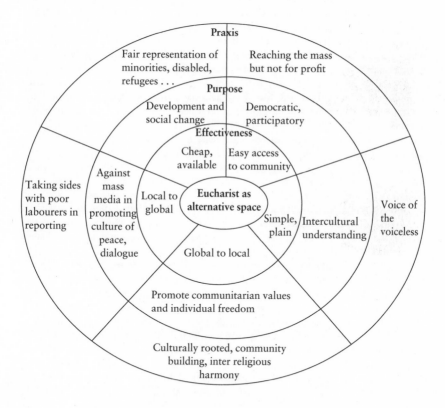

Figure 2. Eucharist as an ideal alternative space

Notes

1 <http://www.hinduonnet.com/fline/fl1617/16170380.htm>.

2 <http://www.hinduonnet.com/2001/07/31/stories/04312236.htm>; <http://www.hinduonnet.com/fline/fl1616/16160210.htm>.

3 <http://www.hinduonnet.com/thehindu/2000/07/07/stories/0407223b.htm>.

4 <http://web.amnesty.org/library/Index/ENGASA200142000?open&of=ENG-398>; <http://hrw.org/english/docs/1999/08/06/india1017.htm>.

5 Long ago, the churches, temples and mosques played a major role as the centre of the community. They provided values, worldviews and attitude to their members – particularly to the children. Nowadays it is the mass media, particularly television, that has taken over this role in providing values and worldviews to children and even to adults. Interestingly, it is not merely the local media but the global media which is playing this role of a teacher, priest and parent, argues Gregor Goethals. Due to economic interests and the concentration of global media in the hands of a few rich moguls, they promote a neo-liberal ideology that suits their business of competition, survival and success. This has led to the commoditization of values, people's lives, service, faith and religion. Even the public sphere is shrinking into a private and personal space where everything can be bought and sold. Only those things that are saleable can be transmitted through mass media. In such a context, there is often no public sphere where the basic human values are often neglected or rejected for the churches.

6 First of all there are many definitions of globalization. I give one or two for simplicity in defining the word. Mowlana defines globalization 'as a process of structuration that encompasses homogenization and heterogenization – process in which agencies operate under different temporal sequences interact to connect and alter varying structures of social existence to create a structurally oligarchic, but interconnected, world', *Global Communication in Transition: The End of Diversity?* Thousand Oaks, CA: Sage, 1996, p. 198. Mohammadi also identifies globalization 'as the way in which, under contemporary conditions especially, relations of power and communication are stretched across the globe, involving compressions of time and space and a recomposition of social relationships', *International Communication and Globalization*, London: Sage, 1997, p. 3. From different perspectives the word is critically defined. For Traber, globalization is undoubtedly a continuation of Western imperialism whether economic, political or technological or broadly cultural. The globalization of the mass media in terms of professional techniques is an accomplished fact (*Globalization, Mass Media and Indian Cultural Values*, New Delhi: ISPCK, 2003). Globalization of the media for Chomsky means huge increases in advertising, especially foreign commodities. It also means a much narrower concentration of media sources. It will reflect the points of view of those who can amass the huge capital to run international media. Diversity and information will decline, media will get more and more advertiser-oriented ('An interview with Noam Chomsky', *Third World Network*, 1 July 1996).

7 See George Gerbner, Hamid Mowlana and Kaarle Nordenstreng, eds, *The Global Media Debate, Its Rise, Fall and Renewal*, Norwood: Ablex Publishing Corporation, 1993.

8 Wolfgang Kleinwatcher, 'Three Waves of the Debate', in Gerbner et al., *The Global Media Debate*, pp. 13–14.

9 Robert A. White, 'The New Order and The Third World', in Gerbner et al., *The Global Media Debate*, pp. 21–34 (22–3).

10 Sean MacBride and Collen Roach, 'The New International Information Order', in Gerbner et al., *The Global Media Debate*, pp. 3–12 (5).

11 Anthony Smith, *The Age of Behemoths: The Globalization of Mass Media Firms*, New York: Priority Press, 1991, pp. 21–37.

12 Chris Arthur, *The Globalization of Communications: Some Religious Implications*, Geneva: World Council of Churches. 1998, p. 6.

13 Tissa Balasuriya, 'Recolonization and Debt Crisis', in Jagadish Gandhi and George Cheriyan, eds, *Globalization: A Challenge to the Church*, Chennai: Association of Christian Institutes for Social Concern in Asia, 1998, pp. 8–12.

14 See George Cheriyan, 'Globalization – A Conspiracy of the Rich Against the Poor', in Gandhi and Cheriyan, *Globalization: A Challenge to the Church*, pp. 63–74; M. A. Oomen, 'Globalization and Decolonization: The Contemporary Challenges', in Gandhi and Cheriyan, *Globalization: A Challenge to the Church*; M. S. Varadhan, 'Opportunities', *The Hindu*, 15 October 1997, Supplement.

15 In the 1960s, alternative media was understood in the Latin American region as an indispensable weapon of political communication to combat disinformation and misinformation to connect members, and to spread political ideology. Such media were basically inspired by Leninist and Gramscian writings about the role of intellectuals in revolutionary action and thus were identified as revolutionary media. Taking Paulo Freire's concept of alternative communication some of the Catholic churches have supported and developed grassroots communication among poor communities. See A. O'Connor, 'People's Radio in Latin America: A New Assessment', *Media Development*, 2 (1989), pp. 47–53. In the 1970s, the oppressive regimes that tended to asphyxiate the public sphere and let the state and the market rule made the people at the margins find their own alternative means of communication. See B. Kucinski, *Jornalistas e Revolucionarios nos Tempos da Imprensa Alternativa*, Sao Paulo: Scritta editorial, 1991, p. xiii. The alternative media operated as a corrective mechanism to the mainstream media and became the expression of the public (Pereira Rodrigues, 'Vive a Imprensa Alternativa. Viva a Imprensa Alternativa', in R. Festa and C. E. Lins Da Silva, eds, *Comuncacao Popular e Alternativa no Brazil 53 76*, Sao Paulo: Paulinas, 1986, pp. 55–6). It brought the alternatives and the oppositional groups together (Raymond Williams, *Marxism and Literature*, Oxford: Oxford University Press, 1977, pp.55–6). From the mid 1980s, alternative communication began to play the role of defending democracy and constitutional liberties in Latin America and thus represented the political excluded interests (Simpson Grinberg, ed., *Comunicación Alternativa y Cambio Social*, Mexico City: Premia, 1986). Alternative communication is also known as radical communication, people's media or community media, grassroots media or democratic media. Having been used in diverse ways the alternative media have emerged as one of the recently discussed subjects and practices among many communication scholars and practitioners. We need to study the need for having such types of communication in bringing peace and harmony in the society.

16 R. Huesca and B. Dervin, 'Theory and Practice in Latin American Alternative Communication', *Journal of Communication*, 44, 4 (1994), pp. 53–73.

Part 2

Culture and Empire(s)

Introduction

There is an evident 'mood swing' in Part 2 as the focus is on 'Empire and Culture(s)'. Mindful that a postcolonial scrutiny of worship and liturgy is yet to be developed, this part brings a significant contribution to 'edges' in worship and liturgy – with the contributors coming from both colonial and former colonized contexts.

One of the first essays (if not the first) that attempted to carry out the postcolonial scrutiny was a groundbreaking reflection by Stephen Burns and Michael Jagessar entitled 'Fragments of a Postcolonial Perspective on Christian Worship' and published in slightly different forms in both *Worship* and *Black Theology* journals.[1] The authors made a case for moving beyond the notion of inculturation by drawing on insights from postcolonial discourse to scrutinize worship and liturgy. Plumbing liturgical texts, questions that guided the essay include: do the discourse, texts, symbols and imageries perpetuate bondage and notions of empire? What do the symbols, the language and the shape of our liturgical worship spaces communicate with regard to empire and the politics of location? In this piece, the authors problematize the issues of language, imageries and representations in liturgical texts and symbols with specific reference to a particular liturgical event and text. Authors in this section amplify these concerns.

In 'Liturgical Explorations in a Postcolonial Context', David Joy builds on the essay by Burns and Jagessar in his critical engagement with the liturgy of the Church of South India, raising key theological and hermeneutical issues. His discourse is appropriately grounded in a discussion around three 'native' and culturally appropriated liturgical texts as he evaluates Indian attempts to shake off the colonial inheritance as related to worship and liturgy.

The second essay, 'Hymns Old and New: Towards a Postcolonial Gaze', moves the scrutiny over to hymns. Hymns and hymn books are fundamental to the Christian faith and the propagation of it. Yet, nowhere in the revisions of hymn books have any attempts been made to question lyrics, to reflect on the theology that informed these, to locate hymnals in the context of British imperial history and to use tools such as the postcolonial optics to enable the scrutiny. Jagessar and Burns, therefore, scrutinize hymns of the Church for their hegemonic link with the colonial agenda using the postcolonial optic.

The third essay in this section is by Anthony Reddie, a Black British theologian. While Reddie's gaze in 'Liturgy for Liberation' is not specifically postcolonial, he inhabits the space and writes from the perspective as one whose heritage has been shaped in the colonial context of the Caribbean (and specifically Jamaican) history and as a Black British citizen. Employing the medium of drama, Reddie provides readers with a sketch that gives agency to and enables oppressed people to employ the story/vision of the gospel of Jesus for their ultimate liberation. He uses the silences in the specific text to reflect on the silenced or subaltern voices.

Postcolonial disapora studies, however, is yet to give agency to the condition of today's refugees and asylum seekers.[2] The question is: how are our liturgical practices intervening with an ethical and ideological commitment that is shaped by a generous, open and inclusive morality? The final essay by Susanna Snyder offers a timely and powerful reflection on the experiences of persons in the 'newer' diaspora, those seeking asylum. Noting the importance of faith and faith communities in the lives of many asylum seekers, Snyder is concerned about the paucity of reflections among Christians of how asylum seekers worship in Britain and, more importantly, of how the issue of asylum is explored in Christian liturgies. While the essay does not scrutinize the text from a postcolonial perspective, it does raise significant issues to be pursued and interrogated through this optic.

Notes

1 'Fragments of a Postcolonial Perspective on Christian Worship', *Worship*, 80 (2006), pp. 426–53; 'Liturgical Studies and Christian Worship: The Postcolonial Challenge', *Black Theology: An International Journal* 5 (2007), pp. 32–59; see also Michael N. Jagessar and Stephen Burns, *Christian Worship: Postcolonial Perspectives*, London: Equinox Press, 2009.

2 R. S. Sugirtharajah, 'Postcolonial Biblical Interpretation: The Next Phase', in Fernando F. Segovia and R. S. Sugirtharajah, eds, *Postcolonial Commentary on the New Testament Writings*, London and New York: T&T Clark/A Continuum Imprint, 2007.

4

Liturgical Explorations in a Postcolonial Context

DAVID JOY

Introduction

The liturgy of a worshipping community should necessarily reflect its sociocultural groundings within the wider sociocultural aspects of the community's lives. It is, in this context, appropriate to evaluate and analyse the liturgical movements and recent trends in the Indian post-colonial context. This article will analyse two recent liturgies and evaluate their postcolonial/anti-colonial/pro-colonial standings, highlighting the major insights and foci of those liturgies. Such an evaluation will locate the identity of the worshipping communities in a postcolonial context.

Postcolonialism and liturgy

In the postcolonial world, liturgical affirmations are always part of the mindset and life struggles of the people. Michael Jagessar and Stephen Burns perceive that the postcolonial critique of liturgy is beyond the traditional concept of inculturation. They argue:

> In our view, a postcolonial perspective on Christian worship, liturgical studies, hymnody etc will clearly want to build on the notion and practice of inculturation. However, a postcolonial reading will want to include more than that. Significantly, it will also be critical of and question the very notion of inculturation, how it is employed and whether it is another form of hegemonic control, empire building and colonization.[1]

Their attempt to prescribe some parameters for evaluating the existing liturgies should be considered as an exuberant endeavour to pave a new way for people of the margins to articulate and find a space. Most of the mainstream churches continue to use the liturgy of their global partners with some critical look on it. For instance, the Church of South India, one of the largest united churches in the world, uses the Book of Common Worship for her main worship services. However, the Church of South India now has an updated and contextual liturgy and lectionary dealing with contemporary themes and topics. Therefore, this study will explore some key elements in the liturgies of the recent past dealing with a postcolonial mindset and ideology. In the life of the Church, the liturgy and liturgical movements are very significant as they reflect the theological and doctrinal dimensions of the Church. Michel Amaladoss observes:

> The liturgy can truly be called the life of the church. Without the liturgy there would be no Mystical Body of Christ, in which the divine mission of Christ himself lives and acts. In them He continues His active mediatorship between God and human beings, there He continues to offer to God his own all-sufficient sacrifice of praise and atonement. It is through the liturgy that the redemption of Christ is extended over all time for the constant glory of God and the salvation of souls.[2]

This is probably a traditional view of highlighting the significance of liturgy in the life and mission of any church in the world. Moreover, the liturgy also connects the local church into the web of the global Church. Thus the network of local and global churches continues to expand as the believers grow in proclamation of faith and practice of faith.

At the same time, there are more radical and critical views about the present patterns and schemes of the liturgies currently practised in the Indian church. Many of them do not reflect the life situation of the people as they were adapted from their colonial masters. In a recent well-conducted piece of research, Kuruvilla George laments:

> For the present, suffice it to say that the liturgy of the CSI fails to bring the totality of Christian faith to bear on the life of the worshippers. Conversely, it falls short of mirroring the totality of the life and concerns of the people. In fact it tends to restrict the sway of religion to certain areas of life, leaving a large portion of it to its own devices.[3]

This is not an isolated voice in the Indian churches and theological circles as there are a number of similar voices emerging in support of a radical revision of liturgy. However, what should be the direction in which the liturgical revision should be launched is the major concern everybody seems to have raised. Kuruvilla George states:

> Therefore it is imperative for the CSI to think of a scheme to enrich the liturgy so that it will encompass the various dimensions and vicissitudes of human life. The liturgy needs to become comprehensive enough to incorporate common people, their concerns and their mission, in its scheme. This may be done without imperiling the church's precious liturgical tradition and heritage.[4]

This is a real challenge. In order to understand the concerns and dynamics of the common people a methodology that will really analyse the present situation is required. In a postcolonial context, postcolonial theories are hugely significant in the development of such a methodology.

Mark Lewis Taylor evaluates postcolonial theories in the following manner. He states:

> Overall, postcolonial theory is, in fact, a set of theories, arising from and reflecting on anticolonial liberating struggle against, and within, geopolitical systems that generate large-scale human suffering.[5]

The postcolonial search is part of a global level enquiry for a possible methodology to understand the structures of history and contemporary changes. With this tool of analysis, I propose to analyse portions of the following liturgies.

1 Liturgy for Lord's supper by C. I. David Joy[6]
2 A Liturgy – People's Theatre by Kuruvilla George[7]
3 Justice: A Celebration by Paulson [8]

There are a number of common elements in these liturgies, and it is proposed to attempt to bring out some theological and hermeneutical issues which will help readers to take a theological position in a postcolonial context.

Indian liturgies, culture and challenges

Cultural studies are now gaining momentum as many such enterprises have attempted to consider the cultural shifts and stages of change in a legitimate manner. In many of the recent liturgical explorations in India, native culture and its various elements have been a matter of focus.

It is a very interesting field of study which was launched by some of the contextual theologians of the 1980s, namely, Anthony Mooken-thottam, J. P. Pinto and others. Anthony Mookenthottam's arguments are significant as he proposes to find truth in the Indian scriptures and in the Christian scriptures by citing points of agreement, disagreement or convergence. It will, according to him, lead to the reinterpretation of texts from both Indian and Christian scriptures. Moreover, a new approach may emerge in the light of such an exercise.[9] Similarly, Joseph Prasad Pinto stands for a kind of inculturation through basic communities.[10] However, his perceptions are on the basis of culture and liberation motifs. Therefore, cultural studies can offer a solid path of thought in terms of creating a fresh understanding of the pluriformity of cultures and liberation. Clifford Geertz defines culture as follows:

> Culture denotes an historically transmitted pattern of meanings embodied in symbols, a system of inherited conceptions, expressed in symbolic forms by means of which human beings communicate, perpetuate and develop their knowledge about and attitudes towards life.[11]

It is significant that the notions of culture are transmitted through symbols of human life. Therefore, the signs and symbols in liturgical texts need to be interpreted in the light of the local cultures and religious values. Stanley J. Samartha's contributions in this regard cannot be overlooked as his writings have influenced and continue to stimulate many who believe in the liberative potential of such texts. He argues that:

> The question of language and symbols is one of the important factors in the new perceptions of religious pluralism today. Studies in the structures of language and sociology and psychology of knowledge show how precarious it is to depend on texts and translations to arrive at the truth behind words.[12]

These insights are important in analysing the liturgies of the recent past in the postcolonial context. It is interesting to note that these liturgies clearly bear witness to the presence of postcolonial elements included in the prayers and affirmations.

Analysis of the liturgies from a postcolonial viewpoint

From the viewpoint of culture and religion in a postcolonial context, the suggested liturgies are evaluated. David Joy's liturgy presents a creed which affirms the egalitarian nature of the reign of God without bringing the symbol of empire to the forefront of debate. It reads:

> We believe in God
> Who created the world and blessed it with equal blessing
> and therefore required us to pay equal respect to all creatures
> Who created us, in God's own image
> equally beautiful in our own features
> Who does not discriminate against any people based on colour, feature, race and religious belief. Who is not against any tradition but the tradition of oppression and therefore wants us to stand for the oppressed.[13]

It is interesting to note that the following categories of insights are mainly explicit in the liturgies.

1 Trends in the process of indigenization
2 Critique of the structures of domination
3 Affirmation of a Christocentric faith
4 More lyrics from native cultures

The process of indigenization

The process of indigenization has been a very serious step in the postcolonial Indian context in order to facilitate the exercise of finding a proper and plausible liturgy which will clearly reflect the aspirations of the people of God. In 1987, the United Theological College published two very significant monographs, namely *Christian Faith and Multiform Culture in India* and *Worship in Indian Context*. Both volumes affirmed the fact that any meaningful understanding of Christianity in the Indian context should stand firm for indigenization and inculturation. Since then, the United Theological College in Bangalore has passionately promoted various indigenous elements in the liturgies. It has certainly made an impact on the worship services of the churches. Stanley J. Samartha contends:

Christian theological reflection in India obviously cannot take place in isolation. It has to take into account what is happening in different parts of the Church in the world. At the same time, it cannot go on as if, in its long centuries of religious life in India, there has been no theological reflection whatsoever on serious issues in inter-religious relationship. The Hindu response to religious pluralism should become very much a part of Indian Christian theological reflection on this matter. Thus, the interplay of these two factors, namely, the ferment within the world Church and the experience of religious life lived pluralistically in India, provides the context for these reflections.[14]

The search for the living contexts of the worshipping community should continue to be reflected in liturgies emerging in a postcolonial world. The three liturgies mentioned in this article do not sufficiently reflect these elements. However, Kuruvilla George's People's liturgy is exceptionally good in upholding the idea of people's full involvement in the indigenizing process.

Critique of the structures of domination

It is a recent trend among young liturgists in postcolonial contexts to question the structures of domination. D. L. Paulson argues:

> Sisters and Brothers, God who is known through many signs and ways, invites us to worship in life and truth. We were not born at the same time and do not know when we will die, but in the space in-between we are drawn together as co-creatures to build our relationship with God and with ourselves. Let this worship strengthen our relationship further and restore the lives of all those whom we try to separate.[15]

In the liturgy of Paulson, there is a clear sense of questioning the structures of domination in terms of race, culture and politics. In David Joy's liturgy, the creed reflects a mode of protest and resistance in terms of the forces of domination in a postcolonial context. These two factors need to be understood in the light of the changes and developments in the religious field both in colonial and postcolonial worlds. G. Aloysius evaluates the situation thus:

> From the point of view of religion in society, the 19th century needs to be seen not only merely as one of crisis but also of resurgence. If a gen-

eral decline of interest and involvement in things religious – [egs.] weakening of authority, fall in Church attendance, irreverence towards age-old dogmas and rituals, the spread of irreligious and atheistic thought – could be observed, a different kind of religious upheaval, fairly widespread – the mushrooming of cults, sects and denominations, a renewed interest in the Bible . . . also need to be taken into account.[16]

In spite of these fluctuations and changes, the attention on the Bible in liturgical exploration remains unchanged. It is very clear in David Joy's liturgy as he uses direct quotations from the Bible in prayers. This is a conscious effort to stand firm with the support of the Bible in questioning the forces of domination and exploitation.

R. S. Sugirtharajah argues that the Bible was misinterpreted and misused in a colonial context to subjugate the other and it is high time to recognize the harmful effects of such misuse, and to take seriously the Bible's critique of violence. He states:

The Hebrew scriptures seem to suggest that empires, because of their military strength and the power that comes with it, are more than likely to behave arrogantly. Discrimination, oppression, inhumanity, cruelty and all forms of barbarity are no less barbarous because they are carried out by nations chosen as God's instrument. Presidents and prime ministers who seek biblical support from the messianic role of empires do well to realize that the same Bible has another harrowing message. Empires are an unreliable way of solving the world's problems, and those who take the sword will inevitably die by it.[17]

Thus, this liturgical use of biblical texts for promoting solidarity and justice can be counted as a hallmark of postcolonial liturgy. It is absolutely necessary for a postcolonial liturgist to take a position in favour of the marginalized and the alienated ones in a postcolonial world.

Michael Prior, in his book *The Bible and Colonialism: A Moral Critique*, takes a firm position on using texts in the liturgy and lectionaries. While analysing the lectionaries and liturgies he observes that many of the potential passages in the Bible which deal with the issues of land, ethnicity and so on have been omitted from the liturgy and lectionary for many years.[18] Branding the issue as 'liturgical "Censoring" of the Word of God', Prior states:

It appears, then, that the worshipping community recognizes in practice the difficulties which the land traditions of the Bible pose for faith and Christian living. Since the Church's purpose in selecting readings from the scriptures is to enlighten and stimulate the faith of the community and invigorate its practice, one readily appreciates its prudence in overlooking those traditions which have provided theological underpinning for various forms of colonialism, and which scandalize most people today. One notes a corresponding ascesis in the use of the Exodus paradigm among liberation theologians.[19]

Prior is absolutely right in pointing out these recent tendencies in the liturgical movement. Liturgists in the postcolonial world should be urged to offer due importance to the Bible in preparing the liturgy by keeping the values of justice and reconciliation uppermost.

Affirmation of Christocentric faith

All three liturgies mentioned in this article are firmly rooted in Christology. A Christocentric approach is absolutely necessary in a postcolonial context, since the marginalized and the alienated ones find their identity in Christ. Hans Schwartz's 2005 book *Theology in a Global Context* uses two interesting phrases while describing the significance of Jesus Christ, namely, 'Relating Christ to the world' and 'Emergence of new voices'.[20] These expressions clearly indicate the trend in modern Christology which takes the living context of the followers of Jesus into account when the identity of Jesus Christ is redefined. The significance and relevance of Jesus Christ in today's world can be demonstrated as the life and message of Jesus Christ continue to empower the marginalized and the despised in society. Hence, there are many contextual expressions of Christology in various contexts. Those Christologies are reflecting in diverse ways the sociocultural and religio-political struggles of the subaltern people in the world.

With the introduction of Marxist ideology in the process of reading the Bible, many biblical interpreters began to use insights from liberation theology which originated in the military context of Latin America. Unlike other contextual theological methods, this theology considered the strategy of resistance as a pattern of hope. There is no unilateral approach in presenting the image of Jesus Christ in the writings of liberation theologians. For instance, the works of liberation theologians in the Asian context express a rainbow of images of Jesus in their presentations such as Jesus with Asian culture and cross (C. S. Song), contextual Jesus (Tissa Balasuriya), Jesus with Justice of God (Samuel Rayan), Jesus among the alienated ones (H. M. Katoppo), Jesus and Minjung (Kim Yong-Bok) and so on. Since the images and reflections on Jesus are many in liberation Christology, the liturgies too reflect many such images in their prayers. Sebastian Kappen from India used insights from liberation theology to contextualize Jesus in order to present Jesus with a relevant meaning in the Indian context. Sebastian Kappen's attempts to engage the Jesus tradition with some positive insights of Marxism could be considered as the foundation for the emergence of liberation theology in India.[21] Thus many of the contemporary liturgies in India reflect the insights of liberation theology and related theological and ideological affirmations. Paulson's and Joy's liturgies have a clear focus on liberation with a special emphasis on Christ.

More lyrics from native cultures

As has already been mentioned, there are a number of lyrics and bhajans used in these liturgies. Since the native language and culture had been subjugated by the colonial forces, there are few such lyrics and bhajans in the mainstream liturgies. However, it is becoming a common movement in the Indian Church to incorporate more lyrics and cultural elements in their worship resources. This was a major conflict during colonialism, as many local cultures and communities tried to place themselves within the framework of religious expressions led by the Protestant missionaries, with minimal success. Hephzibah Israel argues that there were many institutions of hegemony engaged in the process.[22] However, the natives did not get adequate participation in terms of their language and culture in the exercise of worship and liturgy.

While admitting the significance of music in worship, Lawrence E. Mick argues for a careful design with the help of all possible environments for worship.[23] In all three liturgies evaluated in this article, there are a number of bhajans and native lyrics included. Thus, it is argued that, in a postcolonial context, it is hugely significant to have native music in the liturgies, as these pieces will certainly reflect the liberative potential of the people of God in a postcolonial context.

Conclusion

From the above discussion, it is argued that, in a postcolonial context, there should be a very special attempt made to incorporate the aspirations of the people of God. In all three liturgies, by David Joy, D. L. Paulson, and Kuruvilla George, there are a number of common elements which are closely associated with postcolonial reflections and insights. The inclusion of more native lyrics reflects the aspirations of the natives. A strong Christocentric affirmation in the liturgies shows that the people of God clearly accept the eternal hope delivered through Christ. The Bible and other resources invariably help the worshippers to continue their life in solidarity with the poor and the marginalized. These are some of the trends in the postcolonial Indian context in terms of experimental liturgies.

Notes

1 Michael Jagessar and Stephen Burns, 'Liturgical Studies and Christian Worship: The Postcolonial Challenge', *Worship*, 80 (2006), p. 428.

2 Michel Amaladoss, *Our Life in Christ*, Collegeville: Liturgical Press, 1939, p. 50.

3 Kuruvilla George, *From People's Theatre to People's Eucharist: Recovering the Drama of Christian Worship*, Delhi: ISPCK, 2002, p. xxi.

4 George, *From People's Theatre*, p. xxii.

5 Mark Lewis Taylor, 'Spirit and Liberation: Achieving Postcolonial Theology in the United States', in Catherine Keller, Michael Nausner and Mayra Rivera, eds, *Postcolonial Theologies: Divinity and Empire*, St Louis: Chalice Press, 2005, p. 42.

6 C. I. David Joy, 'A Eucharistic Liturgy', *Masihi Sevak* 3 (2002), p. 45.

7 George, *From People's Theatre*, pp. 315–27.

8 D. L. Paulson, *Trial Sermon and Worship*, Bangalore: UTC Archives, no date.

9 Anthony Mookenthottam, *Towards a Theology in the Indian Context*, Bangalore: ATC, 1980, pp. 8–9.

10 J. P. Pinto, *Inculturation through Basic Communities: An Indian Perspective*, Bangalore: ATC, 1985, p. 43.

11 C. Geertz, *The Interpretation of Cultures*, London: SPCK, 1975, p. 89.

12 Stanley J. Samartha, *One Christ – Many Religions: Toward a Revised Christology*, Maryknoll: Orbis, 1991, p. 5.

13 David Joy, 'A Eucharistic Liturgy', p. 45.

14 Stanley J. Samartha, 'The Cross and the Rainbow: Christ in a Multi-Religious Culture', in Somen Das, ed., *Christian Faith and Multiform Culture in India*, Bangalore: UTC, 1978, pp. 16–17.

15 Paulson, *Trial Sermon and Worship*.

16 G. Aloysius, *Religion as Emancipatory Identity*, Delhi/Bangalore: CISRS, 1998, p. 1.

17 R. S. Sugirtharajah, *The Bible and Empire: Postcolonial Explorations*, Cambridge: Cambridge University Press, 2005, p. 189.

18 Michael Prior, *The Bible and Colonialism: A Moral Critique*, Sheffield, SAP, 1997, p. 273.

19 Prior, *The Bible and Colonialism*, p. 278.

20 Hanz Schwartz, *Theology in a Global Context*, Grand Rapids: Eerdmans, 2005, pp. 380, 472.

21 Sebastian Kappen, *Jesus and Freedom*, Maryknoll: Orbis, 1977, p. 46.

22 Hephzibah Israel, 'Cutchery Tamil versus Pure Tamil: Contesting Language Use in the Translated Bible in the Early Nineteenth-Century Protestant Tamil Community', in R.S. Sugitharajah, ed., *The Postcolonial Biblical Reader*, Oxford: Blackwell, 2006, pp. 269–83.

23 Lawrence E. Mick, *Liturgy and Ecology in Dialogue*, Collegeville: Liturgical Press, 1997, p. 67.

5

Hymns Old and New:
Towards a Postcolonial Gaze

MICHAEL N. JAGESSAR AND STEPHEN BURNS

> Rule now on earth from realms above
> Subdue the nations by thy love . . .
> And all the earth, redeemed by thee,
> Shall know a glorious liberty
>
> ('O Christ the Lord, O Christ the king', R. T. Brooks 1918–85,
> as found in the *New English Hymnal*)

Locating our conversation

Imperializing texts assume 'many forms' and 'shapes' and those from the pen of hymn writers are no exception.[1] In our article on 'Fragments of a Postcolonial Perspective on Christian Worship'[2] we noted that hymnody, among other elements of our worship, requires critical attention. While the focus in that earlier essay was on liturgy, this essay is an attempt to engage in a similar critical conversation with regards to our hymns and hymnals. As Charlotte Kroeker notes, church music 'is in the service of the liturgy' and 'at its best is a way to understand theology'. In other words both liturgy and theology matters and hymns may play a crucial role in both.[3]

In the earlier article, we located the problematic by raising some questions that are also applicable to the conversation we intend in this present essay. Among those questions were the following: Do the discourse, texts, symbols and imageries [of the hymns] perpetuate bondage and notions of empire? How do they represent black peoples, ethnic minorities, the Other, gender and sexuality? What do symbols and language communicate vis-à-vis the agenda of empire/colonialism and the politics of location? When is inculturation and the appropriation of other people's songs and music another form of exploitation or a new kind of colonialism? These framing questions ought to enable our critical scrutiny of hymns and hymnals of Christian communities.

A postcolonial gaze at hymns, hymnals and hymnody is both exciting and daunting. It is exciting because of the need to highlight the link between the European colonial agenda and the expansion of European Christianity and also because there is an urgent need for such a scrutiny. The daunting nature can be located in the demands of the undertaking given that such a gaze is yet to be developed and we are working into a hugely underdeveloped area within the inevitable limitations of a short essay. Hence, with regard to the latter, our undertaking can only be considered tentative and as part of a longer process.

We bring to this task our own interest in a variety of disciplines and a heart for interdisciplinary conversations that can fund creative and transforming discourse. Stephen Burns is a white male English Anglican clergyman who is not only a specialist in liturgical theology but also a competent contextual theologian with interests in intercultural theologies and postcolonial criticism. Stephen is very interested in dialogue across disciplines. Michael Jagessar, a member of the Caribbean (Indo) diaspora, is even more eclectic. A male minister of the United Reformed Church, Michael's interest and expertise lies in theologies, interfaith studies, ecumenics and Caribbean literature. So while Stephen writes as one from within the heart of empire (Britain), Michael does so from the perspective of a region (Caribbean) that features significantly as a colony of Great Britain.

Employing the postcolonial gaze: singing via a different optic

As this is an attempt to scrutinize hymns and hymnals through the post-colonial optic it is important that we clarify what we mean by the term 'postcolonial' and how we hope to use it to realize our task. Post-colonialism, it has been noted, is not about the demise of colonialism as 'post' as it embodies both 'after' and 'beyond'. It is not about historical chronologies but more about a critical stance, oppositional tactic or subversive reading strategy. Hence, in the context of biblical studies and theological discourse R. S. Sugirtharajah asserts that 'postcolonial' shelters a range of distinct but related meanings. Historically, 'it encapsulates the social, political and cultural conditions of the current world order, bringing to the fore the cultural, political and economic facts of colonialism, and aiding the recognition of the ambiguities of decolonialization and the ongoing recolonialization'. As a 'critical discursive practice', the postcolonial critique 'provides openings for oppositional readings, uncovers suppressed voices' with its primary concern that of victims and their state. A third way the term is employed is related 'to the political and ideological stance of an interpreter who is engaged in anti-colonial and anti-globalizing theory and praxis'. Employing this, for instance, in the scrutiny of the Bible, the aim will be 'to uncover colonial designs in both biblical texts and their interpretation', with then attempting 'to read the text from such postcolonial concerns as identity, hybridity and diaspora'.[4] Thus according to Christopher Duraisingh, the postcolonial optic affirms 'a new mode of imagining, a new cultural logic, posited over against the euro-centric monologic and the colonial manner of thinking and visioning reality'.[5]

So applied to the task before us – hymns, hymnals and the theology they espouse – the postcolonial optic allows us to undress the 'colonial designs' in our hymns and endeavour to read their theology from themes such as identities, power, hybridity, cultures and so on. This critical engagement is also geared at offering 'viable critical alternatives'.[6] Therefore, in this paper, we turn a postcolonial theological focus on hymnody, and suggest two main lines of enquiry. First, we ask about what hymns may say, questioning aspects of their language and suggesting the need to recast and revision certain elements of hymn-texts. Second, we ask about how hymns are used, and in particular comment on the ambiguities of appropriating 'world church' hymnody into dominant Western liturgical contexts.[7]

Sounding empire: hymns, theology and imperialism

That European colonialism carried the hymnody around the world and that much of European hymnody advances the cause of European colonialism should be of no surprise to readers. In *Imperialism and Music: Britain 1876–1953* (2001), Jeffrey Richards shows how a wide range of musical forms (which includes hymns) gave expression to British national identity at home, as well as extended its reach overseas through British imperialism. Among other things, Richards shows how Victorian hymns were imperialistic, with even the masses interested in empire. His chapter on imperial hymns locates the centrality of empire and Christian militarism in a great deal of Christian song.[8]

European Christians found in what is sometimes referred to as the 'Great Commission' (Matthew 28.18–20) inspiration for conquering foreign lands and their peoples. Hence, the missionaries who came out of the milieu that celebrated the expansion of European nations to the ends of the earth had no difficulty articulating that Christianity, expansion and civilization went together. Hence, mission was an opportunity for extending the Christian gospel outside England and, by extension, meant the expansion of the British Empire.[9] Christianizing and civilizing became euphemisms for enslavement, domination and exploitation, and the theology that the established and historic churches sang underscored this. The point is that many European ecclesial traditions – their ethos, hymns, Bibles, interpretations, liturgies and doctrines – went hand in hand with the colonial enterprise to affirm production, control and domination consciously or unconsciously. Ellerton's hymn written for the Queen's jubilee (1887) sums up the tenor of the time:

Dusky Indian, strong Australian,
Western forest, Southern sea, None are wanting, none are alien,
All in one great prayer agree –
God save the Queen!

But before him, Isaac Watts (1674–1748) penned these telling lyrics:

Sing to the Lord with joyful voice
Let every land his name adore
The British Isles shall send the noise
Across the ocean to the shore.

Our colleague John Hull has done some critical work on the hymns of Isaac Watts. While Hull does not claim to be doing so from a postcolonial perspective, his contribution falls within the kind of scrutiny that is in focus in this essay. Hull underscores the fundamental point that Watt's hymnic 'theology of Britain' includes among its features the identification of Britain as God's 'chosen isle' and identifies the triumphant armies of the Psalms with British troops abroad. Further, Watts' tactic in his psalm 'translations' is often to transfer the powers of the Hebrew monarch to Jesus and in turn to the British monarchy. At just the time at which the value of imports from India to Britain at least doubled – the same era in which the first Christian church and the Bank of Calcutta were opened within a decade – Watts 'translated' his Psalms of David:

Behold the Islands with their kings,
And Europe her best tribute brings;
From north and south the princes meet
To pay their homage at his feet.

There Persia, glorious to behold.
There India shines in eastern gold,
And barbarous nations at his word
Submit, and bow, and own their Lord.

Although these verses were edited out of editions of his Psalms of
David by the nineteenth century, the legacy of empire remains even in
his most durable hymns. 'When I survey the wondrous cross' smacks of
parallel activities of 'surveying' the 'glorious' 'wonders' and exotic
'charms' of other nations, 'counting' their value and 'gaining richly'
from them. Although 'When I survey' suggests a turning from the ultimate significance of commercial domination, the imagery of the hymn is
saturated in the idea and practices of empire.[10]

A similar observation can be made of many of the hymns of Methodism. The introductory sentence in the 1933 British *Methodist Hymn-
book* notes 'Methodism was born in song', reflecting John Wesley's own
words in the preface of *Psalms and Hymns* (1737) in which he noted that
a hymnal ought to 'contain all the important truths of our most holy
religion', embody 'experimental and practical divinity' and capture the
'spirit of poetry' which becomes 'the handmaid of piety'.[11] No wonder
scholars speak of the Methodist hymnal as embodying Methodist theology.[12] If, as Methodists claim, the theology of this particular ecclesial
tradition is summed up in the hymns Methodists sing, then the hymns of
the Wesleys are also worth scrutinizing as these evolved at the peak of
British imperialism. One wonders whether John Wesley's claim that the
'world is my parish' is an echo of the English vision of conquering the
corners of the world. And lest we forget, Charles Wesley (1707–88)
taught Methodists to sing:

Thy sovereign grace to all extends
Immense and unconfined
From age to age it never dies
It reaches all mankind [*sic*].

As well as,

O for Thy truth and mercy's sake
The purchase of Thy passion claim!
Thine heritage, the nations, take
And cause the world to know Thy name.

On the surface these words of Charles Wesley may not be speaking of empire. Indeed, Wesley may have read the moral philosophers of his time, felt convinced about the impending judgement of the world for its sins and held that Christ died for all human beings. Yet, for him the natives in the far-flung corners of Africa had to be converted before they could be 'civilized' and hence become moral beings. Moreover, he saw this as 'the task thy wisdom has assigned/O let me cheerfully fulfil'.[13] With a heart 'full of Christ', as 'ransomed servant(s)' and 'docile, helpless, as a child',[14] the Wesleys saw Jesus 'firing up the nations' as 'soldiers of Christ, arise'.[15]

The problem is that the Wesleys worked (understandably so) within the confines of a white British mindset that contemplated a process that would lead the enslaved Africans or native Americans to becoming human by moving from what was termed their natural state to one of enlightenment: inculcating Christian virtues would result in this civilizing process. Those virtues were soaked with British/European values. Totally de-culturalized, a new identity would be created for the natives and the enslaved. Redeemed through Christian (British) conversion, the new creature (at last properly human) would become a more manageable workforce to the benefit of society, that is, the imperial treasury and its agents. And this mindset culminates in the image that all will live happily ever after in the emerging capitalist model of mutuality between landlords and tenants.[16]

It is no wonder that the hymns of Charles Wesley are steeped with the notion of submission, meekness and docility, proposed as the way of Jesus. And it is also not surprising that Methodism, especially at the latter part of the Wesleys' lives, was more missionary in orientation than emancipatory. For in the final analysis, whether it was empire or not, the underlying premise was that of a superior group of people either ruling an inferior lot or a superior group of souls filled with chalky light bringing enlightenment to natives in their natural state of ignorance.[17]

What the foregoing underscores is that the colonial legacy pervades much Christian hymnody used in the West. And unfortunately this is not something confined to the past as many of those hymns are sung even to this day just as some of the newer ones reinscribe the notions of empire, among other baleful things. To an extent some hymns have been sanitized to express sentiments and theology that reflect contemporary issues. Yet, many of these hymns have been sung for over 200 years and the sentiments and thoughts they embraced were what the British took with them to India, Africa, the Caribbean and the dominions. Globalization today is ensuring the perpetuation of these sentiments and even if

Christianity is growing in lands of the 'south', many of the hymns that are sung in these places, as a result of years without any critical scrutiny of the inherited Eurocentric versions of Christianity, have remained untouched in terms of the theological notions that they espouse. As one stark example, one of us (Stephen) remembers singing hymns from Sankey and Moody's *Sacred Songs and Solos* as one of only two white members of a congregation (the other being the 'imported' preacher) in a remote Aboriginal community in central Queensland. The Aboriginal Inland Mission congregation used this hymnal as recipients of a legacy of earlier missionary activity closely allied to lamentable forms of imperialism.

Hymns, hymnals and their revision: a postcolonial gaze

A number of questions may rightly be asked: for instance, why this harping back to those hymns written during a particular era? Are we not constantly revising our hymns and hymnals by adding newer ones that reflect contemporary sentiments? Do modern hymn writers operate with notions of empire and imperial grandeur? These are pertinent questions and to them we now turn as we attempt a brief tour of some of the post-Reformation history of hymn writing and a closer scrutiny at the revising of hymnals.

Hymnals and hymns: a brief overview

Hymns and hymn singing have a long and interesting history. In the Western world, the Protestant Reformation played a significant role in the development of hymns and congregational hymn singing.[18] On the English landscape the person most closely associated with the development of English hymns is Isaac Watts (1674–1748) with his first hymnal appearing in 1707. Watts wrote over 600 hymns. After him came perhaps the greatest hymn writer of all time, Charles Wesley (1707–88), who wrote approximately 6,500 hymns. Hymns, for some, have the ability to transgress boundaries of gender, generation, ethnicity and class.[19] For others, hymns are our 'confessional documents' serving as the 'container' of and formative influence on much of our faith. Hence, Albert van den Heuvel wrote: 'tell me what you sing, and I'll tell you who you are'.[20] Indeed: hymns do not simply lie on the page as empty words; they come to life because they are sounded and what is sounded is never value free. What they represent is linked to some agenda. Hymns were and are used to convey theological notions and teachings of the Christian faith. And hymn writers are historically, culturally and socially located: they write according to particular doctrinal viewpoints and their views reflect their time and contexts (as we have seen in relation to Watts and the Wesleys). Significantly, many hymn writers whose works are still sung lived and wrote during the high noon of European, and for our purposes British, colonial expansion. In fact, it was during this period that what we have inherited as hymnodies rapidly evolved. As such they need to be interrogated for their ideological content.[21] Here the issue of representation in hymns becomes a critical one. Who is representing whom, what is being represented and how these representations reinforce systems of inequalities and subordination and the sustaining of colonial and neo-colonial projects are critical questions in the process of interrogating our hymns (past and present).

Scrutinizing the revision of hymns and hymnals: examples and questions

As we noted, the concern may rightly be raised as to the value of such an exercise given that our hymns and hymn books are constantly being revised. Indeed, we no longer sing about the rich in the grand hall of their castle, the poor below at their gates and that God made them that way and ordered their state. But do we ever question what the singing of that hymn for generations has done to our Christian ethos, doctrines and theology? What is the link with such theology and some of the newer hymns of the 'prosperity gospel' sort that creep into our hymnals and worship (whatever the cultural garb)? Sugirtharajah reminds us that in the minds of 'most European theologians at the time, the empire was a matter of divine dispensation, and, as such, beyond ultimate criticism'.[22] Furthermore, many of our ecclesial traditions find it much safer to hold on to narrow and rigid frameworks as these are supposed to 'keep their doctrines intact' and 'their institutions safe'.[23] This may be one reason why a contemporary hymn writer such as Ruth Duck, a leader in the revision of hymns around the significance of gender, writes that her 'emphasis is on recreation, not critique of tradition'. This is a comment that relates to others appearing in a number of the prefaces of revised hymnals. Because critical theological scrutiny is risky, it may require a revision of beliefs, deconstructing/dismantling of tradition and reconfiguring of identity.[24] The prefaces of some of the newer hymnals make interesting reading, especially in terms of their comments on the revision processes employed, the overriding leitmotif and the lenses through which these have been read and carried out.[25] We commend some of these, such as the United Church of Christ's *New Century Hymnal* (1995), in which

> Every effort was made to ensure that all hymns speak to and for all God's people, equally. This resulted in the examination of language from racial, ethnic, and sociocultural perspectives, and the review of language that could be diminishing to people with physical disabilities. Consideration was also given to imagery to assure that it relate to the scientific understandings of a coming generation.[26]

However, what is largely and too often passed over in the revision processes is the connection between hymns, the colonial agenda and empire language (past and present) and the possible implications of the paucity of critical scrutiny of the theology, the militaristic/triumphalistic language and tone, cultural arrogance/superiority and the continuing perpetuation of hegemonic notions. Pete Ward's critical evaluations of recent generations of the 'choruses' that emerged in evangelical and charismatic circles but now traverse many church styles includes an important critique of increasingly prevalent militaristic imagery, and needs to be applied not only to the maturing genre of the chorus but also to the wide breadth of inherited hymnody.[27] The revision of hymn books and the development of new styles of Christian song are both yet to engage properly with tools such as the postcolonial optic as one the lenses through which to scrutinize how and what we sing of the faith. For if, as John Bell notes (in a similar comment to that of Albert van den Heuvel cited earlier), 'congregational singing is an identity-shaping activity', and that our communities are defined 'by the songs that we sing',[28] surely hymn writers and hymnal revisers need to ask hard questions around whose and what kind of identities and who does the defining and for whom? Of course, it may be that this is not the kind of scrutiny that hymnody committees and hymn writers are interested in. And to be fair to John Bell, he does go on to express his dismay over the multiplicity of images related to soldiers, warriors and a 'tamed' Christ in our hymns, including modern ones. Bell bemoans the lack of words such as 'midwives', 'kitchen' and 'economics'. What Bell misses, however, is how many hymns may not have used a word like economics, but were shaped under colonial influences by a certain kind of 'economics' that was supposed to give Europeans the God-given right to discover and exploit distant isles and lands under the pretence of bringing natives 'light' while exploiting the resources of these lands. Economics was very central in Livingstone's three C's – Civilization, Commerce and Christianity.

But, let us delve some more into the subject of revision and the optics through which hymnal revision has been engaged. Obviously, the editors of *The New English Hymnal* (much used in some English Anglican settings), even in its fourteenth impression of 2002, never thought of the postcolonial optic informing their task and indeed saw it fitting to retain 400 of the 656 hymns printed in the original version (1906). Likewise, the editors of the United Reformed Church's *Rejoice and Sing* (1991) while revising hymns to be gender inclusive never bothered to scrutinize the hymns of Isaac Watts and the others for their imperial overtones and connections with British imperial history. In their view, its hymns 'enabled congregations to express together their worship and praise, their wonder at the almighty power and grace of God'.[29] Hence, the diverse and multicultural nature of these congregations and the implications of Watts' link with British imperial history lay buried in the pages of the hymnal.

Should we then be surprised that during his 1997 election campaign, Tony Blair, heavily influenced by a British Christian ethos, could say that he was a proud British patriot[30] and in another address at the Lord Mayor's banquet articulated his vision for Britain and the world by noting how proud he was of British history, and the fact that Britain had an empire should propel the nation to a more active global view and role?[31] Presently, we are trying to pick up the pieces in Afghanistan and Iraq as a result of such patriotism. George W. Bush, his 'com*patriot*', is even more blatant by entitling his memoirs *Charge to Keep*, the title of which is a phrase taken from a well-known hymn by Charles Wesley. Bush's favourite hymn speaks of the charge in terms of 'a God to glorify' – not about an empire to build by annexation – but Bush is not so far away from the high 'churchmanship' and Tory mindset of the Wesleys – a mindset that relished certainty of a God-given right to bring the gospel to the dumb heathens!

Perhaps most interesting is *Hymns Ancient and Modern* (Revised, 1981), in the preface of which the Proprietors ('a body of Church of England clergymen') noted the significant place of their hymnal as 'something of a national institution' and that their revision was intended at 'preserving the general tone and character which the book has always had'.[32] Hence, while some alterations have been made, the intention is that the hymnal will not break 'fresh ground or explore novel ideas' but that the revision 'will find the same endearing and enduring qualities as in the old' and very much 'in keeping with English Christianity'.[33] These are interesting lines: Is there a yearning here to return to what is imagined to be some supposed 'pure' state of English Christianity? What or whose version of English Christianity did these Proprietors in 1981 work with? With the presence of peoples from former colonies, newer migrants in England and the engagement with other cultures and religions, certainly English Christianity needs to be redefined and perhaps draw more of the 'hybridity' that has in reality always been part of its story, albeit not always told. As Sugirtharajah reminds us: 'In an ever-increasing multi-cultural society like ours, where traditions, histories and texts commingle, interface, a quest for unalloyed pure native roots could prove not only to be elusive but also to be dangerous.'[34]

Common Praise (2000), the new edition of *Hymns Ancient and Modern* (first published in 1860-1 and since then used throughout Britain and its colonies), is also both a national and imperial text. Yet the committee responsible for its revision, while noting all the significant historical developments since the hymnal's birth, fail to mention the relationship between the hymns and British imperialism, despite the fact that during the period through which this hymnal evolved 'empire was central to English domestic life and popular consciousness'.[35] While it was noted that the Church has become more ecumenical, there was not a word about the *Windrush* generation and how the churches have become more multicultural. And, while the committee has attended to the archaisms of some hymns and the problematic related to gender-inclusive language, the editorial policy was intentionally 'conservative', 'respecting the integrity of the text, the author's known intentions, and the poetry of the original'.[36] What is interesting about these reasons is that they serve to remove any attempt to critically scrutinize hymns and the ideology that may have influenced the hymn writer. From a post-colonial stance one will want to ask why 'conserve' even good poetry when the integrity of a text may be questionable because of its implicit or explicit arrogance, marginalization of peoples or groups and the locating of Eurocentric Christianity above all else (especially that which is native). Take, for example, the hymn 'Dear Lord and Father of Mankind' by John Greenleaf Whittier (1807-92). This hymn reacts to a practice in Hindu worship in which the Vedic priests consume a drink (soma) for a deep religious experience with the divine. Finding such a practice repulsive, especially its aspect of religious frenzy, Whittier, a calm Quaker, responds to this Hindu practice by asking the God of Jesus to forgive such foolish ways and replace them with higher religious devotion characterized by 'quietness', 'purity', 'order' 'deeper reverence', 'simple trust'. Certainly, the integrity of text and intentions of the author should be respected; yet the influence of this hymn – sung for generations – on the psyche of people cannot be imagined to be value free for the author, in its uses, or in terms of how readers may perceive the hymn. The intentions of a hymn writer (known or unknown) are complex because writers are always socially, culturally and politically located. Within the colonial mindset, Whittier's hymn – like many others – 'offered a simple choice between truth and falsehood' – in other words 'if one is right, the other is invariably wrong'. Counter to this, a postcolonial optic will not offer a forced choice 'between truth and truth' nor agency to one perspective by negating the other.[37] The fact that hymns significantly shape our identity and define who we are (as noted earlier) is not neutral; it can be either positive or negative. Hence, the need to interrogate hymns, not merely engage in singing poetic lines.

Even so, the generally more inclusive *Common Ground* (1998) never thought of slapping imperial overtones as one of its restrictions to determine whether hymns would find their way into this hymn book 'for all the churches'. In fact, readers are told that *Common Ground* is a 'unique' publication, as it 'takes over 20% of its material from nations in the southern hemisphere'.[38] Perhaps, this should read more like 'hijacking over 20%', as the naming or representing of this transaction as 'world church music' is one given by the West for music 'taken' from the southern hemisphere and often sold for a neat sum. Is this a case of 'expanding markets and securing new clients'?[39] As part of this, there are important questions to be asked related to Western churches' copyrighting of materials that have emerged from other cultures, which may amount to another form of exploitation and neo-colonialism.[40] Certainly, one can ask: how different is this from buying up fruits cheaply from all over the former colonies and then processing them and repackaging them either as dried fruits or canned to be exported back to these countries for prices that the natives themselves cannot afford? This is not even to mention how unrecognizable and tasteless the thing has become. One of us (Michael) recalls attending a conference where a hymn writer/musician was teaching a group of ministers new world songs/music. Among the participants was a Ghanaian minister who protested that he could not recognize the way the song (which came from his country of birth) was sung – much to the displeasure of the leader. This was a clear case of using 'world church' hymns without appropriating concerns of context from which they come and sensitivity to people of those contexts who are now part of Western communities.

One therefore wonders about the view that the inclusion of 'world church music' affirms that our churches have become more inclusive, multicultural and global. Indeed, one needs to interrogate all the rhetoric surrounding multiculturalism. This would suggest it is 'a project of the colonizing, dominant culture . . . a monocultural Anglo version of multiculturalism that wants to host, invite, and include' or incorporate 'the other' in 'otherwise Anglo realities and structures'.[41] The question of when inculturation and the appropriation of other people's songs and music becomes another form of exploitation or a new kind of colonialism is a very important one, not least because imperialism finds interesting ways to reclothe itself so that we need to be ever vigilant. Here the concern of Myke Johnsont (writing in a different context, that of the cultural appropriation of Native American symbols and ceremonies) remains valid: Johnsont raises the question of 'cultural appropriation' as a 'form of racism' and a 'weapon in the process of colonization' – especially in the context of the powerful and powerless.[42] Our concern does not lead us to the view that music and hymns should not be shared: we live in too complex a world in which cultures and people transcend boundaries and are constantly in dialogue, and moreover, the realities of colonialism mean that destinies are intertwined and many of us straddle multiple identities. We have no difficulty with the view expressed by Michael Hawn that a variety of musical styles and hymns from around the world can deepen worship and our understanding of the incarnation of Christ.[43] Our unease is that if we do not read such sharing through a postcolonial gaze, we may not be asking the critical questions as to how this is done, who initiates and who permits it, how it is named and how it might become accessible to all.

A further related question, borrowing from Sugirtharajah, is how much of the incorporation of the 'world church hymns and music' is about 'disturbing and dislodging' an imperial agenda?[44] Is it possible to grow 'cultural sensitivity' and yet not experience 'another culture from within'?[45] Hence the question: how can the singing of a South African and Latin American liberation song speak to a still largely white European audience whose nations thrive on cheap labour, global capital and continuing impoverishment of poorer countries and sections of people within its own border? How can 'world church' words and music come alive in a transforming way and not sound patronizing? There is certainly the danger, to borrow from John Witvliet, of indulging in 'ethno-tourism' while safely basking in our own comfort zones![46]

Sound theology: examples of good practice

Notwithstanding our concerns, we are pleased to note that hymn books and hymns have been and are being constantly revised. We affirm the practice of bringing together new hymns by contemporary hymn writers alongside older ones, whose language and images can, when necessary, be revised. We delight that it is increasingly common for hymn books to be reviewed in terms of education in feminist and expansive language concerns, and we are heartened by the likes of Brian Wren's work to reconfigure notions of masculinity[47] as part of the task of raising awareness of the significance of gender, which is not only a matter of how women are portrayed. We enjoy many of the ways in which perhaps the most daring contemporary hymnal, *The New Century Hymnal*, has revised and expanded the hymnody of many contemporary Christians, and we note with particular appreciation that it includes a rare 'litany of light and darkness' in which darkness is not simply associated with fear and dread:

> It is only in the darkness that we can see the splendour of the
> universe – blankets of stars, the solitary glowings of distant
> planets.
> It was darkness that allowed the magi to find the star that guided
> them to where the Christ-child lay.
> **You are with us, O God, in darkness and in light.**
> In the darkness of the night, desert peoples find relief from the cruel,
> relentless heat of the sun.
> In the blessed desert darkness, Mary and Joseph were able to flee
> with the infant Jesus to safety in Egypt.
> **You are with us, O God, in darkness and in light.**
> In the darkness of sleep, we are soothed and restored, healed and
> renewed.
> In the darkness of sleep, dreams rise up. God spoke to Jacob and
> Joseph through dreams. God is speaking still . . .[48]

This litany offers a counter-voice to a deep and worrying tendency in much Christian song to make uncritical correlations between light and darkness and desirable and undesirable things respectively. Like Brian Wren's 'Joyful is the Darkness', inspired by the line in one of his better-known hymns, 'Bring Many Names', the litany of light and darkness is among too few potential fragments of 'oppositional reading' to the usual currency of the metaphor of darkness.[49] In our view, recasting light and darkness imagery is a crucial strand of developing a postcolonial voice in the hymns Christians sing, and represents a constructive challenge to be set alongside the schooling in the critical gaze we attempt throughout this essay.

Notes

1 Musa Dube, 'Reading for Decolonization (John 4.1–42)', in Musa Dube and Jeffrey L. Staley, eds, *John and Postcolonialism: Travel, Space and Power*, London and New York: Sheffield Academic Press, 2002, p. 56.

2 Michael N. Jagessar and Stephen Burns, 'Fragments of a Postcolonial Perspective on Christian Worship', *Worship*, 80 (2006), pp. 426–53; see also Michael N. Jagessar and Stephen Burns, 'Liturgical Studies and Christian Worship: The Postcolonial Challenge', *Black Theology*, 5 (2007), pp. 38–53.

3 Charlotte Kroeker, ed., *Music in Christian Worship*, Collegeville, MN: Liturgical Press, 2005, p. x.

4 R. S. Sugirtharajah, *Postcolonial Reconfigurations: An Alternative Way of Reading the Bible and Doing Theology*, London: SCM Press, 2003, p. 4.

5 Christopher Duraisingh, 'Towards A Postcolonial Re-Visioning of the Church's Faith, Witness and Communion' in Ian T. Douglas and Kwok Pui-lan, eds, *Beyond Colonial Anglicanism*, New York: Church Publishing, 2001, pp. 337–67 (337).

6 Sugirtharajah, *Postcolonial Reconfigurations* , p. 4.

7 Hence, while C. Michael Hawn will ask of hymns the following four questions: 'What does this song mean for me? . . . What does this song tell me about the God who became human? . . . How does this song help me intercede before God on behalf of the world? . . . How does this song help me welcome the stranger and make more room at the table?', the postcolonial scrutiny will want to go further to ask questions related to the imperial motives of hymns. See C. Michael Hawn, *Gather into One: Praying and Singing Globally*, Grand Rapids, MN: Eerdmans, 2005, p. 30.

8 Jeffrey Richards, *Imperialism and Music: Britain 1876–1953*, Manchester: Manchester University Press, 2001.

9 Ian Bradley, *Abide With Me: The World of Victorian Hymns*, London: Bloomsbury Press, 1997, p. 108.

10 John M. Hull, 'Isaac Watts: Experiential Educator to Nationalist Theologian and Hymnwriter', *Panorama: International Congregational Journal of Comparative Religious Education and Values*, 14 (2002), pp. 91–106 (xx).

11 *Hymns and Psalms*, Peterborough: Methodist Publishing House, 1983, p. ix and p. xii.

12 For example, Gordon Wakefield, *Methodist Spirituality*, Peterborough: Epworth Press, 1999, p. xx.

13 *Hymns and Psalms*, p. 381.

14 *Hymns and Psalms*, p. 737.

15 *Hymns and Psalms*, p. 719.

16 See Orlando Patterson, *Slavery and Social Death: A Comparative Study*, Cambridge, MA: Harvard University Press, 1986, pp. 56–8.

17 Cf. Sugirtharajah, *Postcolonial Reconfigurations*, p. 147.

18 See Richards, *Imperialism and Music*.

19 Bert F. Polman, 'Forward Steps and Side Steps in a Walk-Through of Christian Hymnody' in Kroeker, *Music in Christian Worship*, p. 65.

20 As quoted by C. Michael Hawn, 'Reverse Missions: Global Singing for Local Congregations' in Kroeker, *Music in Christian Worship*, p. 107.

21 Cf. Edward Said, *Orientalism: Western Representations of the Orient*, London: Routledge and Kegan Paul, 1978. Said's monumental work together with Frantz Fanon's writings have greatly influenced postcolonial scholarship.

22 Sugirtharajah, *Postcolonial Reconfigurations*, p. 148.

23 Sugirtharajah, *Postcolonial Reconfigurations*, p. 121.

24 Ruth Duck, *Circles of Care: Hymns and Songs*, Cleveland, OH: Pilgrim Press, 1998, p. ix.

25 Samuel J. Royal makes the observation: 'Hymnal editors and editorial committees for compiling hymns do, to an extent, play significant roles in the determination of what hymns will rise to the pews . . . hymnal editors possess and exercise considerable influence in shaping the definition of the congregational hymn.' *Essays of John Wesley and His Contemporaries: The Texture of the 18th-Century English Culture*, Lampeter: The Edwin Mellen Press, 2007, p. 155.

26 *New Century Hymnal*, Cleveland, OH: Pilgrim Press, 1995, p. ix.

27 See Pete Ward, *Growing Up Evangelical*, London: SPCK, 1994, Chapter 5, and more recently his *Selling Worship*, Milton Keynes: Paternoster Press, 2005.

28 John Bell, '"Sing a New Song": Interview with Christian Century' in *Christian Century* 123/15 (25 July 2006), pp. 20–3 (p. 20).

29 United Reformed Church, *Rejoice and Sing*. Melody Edition. Oxford: Oxford University Press, 1991, p. v.

30 Inderjeet Parmar, '"I am Proud of the British Empire": Why Tony Blair Backs George W. Bush', *The Political Quarterly* (2005), pp. 218–31 (p. 226).

31 Parmar, 'Proud', p. 226.

32 *Hymns Ancient & Modern Revised*, Norwich: Canterbury Press, 1981, p. vi.

33 *Hymns Ancient & Modern Revised*, p. viii.

34 Sugirtharajah, *Postcolonial Reconfigurations*, p. 123.

35 Sugirtharajah, *Postcolonial Reconfigurations*, p. 143.

36 Hymn Book Committee, *Common Praise*, Norwich: Canterbury Press, 2001, p. ix.

37 Sugirtharajah, *Postcolonial Reconfigurations*, p. 125.

38 Church of Scotland, *Common Ground: A Song Book for All the Churches*. Words Edition. Edinburgh: St Andrew's Press, 1998, p. 5.

39 Juan M. C. Oliver, 'Just Praise: Prayer Book Revision and Hispanic/Latino Anglicanism' in Ruth A. Meyers, ed., *Prayerbook for the 21st Century*, New York: Church Publishing, 1996, pp. 256–85 (p. 266).

40 See Karen Westerfield-Tucker, 'A Decade of Christian Song', *Studia Liturgica*, 31 (2001), pp. 193–210.

41 Oliver, 'Just Praise', p. 267.

42 Myke Johnsont, 'Wanting to be Indian: When Spiritual Searching turns into Cultural Theft', Joanne Pearson, ed., *Belief Beyond Boundaries: WICCA, Celtic Spirituality and the New Age*, Aldershot: Ashgate, 2002, pp. 277–94 (p. 281). Our addition in brackets.

43 Hawn, 'Reverse Missions', pp. 102–03.

44 R. S. Sugirtharajah, ed., *Vernacular Hermeneneutics*, Sheffield: Sheffield Academic Press, 1999, p. 12.

45 Westerfield-Tucker, 'Decade of Christian Song', p. 267.

46 John D. Witvliet, 'The Virtue of Liturgical Discernment' in Kroeker, *Music in Christian Worship*, p. 95.

47 Brian Wren, *What Language Shall I Borrow? God-talk in Worship: A Male Response to Feminist Theology*, London: SCM Press, 1990.

48 *New Century Hymnal*, p. 880.

49 June Boyce-Tillman's work is important. See most recently her *Unconventional Wisdom*, London: Equinox, 2008.

6

Liturgy for Liberation

ANTHONY G. REDDIE

The following meditation was conceived as a reflective piece that attempts to get 'inside' and 'under' a familiar biblical text. The aim of this piece is to give voice to and enable oppressed people to use the story/vision (of the gospel) for their ultimate liberation.[1] This work enables black people, in particular, to claim the gospel of Jesus Christ as their own. The meditation proceeds on the basis of imaging a real, marginalized and angry person within the heart of a gospel narrative.

In writing this piece, I have tried to reflect upon where there are silent voices in the story. What would happen if we gave voice to a presence within the narrative that appears to be nothing more than a 'plot device' to enable this particular account to gain some prescience for being a helpful pedagogical tool? How is the story opened up through the insertion of the real emotions, anger and frustrations of the marginalized?

It is my belief that central to the transforming impact of the gospel on people's lives is the need to enable individuals to see themselves as being central players in the narratives of salvation. What would happen if a seemingly insignificant person became the centre of the story?

The crucial learning that results from the theological imagining is the sense that marginalized and oppressed black people begin to see themselves as subjective agents in their interaction with oppressive authority, by means of re-imaging themselves within the sacred narrative of God's involvement with God's all – with all people. In effect, they learn to see themselves not as distant spectators in God's story, but as central players.[2]

This meditation and the educational and theological process implicit within it is a deeply political and ideological act. For this process of self-actualization is one that runs counter to the thrust of our so-called 'New World Order'. If broader society largely confines black people to subservient and demeaning roles, then why should we necessarily expect these selfsame people to imagine themselves in central, defining positions within biblical narratives? This piece of reflective and imaginative theological writing is one that seeks to overturn the top-down, racist, classist, sexist and heterosexist predilections of the world by seeking to give narrative agency and voice to one who is often viewed as other and marginal to all that matters in the world. In effect, it is a way of talking of liberation.

Talking of Liberation
(Based on Luke 18.1–8)

Voice
I sat and waited. I'm sick of the waiting. I have almost lost my voice shouting at the window. I've been here for hours and I am sick of this waiting. I know he's in there and I know that he can hear me. He's trying to pretend that I'm not here. I know his game, but it's not going to work.

Black people have struggled against seemingly unequal forces for centuries. Forced removal, captivity, negative propaganda, frustrated external control and desperate material poverty; we have waited and continue to wait for our liberation. When will the waiting end? When will our cries for justice be heard?

There is a moment's silence

A Prayer
Creator God, who is Mother and Father to all of us, we thank you this day that we have the opportunity to come together, to give thanks and praise to you. We remember this day that we are members of your family, the family of God. A family that stretches from east to west, north to south. From rich to poor, from black to white. We thank you for the diversity you have created in this world, and pray that all members of it, and God's family, may be valued and supported, as you commanded. *May your will be done . . . On earth as it is in Heaven.*

Voice
I began to throw stones at the window . . . Small stones at first, then bigger ones and eventually, almost boulder size. The man inside had to acknowledge me now. Now he heard me. Now he wanted to talk. Began to call me a vandal. An uncouth thug and worse. But all I want is justice. How comes I get labelled when all I want is to get what is owed to me. To get what I deserve. Is that too much to ask?

Such is the inequitable system in which black people have existed for several hundred years we now find ourselves on the receiving end of the negative barbs and assertions of others. We are victims and yet our cries for justice remain unheard and we get the blame for the condition in which others have placed us.

There is a moment's silence

A Prayer

We remember those within the worldwide family of God, who suffer daily the pains of hunger and poverty. We think especially of those who are stigmatized and ridiculed for simply attempting to find a way of establishing their very existence and presence in the world. We pray for those whose silence is increased by the tendency of the powerful elite to ignore and pillory them. So while the majority of the family experience sad and inhuman conditions, the comfortable minority have more than they need and enjoy that which the majority can only imagine. This is not your intention for the world you created. *May your will be done . . . On earth as it is in Heaven.*

Voice

The police came by, asking me to move on. I was creating a disturbance. Now that's rich, I thought to myself. I'm fighting for justice and the man whose job it is to see that I get it is ignoring me; but yet I'm still the one at fault. How can that work?

It is the easiest thing in the world to blame others for the condition in which they find themselves. The powerful create the system and then impose it on those who are weaker than them. The powerful then police and administer this inequitable state of affairs. And finally, in perhaps the worst irony of all, they blame the powerless for creating their own misery. The best trick of all is to wrap this cheap notion of injustice within the warm cosy glow of so-called Christian morality. It's so easy to do. Even good Christian Prime Ministers do it – linking African poverty to poor governance and corruption. Who taught them how to be corrupt in the first place?

There is a moment's silence

A Prayer

We think this day of the hard places in the world. The places of conflict and turmoil. The places of struggle and oppression. We think of countries where one group of the population is in opposition with another. Those countries where a minority of the population is persecuted by the majority. Those places in the world where human rights and human dignity for all people are not in evidence and there is no sense of justice. This was not your intention. *May your will be done . . . On earth as it is in Heaven.*

Voice
So there I stood, refusing to be moved. If they think that I'm going quietly then they simply don't know anything about me. I've been here too long, seen too much, faced too much heartache and pain to give in and give up now. I am going to get him inside to deal with me. He will deal with me. He will. He will.
The struggle for liberation has taken on many forms and phases. Slavery gave way to colonialism, which in turn moved into economic slavery and dependence; and now there is AIDS. We are still shouting at the people who can give us justice. Our prayers continue and we are still waiting.

There is a moment's silence

A Prayer
The worldwide family of God is made up of people both far away and closer to home. We remember the people within our country, who are marginalized. Those who are on the edge of society. Those who have no stake. Those who are left to fend for themselves, to carry the stigma of hurtful labels, snide remarks and societal indifference. Help us to remember that your family is made up of all people, and not just the ones we think or consider to be suitable or acceptable. Your Son Jesus died that we all might live, and live life to the fullest. This is your intention.

Voice
And so, I'm still waiting. My standing here has caused difficulties for so many people. The authorities have been doing their best to smear me in the press. They've dug up distant relatives and paid them cash to dis me in public – I can't remember half the things I'm supposed to have done. These people? Why don't they just deal with me? I have a right to be heard and I'm not going away. I don't care how many of my former lovers they dig up to trash my reputation; I will be heard. They will listen to me. I've come too far to be humbled and dismissed now.

The continued challenge for the powerless is to continue to 'hang in there' and not succumb to despair. The struggle is one that demands endless patience and fortitude. It is the challenge to keep hope alive and to believe that some day in the realizable future, justice and equity will prevail. It is a belief in a form of hope beyond hope. A belief in the power of God to change hearts, to humble the powerful, in partnership with the powerless, to bring about a new reality for all who are on the outside, railing against the doors of injustice in order to be heard.

There is a moment's silence

A Prayer

We bring before you, Creator God, the much loved men and women whose presence illuminates our lives, and who bring a sense of joy to all who come into contact with them. We remember what these people have done. We remember their gifts and insights. The way they often possess the gift for bringing disparate people together. People who might normally look upon one another with suspicion and scorn. For their gift of finding the best in people and encouraging those individuals to share their best with others. Creator God, we ask that your peace be with these unique individuals, and the families who sustain and support them in their ongoing lives and ministries. *May your will be done ... On earth as it is in Heaven.*

Voice

At last ... The door opened and out he came. Full of arrogance and indignation. 'Did I know how much trouble I had caused? Was I aware of how bad I had made him look?' I don't know how I didn't burst out laughing! After all I've been through and all he had to say was how I had made him look! 'You really are on a different planet to me,' I thought. So there we stood, each glowering at the other. He was so angry. For a moment, I was really scared. 'Look what you've done', I thought to myself. But then I remembered everything I've been through. The hardship and the endless waiting! Then I stopped being scared. He motioned for me to follow him inside. I took a deep breath and followed him in ... At last!

And so the struggle goes on. We wait, trying to hold onto patience, but most importantly, determined not to lose our dignity. We wait and then, finally, once in an isolated while, someone comes from the inside and condescends to meet with us. They offer cheap platitudes or veiled threats; often both in the same breath. We are told how difficult we have been and how this really isn't the way in which things are done in the polite and refined world in which we live. Or do they mean themselves? Talks take place, not because there is a sudden thirst for justice after the arid sterility of the desert of injustice. Rather, it is the fact that the public relations people have been on to them and assured them this is not playing well in the media, that they should begin talks and be seen as flexible and compassionate. The dance of charade and mutual suspicion continues. And black people across the world continue to wait.

There is a moment's silence

A Prayer

Forgive our failures to listen to your world and to learn from it. We think of those who misunderstand us or cross the boundaries that we want to make. Help us to avoid the temptation to hide inside our comfortable walls of complacency. The whole world is yours and the created things within it. We give thanks, Creator God, for this beautiful world you have made. We respect it and the people of your family who live within it. In your name we pray. AMEN

Notes

1 See Thomas Groome, *Christian Religious Education*, San Francisco: Jossey-Bass, 1999.
2 See Anthony Reddie, *Growing into Hope: Liberation and Change*, Peterborough: Methodist Publishing House, 1998, pp. 8–9.

7

'Strangers' in the Sanctuary:
Asylum Seekers, Faith and the Church

SUSANNA SNYDER

Introduction

Asylum seekers are among the most marginalized people in British society. They come to Britain seeking refuge from violence or political abuse in their home countries, yet often find themselves experiencing more hardship, hatred and insecurity here. Each year, about two-thirds of asylum applications made to the Home Office are ultimately refused and public hostility is prevalent.[1] One post 7/7 headline read, 'Gratitude! Their families came here seeking asylum and were given homes, schooling and all the benefits of British life. How do they repay us? By trying to blow us up.'[2] Another back in 2003 claimed, 'Asylum seekers eat our donkeys'.[3] While their claims are being processed, most asylum seekers are provided with basic accommodation and a small weekly allowance for essentials.[4] However, this meagre support is withdrawn if a final appeal is unsuccessful and asylum seekers then find themselves destitute. Many find it impossible either to return home or look forward and build a future. Kadir, a 25-year-old man, tells of how he fled Sudan after his village was attacked and his family murdered. He arrived in the UK in December 2005 and when his final appeal was refused, he had little choice but to live rough. He is now anxious and ill:

> I feel depressed and hopeless. I feel less than human – like an animal. I hate myself. I left my country to escape imprisonment, suffering and death. Here I fear hunger and homelessness . . . I wouldn't have to ask any more questions if I was dead.[5]

It has been estimated that in Birmingham alone, there are between 1,000 and 2,000 destitute asylum seekers.[6]

For many asylum seekers, faith is an important source of sustenance and energy. Religious networks often play a significant part in enabling people to make their journey in the first place, and they continue to provide a sense of identity and emotional and spiritual support in the new country. Indeed, Peggy Levitt has explored the role of religion in the migration process and suggests that faith is often used by migrants to 'delineate an alternative cartography of belonging'.[7] Religious networks can encourage and facilitate migrants' entry into the local community and prayer and scripture reading frequently provide a comforting anchor or spring of hope. Other researchers have shown how Guatemalan Mayan migrants use their Catholic faith in processes of decision making, preparation, journeying, settlement and forming transnational linkages and how Islam has provided an important source of stability for Somali refugee women trying to reconstruct their lives in Melbourne.[8]

What is more, many churches and Christians offer significant practical, day-to-day support for asylum seekers, plugging the gaps in statutory support. In Birmingham for example, *Restore*,[9] an ecumenical Christian body, organizes one-to-one volunteer befriending, a summer holiday programme for children and awareness-raising sessions. It also provides information and support for a variety of local church groups, which in turn undertake everything from providing English classes, clothes and food to campaigning against destitution. Across the UK, Christian volunteers accompany asylum seekers to court hearings and MP surgeries, visit people held in removal centres and offer basic practical advice and emotional support.

Given the importance of faith and faith communities in the lives of many asylum seekers, it is surprising that there has been little discussion among Christians of how asylum seekers *worship* when they come to Britain. How, for instance, are asylum seekers engaging in church services? How is the issue of asylum seeking explored in Christian liturgies?

In this chapter, I offer some tentative and unsystematic thoughts on these issues. These thoughts arise from my experience of worshipping and talking with asylum seekers in various contexts in the UK and are focused on asylum seekers' engagement with mainstream Christian denominations.[10] I am self-consciously writing as a middle-class, white, ordained, British woman and, while recognizing that it is inherently problematic, I use 'they' to refer to those seeking asylum according to the UN's 1951 Convention on Refugees and 'we' to refer to members of the UK host population.[11]

Two kinds of approach

Offering the 'standard'

One approach to asylum seekers within the church is to welcome them into our ordinary, standard Sunday services. This approach has its merits.

Many asylum seekers have come from countries with a colonial European past and are therefore familiar with the traditional services brought by missionaries. Some have grown up in the Roman Catholic tradition, others within Anglicanism or Methodism. At a time when everything else is in flux and people are experiencing uncertainty and insecurity, to come to a 'bog standard' or traditional service – to have the security of receiving communion in a recognizable manner and hearing familiar biblical passages – can be comforting and helpful. It provides a known and normalizing space where people seeking asylum can just be human beings, rather than being labelled and identified as 'asylum seekers'. It provides a space where they can worship as they have been used to doing so regularly at home.

However, there is perhaps a danger to be aware of with this approach. If all we are doing is going on 'as usual' it may be very easy for us to exclude newcomers, especially if they appear strange or different. Asylum seekers can attend services without being spoken to or only being acknowledged by a few members of the congregation who make a special effort to seek them out. While some churches do seem to manage to include asylum seekers fully in their church lives, others seem to welcome asylum seekers only to the extent that they are allowed to be present in the congregation. In these places, few congregation members acknowledge asylum seekers' presence and fewer still go out of their way to get to know or support them. This is often not a matter of deliberate exclusion, but rather exclusion by accident. People may be worried about what to say to those who have been through traumatic events or whose English is not fluent, or they may have absorbed negative opinions about asylum seekers from the press.

However, this is not an entirely new problem. In the 1950s and 1960s, many Christians came to Britain from the Caribbean and tried to become part of existing Anglican, Methodist, Baptist and Roman Catholic congregations. Often, they were made to feel very unwelcome when ministers and lay members explicitly stated that they did not want black people in 'their' church. Where black people were 'invited' in, they still frequently felt at the edge of the community, excluded from central decision-making processes and lacking access to power. It is likely that this racism, rejection and misunderstanding encouraged some black people to leave the mainstream churches.[12] Today, we still need to be aware of racism and xenophobia in our churches and how easily we can succeed in excluding people even if unintentionally.[13]

Matthew Guest has explored the social functions of worship within a community and argues that the way in which we worship has a significant effect on how we relate to one another:

> Worship events are often key contexts in which relations of power are negotiated, as they bring church communities together in a public space. At such events, norms of authority and hierarchy are often implicit in the very structure of devotional practice.[14]

If we wish fully to include and empower asylum seekers in our 'normal' week-by-week worshipping life and avoid simply reflecting the hostility and powerlessness which asylum seekers feel in society, we need to ask ourselves some important questions. Who, for example, is allowed to speak, pray, read and administer the sacrament in our main services? Are asylum seekers and refugees consulted about important decisions? Are asylum seekers' stories and experiences given a space to be heard? If English is not an asylum seeker's first language, are we trying to find ways in which the liturgy, service booklets and conversation may be available in his or her mother tongue? Essentially, are we providing a space where asylum seekers are offered more respect and access to power than they are generally in society?[15]

I am not suggesting that it is at all easy to include asylum seekers in these ways as it requires considerable effort over a long period of time. Moreover, asylum seekers live very transient and unstable lives and are not necessarily interested in taking part in committees or in reading lessons. What I am suggesting, however, is that it is important for us to be aware of and grapple with these questions.

Creating 'supportive bubbles'

Another approach towards worship and asylum seekers which I have encountered is to create separate and specific liturgies around the issue of asylum seeking. These services can include asylum seeker, but more often than not they are attended predominantly by host country 'supporters'.

In these services, the issue of asylum seeking is considered deeply and intelligently and the readings, reflections, stories, prayers and music are chosen around a theme specifically related to seeking asylum. These themes include pilgrimage and journeying, sanctuary, welcome and hospitality and what it means to be strangers in a strange land. These services provide an important, safe and set-aside space for reflection and spiritual refreshment – a supportive 'bubble' – and can be moving and transformative.

In May 2006, for instance, I was invited to offer a biblical reflection for a weekend *Restore* was organizing for asylum seekers and their supporters in Birmingham. I spoke about Abraham and his identity as a wanderer and stranger, and about Hagar and God's presence with her even though she had been sent away by Sarah. Then, we all came forward, lit candles and placed them by a bowl of water. This symbolized a prayer for God to be with us or with someone else for whom we were concerned. While offering these prayers, we listened to *Full Force Gale* by Van Morrison – a song about life's wandering journey and finding one's home, rest, roots and 'sanctuary' in God. I found this short time of prayer after the reflection deeply poignant and encouraging, and people from both Christian and Muslim backgrounds, asylum seekers and members of the host community took part.

A short interfaith reflection I attended at St Mary Magdalene Refugee Project on Holloway Road, London, was inspiring and refreshing in a different way. Every Friday, the project co-ordinator arranges chairs in a circle and creates a space for prayer. On the occasion I was there, we passed a candle around in silence offering our own prayer while meditative music was played in the background. Closing reflections and prayers at meetings of the London Churches' Refugee Forum have also created an important space for affirmation and re-commitment for those working alongside asylum seekers.

As well as these intimate, meditative and informal liturgies, there are also longer and more formal services, which have been created around the theme of asylum seeking or migration more generally. Every December in Britain, there are services held on Migration Day and Christians from different denominations work together to compile them. In Australia, the National Council of Churches produces a complete and downloadable liturgy for their Refugee and Migrant Sunday in August. There is also a liturgy on the theme specifically designed for children.[16] The Iona Community has published a 'Refugee Evensong' and Michael Jagessar has written a 'Service of Word and Table' around the theme of seeking asylum. Here, Jagessar interrupts and juxtaposes the narrative of the Eucharist with the narrative of 'every refugee and stranger in your midst'.[17]

All of these services, the small intimate ones and the larger, more formal occasions draw on a range of readings, prayers, poems and reflections. Popular biblical passages include Matthew 25.35, 'for I was hungry and you gave me food, I was thirsty and you gave me something to drink, I was a stranger and you welcomed me', Hebrews 13.2, 'Do not neglect to show hospitality to strangers, for by doing that some have entertained angels without knowing it', and Psalm 137.[18] Other materials are drawn from a variety of sources, two of which are particularly rich and helpful. The Jesuit Refugee Service gathers together confessions, readings, reflections and intercessions written by refugees all over the world and those who support them. Some of these can be found in their publication, *God in Exile*, while below are examples from their website.[19]

Prayer by Victor Hategekimana, a refugee at the JRS Kampala English language school

Lord, turn your eyes towards us:
We are far away from our countries;
We are like prisoners without liberty –
Which is why we say we are not free.

Life is full of all kinds of difficulties:
Poverty, hunger, disease and despair!
We try our best to make ends meet,
But life remains insupportable.

In the Refugee Agencies we get all sorts of problems,
Because we can not use the language they use:
Some among us are assisted:
Others thrown out, neglected, told to come back tomorrow:
Life becomes a mountain insurmountable:
To mount our Calvary becomes impossible.
We are wondering what will come tomorrow,
But we remain without hope of tomorrow.

All this you see and you keep in mind,
But, about it, Lord, you do not say anything.

Lord, we are begging your mercy:
Bring into the hearts of your people peace;

We want to be freed from being refugees!
Lord, turn your eyes towards us.

A Christian Response, JRS Australia based on Matthew 25.37

I was a refugee
and you blamed the communists
for causing the revolution.
I was a refugee
and you said the West
shouldn't have interfered;
I was a refugee
and you launched
another satellite;
I was a refugee
and daily you built
five nuclear weapons;
I was a refugee
and you told me to wait;

I was a refugee
and you accused me
of being an 'economic migrant';
I was a refugee
and you said *we prefer people
who speak good English*;
I was a refugee
and you said *we only accept people
who are sponsored by parents or children*;
I was a refugee and you said *we've got compassion fatigue.*

The second particularly useful sets of resources are the anthologies compiled by Geoffrey Duncan. *Entertaining Angels: A Worship Anthology on Sharing Christ's Hospitality* contains a wealth of material on the theme of refugees and asylum seekers drawn from all over the world, including confessions, ideas for Refugee Sunday, a children's liturgy and intercessions. There are responsorial prayers from the Anglican Church of Canada which involve the use of visual symbols, a reflection from South India and responses based on material from the Christian Conference of Asia.[20] Here are three examples:

A Prayer from CAFOD, England

Lord, no one is a stranger to you
and no one is ever far from
your loving care.
In your kindness watch over refugees
and exiles,
those separated from their loved ones,
young people who are lost,
and those who have left or run away
from home.
Bring them back safely to the place
where they long to be
and help us always to show your kindness
to strangers and to those in need.[21]

'Asylum Seekers' by Ann Lewin, England

They live under the shadow of
A two-edged sword: in a place of safety
And a state of fear. The rules
Ensure we are kept safe; our fear
Defines our hospitality,
Keeps them on edge.
Compassion is constrained
By prudent care.

Could we, instead of seeing problems,
Begin to recognise the gifts they bring,
And be enriched by their humanity?[22]

Refugees – a Confession from the South African Bishops' Conference (adapted by CAFOD)

Lord, we ask your pardon for our ignorance
of the plight of refugees in our country.
Lord have mercy
Lord have mercy.

Lord, we ask for pardon for the way in which our country
has contributed to the wars in other countries
that have produced so many refugees.

Christ have mercy
Christ have mercy.

Lord, we ask pardon for our poor response to those asylum seekers
who sit in detention centres within our country
and for all those children, women and men
who will suffer from our government's policies.
Lord have mercy.
Lord have mercy.[23]

There are also helpful reflections on welcoming strangers and a prayer
for detained asylum seekers in *Seeing Christ in Others*.[24]

This 'supportive bubble' approach can be very helpful and encourages many supporters to continue their vital and positive engagement
with asylum seekers. However, as with the 'offering the standard'
approach, it also has potential drawbacks. First, these liturgies tend to
attract those already involved in supporting refugees and asylum seekers
and there is thus a danger that such services simply end up preaching to
the converted. It is rare to find prayers or reflections like these being
used in regular Sunday services and members of the host community
who do not choose to attend specific asylum seeker-related services may
never hear or engage with this material. Second, although there is some
worship material written by refugees and asylum seekers, most of the
services I have attended have seemed to be more for supporters than
for asylum seekers themselves. When there have been asylum seekers
present, they have seldom led any parts of the liturgy. Is there perhaps a
danger that often we are engaging in liturgy *about* asylum seekers rather
than *with* them?

Third, whereas the 'offering the standard' approach risked asylum
seekers being ignored, the 'supportive bubble' approach risks reinforcing the negative labelling of people as 'asylum seekers'. In services that
are solely focused around the theme of seeking asylum, asylum seekers
are inevitably primarily identified as displaced, disadvantaged people
and all others present as supportive members of the host community.
Robert Winder has pointed out the dangers of this and suggests that
those seeking to support refugees can ironically help to reinforce negative stereotypes. He claims that in the nineteenth century, nationalists
and defenders of Irish immigrants 'added crude glitter to the same
cartoon'. Nationalists amplified the myth of Irish ugliness to emphasize
their own superiority while defenders did the same to highlight the
wickedness of English oppressors. There was thus a 'strange collusion

between enemies and friends'.[25] Today, in a society which insists on labelling people seeking refuge as 'asylum seekers', would it be more helpful and empowering for Christians to create worship contexts in which people seeking refuge in the UK could be known primarily as mothers or doctors or teenagers or Iraqi rather than as 'asylum seekers'?

Being transformed by 'strangers'

The 'offering the standard' and 'creating supportive bubble' approaches clearly both have positive and helpful aspects. However, neither seems to be entirely adequate on its own. Should we therefore be trying to find a way of holding the two approaches together? Should we be making connections between what we do in the 'supportive bubbles' and what we do as 'standard' on Sunday mornings? I would like to suggest simply one way in which this might be possible, a way which involves recognizing the importance of allowing ourselves to be transformed by 'strangers'.

Worship is all about transformation. As Gordon Lathrop has suggested, it should turn us 'inside out'.[26] Or as Robert Hovda has put it,

> Good liturgical celebration, like a parable, takes us by the hairs of our heads, lifts us momentarily out of the cesspool of injustice we call home, puts us in the promised and challenging reign of God, where we are treated like we have never been treated anywhere else.[27]

It should help those present to have a transforming encounter with God. This God is one who is beyond us but who can also be known through others and especially through strangers.[28] Drawing on the Emmaus story in Luke 24.13–35, N. Lynne Westfield suggests that meeting Jesus 'occurs when ordinary strangers, people estranged from themselves and each other, dare to invite each other to the table'.[29] She argues that sharing and risking are vital because in so doing,

> both guest and host allow each other to step across the threshold into Mystery. Mystery gives way to familiarity . . . In the presence of God, invoked by gathered strangers, we are our most connected, familial, human selves. Mystery also gives way to surprise.[30]

Similarly, Philip Sheldrake suggests the importance of journeying across boundaries to encounter God, of being nomads and allowing the 'other' to disrupt and challenge us.[31] 'The presence of God acting in the within of all things is always strange and elusive, overflowing boundaries into what is "other" . . . God is the disruptive action within each person that decentres this illusory centre.'[32]

Asylum seekers are strangers in British society 'par excellence' – they come from other countries, often do not speak English and are excluded from mainstream services. Thus, actively engaging with them surely has the potential to challenge us, to renew our faith, reinvigorate our understanding of God and help us to see in a new way. Instead of seeing asylum seekers either as simply more worshippers for our 'standard' services or as people in need of specific help and separate liturgies, we should perhaps begin to think about how their presence and experience is calling us to transform what we currently do as 'normal' in our main Sunday worship.[33]

First, might asylum seekers help us to recognize and engage with our own identity as strangers and enrich our understanding of what this means? Our fundamental human identity as strangers is a theme woven throughout the Bible. In the Hebrew Bible, the people of Israel live in exile in Egypt, journey to the Promised Land and then find themselves in exile again in Babylon. In the New Testament, Jesus reveals himself to be the ultimate and divine stranger and his early followers described themselves as strangers in this world.[34] Could we therefore begin to explore, through our preaching and prayer, connections between asylum seekers' stories, our own experiences of exile and our faith?[35]

Second, could the presence of asylum seekers among us encourage us to grapple with some of the problematic aspects of the Bible? There are a number of passages which tend to be overlooked in the Sunday lectionary, including those containing negative attitudes towards foreigners. The books of Ezra and Nehemiah are just two examples.[36] The presence of asylum seekers calls us to engage with these passages at the edges of scriptural respectability, to own them as part of our tradition and to struggle with them together as a community.

Third, do the experiences of asylum seekers call us to rediscover the practice of lament as part of our 'standard' worship? In *Praying in Exile*, Gordon Mursell stresses the importance of lament for those in exile:

> [T]he exile must first come to terms with the present, and one way to do that is through lament. In the language of spirituality, lament might be described as the way you respond when faith and experience collide painfully with one another. It is supremely the prayer of the

powerless, of those not in control of what is happening to them. And it is closely linked to memory.[37]

Most of our churches are poor at creating spaces for lament, spaces where traumatic stories or pain can be voiced publicly. We tend to focus more on experiences of blessing and hope than we do on experiences of fear and apparent divine abandonment. However, it is absolutely vital to bring our deep pain, rage and profound unanswered questions before God and one another in all their rawness. The authors of Psalm 22, Lamentations and Job recognized this and, indeed, Jesus himself cried out to God, 'My God, my God, why have you forsaken me?'[38] In creating a space for asylum seekers to voice their lament within worship, we may also give permission to ourselves to do the same.

Fourth, could asylum seekers' presence renew and challenge our understanding and experience of the Eucharist? Tissa Balasuriya argued in the 1970s that the Eucharist had been

> domesticated within the dominant social establishments of the day. Its radical demands have been largely neutralised. Its cutting edge has been blunted . . . Why is it that persons and people who proclaim Eucharistic love and sharing deprive the poor people of the world of food, capital, employment and even land?[39]

He stressed that the Eucharist has to result in liberative action for the oppressed if it is to be authentic. More recently, Nicholas Sagovsky has argued, 'The practice of the Eucharist is a dynamic for the practice of justice, not only within the church but in the wider political arena.'[40] He suggests that celebrating the Eucharist is an enactment of liberation, a symbolic meeting of human need in the sharing of bread and wine which entails a dynamic commitment to meeting human need in every form and an expression of the hope that one day unjust regimes will be overthrown by the reign of God. The presence of asylum seekers at our eucharistic tables reminds us that the Church is not supposed to be a club of socially, economically, culturally or ethnically similar people and that we are not engaged in an exclusive religious practice which has little meaning beyond church walls. Asylum seekers call us to rediscover the Eucharist as a radically socially inclusive and political act. It is an act in which 'the other [should be] encountered and social difference transcended' and where all should be able to experience the hospitality of God.[41] It is an act which should encourage and equip us to go out and strive for justice and equality in our world.

Notes

1 Amnesty International, *Down and Out in London: The road to destitution for rejected asylum seekers*. London: Amnesty International, 2006, p. 5. See <http://www.homeoffice.gov.uk/rds/immigration.html> for the latest Home Office asylum statistics.

2 *The Daily Mail*, 28 July 2005.

3 The *Daily Star*, 21 August 2003. For more on negative press coverage of asylum seekers, see UNHCR, *Refugees*, No. 142, Issue 1, 2006 and The Information Centre about Asylum and Refugees in the UK, *Media Image, Community Impact: Assessing the impact of media and political images of refugees and asylum seekers on community relations in London*. London: ICAR, April 2004.

4 Others are held in removal centres.

5 Case study in a special edition of *The Common Ground*: 'The Stranger Within: towards a more progressive asylum policy', London: Christian Socialist Movement, Summer 2006, p. 14.

6 Richard Malfait and Nick Scott-Flynn, *Destitution of Asylum Seekers and Refugees in Birmingham*, Unpublished Report, 2005, p. 9. See also Amnesty International, *Down and Out*, p. 13.

7 Peggy Levitt, ' "You Know, Abraham Was Really the First Immigrant": Religion and Transnational Migration', *International Migration Review*, 37:3 (Fall 2003), p. 861.

8 J. Hagan and H. R. Ebaugh, 'Calling Upon the Sacred: Migrants' Use of Religion in the Migration Process', in *International Migration Review* 37:4 (Winter 2003), pp. 1145–62; C. McMichael, ' "Everywhere is Allah's Place": Islam and the Everyday Life of Somali Women in Melbourne, Australia', in *International Migration Review* 37:4 (Winter 2003), pp. 171–88. For more on the role of religion in the migration and settlement process, see the special edition of the *Journal of Refugee Studies*, 'Religion and Spirituality in Forced Migration', 15:2 (2002).

9 See <http://www.restore-uk.org/> for more on *Restore*.

10 There is unfortunately no scope here for discussion of asylum seekers' involvement in Pentecostal churches or in Islamic, Jewish and other worshipping communities in the UK. This is an important area for future research.

11 The 1951 UN Convention defines a refugee as someone who 'owing to a well-founded fear of being persecuted for reasons of race, religion, nationality, membership of a particular group or political opinion, is outside the country of his nationality and is unable or, owing to such fear, is unwilling to avail himself of the protection of that country.'

12 See Joe Aldred, *Respect: Understanding Caribbean British Christianity*, Epworth Press: Peterborough, 2005, p. 84; Anthony Reddie, *Nobodies to Somebodies: A Practical Theology for Education and Liberation*, Peterborough: Epworth Press, 2003; Robert Bedford, *Jesus is Dread: Black Theology and Black Culture in Britain*, London: DLT, 1998; John Wilkinson, *Church in Black and White*, Edinburgh: St Andrew Press, 1993; Ken Leech, *Race*, London: SPCK, 2005; and Mukti Barton, *Rejection, Resistance and Resurrection: Speaking Out Against Racism in the Church*, London: DLT, 2005, for perspectives on racism in the mainstream churches.

13 This said, it is worth noting that increasing numbers of immigrants and refugees do not wish to participate in mainstream Christian denominations. Many consciously choose to worship with their own ethnic group in a very specific style.

14 Matthew Guest, 'Sociological Strand – Worship and Action', in Helen Cameron, Douglas Davies, Philip Richter and Frances Ward, eds, *Studying Local Churches: Perspectives on the Local Church*, London: SCM Press, 2005, p. 100.

15 Thomas R. Whelan discusses issues of inclusion in 'Racism and Worship in Ireland' in Thomas R. Whelan, ed., *The Stranger in Our Midst: Refugees in Ireland: Causes, Experiences, Responses*, Dublin: Kimmage Mission Institute of Theology and Cultures, 2001, pp. 53–69.

16 See <http://www.ncca.org.au/cws/rdp/worship_resources>. There are plenty of other good liturgical resources exploring the theme of seeking asylum on this excellent website.

17 'Refugee Evensong' by the Woolman House Community in Neil Paynter and Helen Boothroyd, *Holy Ground: Liturgies and worship resources for an engaged spirituality*, Glasgow: Wild Goose, 2005, pp. 20–4. Michael Jagessar's liturgy is unpublished, but can be downloaded at <http://www.lifewords.info/asylum/reflect/services.html>.

18 All biblical quotations are from the New Revised Standard Version.

19 Jesuit Refugee Service, *God in Exile: Towards a shared spirituality with refugees*, Rome: JRS, 2005. This can also be downloaded at <http://www.with.jrs.net/files/GodinExile.pdf>. The resources can be found on the 'Liturgy Resources' page of <http://www.jrsuk.net>. Permission to use selected texts has been granted by the copyright holder.

20 Geoffrey Duncan, ed., *Entertaining Angels: A Worship Anthology on Sharing Christ's Hospitality*, Norwich: Canterbury Press, 2005. Texts are used with the permission of CAFOD, Romero Close, London, SW9 9TY.

21 Duncan, *Entertaining Angels*, p. 102.

22 Duncan, *Entertaining Angels*, p. 106. Ann Lewin in *Watching for the Kingfisher*, published by Methodist Publishing House. Permission granted by the author.

23 Duncan, *Entertaining Angels*, p. 108.

24 See Geoffrey Duncan, ed., *Seeing Christ in Others*, new edition, Norwich: Canterbury Press, 2002.

25 Robert Winder, *Bloody Foreigners: The Story of Immigration to Britain*, London: Abacus, 2005 [2004]), pp. 212, 468.

26 Gordon Lathrop, 'Liturgy and Mission in a North American Context', in Thomas Schattauer, ed., *Inside Out: Worship in an Age of Mission*, Minneapolis, MN: Fortress Press, 1999, pp. 201–12 (202).

27 Robert Hovda, 'The Vesting of Liturgical Ministers', in John Baldovin, ed., *Robert Hovda: The Amen Corner*, Collegeville, MN: Liturgical Press, 1994, pp. 213–33 (220). See also Don E. Saliers, *Worship as Theology: Foretaste of Glory Divine*, Nashville, TN: Abingdon Press, 1994.

28 See my article, 'The Dangers of "Doing our Duty": Reflections on Churches Engaging with People Seeking Asylum in the UK' in *Theology*, Vol. CX, No. 857, pp. 351–60 for a more detailed discussion on the idea of God becoming known through strangers.

29 N. Lynne Westfield, *Dear Sisters: A Womanist Practice of Hospitality*, Cleveland, OH: Pilgrim Press, 2001, p. 113.

30 Westfield, *Dear Sisters*, p. 114.

31 Philip Sheldrake, *Spaces for the Sacred*, London: SCM Press, 2001.

32 Sheldrake, *Spaces*, pp. 67–8.

33 Duncan Forrester argues for the liberating transformation of Christian worship. He suggests that Christian worship 'cannot be separated from a concern for liberation . . . Worship must be freed, if it is itself to be liberating.' See 'The Liberation of Worship' in Duncan B. Forrester, *Theological Fragments: Explorations in Unsystematic Theology*, Edinburgh: T&T Clark, 2005, pp. 107–08.

34 See, for example, Deuteronomy 10.19; Hebrews 11.13; 1 Peter 1. Stanley Hauerwas famously described Christians as 'resident aliens' in Stanley Hauerwas and William H. Willimon, *Resident Aliens*, Nashville, TN: Abingdon Press, 1989.

35 Julia Kristeva has explored how foreigners reveal to us the stranger within ourselves. See *Strangers to Ourselves*, New York: Columbia University Press, 1991.

36 Daniel L. Smith-Christopher explores a variety of texts which express hostility towards foreigners in 'Between Ezra and Isaiah: Exclusion, Transformation and Inclusion of the "Foreigner" in Post-Exilic Biblical Theology', in Mark Brett, ed., *Ethnicity and the Bible*, Leiden: Brill, 1996, pp. 117–42. For a discussion around exclusivity in Pauline texts, see Daniel Boyarin, *A Radical Jew: Paul and the Politics of Identity*, Berkeley, CA: University of California Press, 1994, p. 24.

37 Gordon Mursell, *Praying in Exile*, London: SPCK, 2005, p. 40. See also Kathleen M. O'Connor, *Lamentations and the Tears of the World*, Maryknoll, NY: Orbis, 2002.

38 Mark 15.34.

39 Tissa Balasuriya, *The Eucharist and Human Liberation*, London: SCM Press, 1979, pp. xi–xii.

40 Nicholas Sagovsky, 'The Eucharist and the Practice of Justice', *Studies in Christian Ethics* 15.1 (2002), pp. 75–96 (87).

41 Sheldrake, *Spaces*, p. 114. See also Stephen Burns, *Worship in Context: Liturgical Theology, Children and the City*, Peterborough: Epworth Press, 2006.

Part 3

Body Theology

Introduction

Liturgy takes place within the body of Christ, the gathered ecclesial community which, in both its brokenness and its risen potential, recall and re-member the broken and risen body of Jesus. Liturgy, then, of all theological disciplines, should be rooted and grounded in sensitive awareness of 'the body': the body politic and the social body, as well as the actual bodies of the women, men and children who come together to make prayer and praise. Yet too often liturgical studies have either assumed a kind of normative (typically adult, male, white, able-bodied, educated and so on) body as the subject of liturgy, or proceeded as if liturgy is really the business of disembodied spirits who neither touch, feel, see, hear nor experience bodily longings or pains.

The essays in this section eschew any idea of a typical, normative body. Each is written from the perspective of a particular body experience and location, sometimes the writer's own (Jane Wallman-Girdlestone), but in one case (Frances Young) that of the writer's son and in another (John Hull), reflecting empathetically from the experience of blindness into the parallel experience of deafness, while in another again (Claire Carson and Nicola Slee), two contrasting experiences of relating to food provide perspectives for a dialogue on eating disorders. From diverse experiences of profound learning disability and linguistic marginalization, visual impairment and the experience of an eating disorder, each of the writers explores the ways in which a highly particular bodily condition has been both the occasion of social exclusion and also of insight into gospel values: of what it means to live and pray as a person inhabiting this particular body, with its unique and unrepeatable pains, limitations, glories and sensitivities. Each offers a critique of the Church's liturgy, highlighting the ways in which both liturgical texts and practices frequently function to impose oppressive meanings of the body on the people of God; in doing so, they create an awareness in the reader of the need for a more expansive and inclusive praxis.

Thus, Frances Young reflects on the meaning that liturgical participation can have for someone, like her son, who has profound learning difficulties and cannot communicate via language; in doing so, she widens the meaning of authentic participation in liturgy for all of us. Jane Wallman-Girdlestone writes about her experience of belonging to the Church from the perspective of visual impairment, playing with the metaphor of 'edges' in interesting ways (notably celebrating rather than seeking to correct the 'blurring' of ecclesial and theological edges), and offering some examples of rituals based on play therapy that are intended to be inclusive liturgies of healing – where healing is understood in its widest sense. John Hull is well known for his critique of biblical and liturgical sources from the perspective of blindness; in his essay for this book, he offers a critique of hymnody from the perspective of deafness as a way of heightening sensitivity within the ecclesial body of the way in which language and imagery can unwittingly wound and alienate those with hearing impairment. Finally, Claire Carson and Nicola Slee reflect on ways in which liturgical rites – particularly, though not exclusively eucharistic rites – can exclude and cause pain to those with eating disorders, and offer some texts that employ metaphors and imagery of food and eating in more liberating and expansive ways.

8

Songs without Words:

Incorporating the Linguistically Marginalized

FRANCES YOUNG

Introduction

Arthur, my eldest son, is unable to use language to communicate, and it is doubtful whether he really understands many words at all, though some he tries to copy and others he apparently responds to. He has profound learning disabilities as a result of pre-natal developmental failure: he was deprived of nourishment and oxygen in the womb because the placenta was insufficient. In his fortieth year, he is entirely dependent, has no mobility or self-help skills. However, he is part of my ministry. He regularly accompanies me to church, usually enjoys being there, and except when distracted by music, makes a lot of inarticulate noise, especially if there is a stimulating echo! This is an attempt at reflection on what this lack of language means for him, as well as for us, and what the implications might be for public worship.

Let me begin with a couple of stories.[1]

First, when Arthur was a late teenager, I was invited to be the study leader for a week at the Othona community. Each morning and evening we gathered for prayers in the oldest place of Christian worship in England, St Peter's-on-the-Wall at Bradwell in Essex, built out of the stones of the old Roman fort of Othona – hence the community's name. Arthur's wheelchair was regularly transported around the edge of a ploughed field so that he could be with us in the chapel. One evening, in the candlelight, the person leading prayers said that he had planned that we would simply spend the time in silence. 'But with Arthur we cannot have silence,' he said; 'so we will create silence by singing psalms.' Guitars and flutes and human voices echoed through the space as we sang from the Othona Psalm-book.[2] One of the psalms (the Othona version of Psalm 131) went like this:

I am too little, Lord,
    to look down on others.
I've not chased great affairs,
    nor matters beyond me.
I've tamed my wild desires
    and settled my soul.
My soul's a new fed child
    at rest on the breast.
My brothers seek the Lord,
    both now and for ever.

As we sang it suddenly seemed as if Arthur was the Christ-figure in our midst.

The second story: sometime back in the 1980s, there was to be a day focusing on disability at the Queen's Theological College. I was asked to preach at the chapel service at the end. Being involved in worship at Queen's was part of my professional life on a weekday, and Arthur had never accompanied me, as he regularly did, and still does, on Sundays. When I suggested I should arrange to bring him this was greeted with some consternation, expressed in the question, 'Why? Was he to be used as a visual aid?' I remember being quite taken aback, but also taking the question seriously in terms of examining my motives – there probably was an element of feeling people should confront the reality of what they had been talking about all day! But the more I thought about it the more I felt that Arthur's presence was essential to what I wanted to say on that occasion, and a compromise was reached: he would be taken out for the sermon, since there remained sensitivity about my talking about him in his presence – although the only thing he would have picked up was recognition of his own name, which he would probably then have repeated over and over again!

The whole incident sharpened up what I needed to say. 'There is no longer Jew or Greek, there is no longer slave or free, there is no longer male and female' (Galatians 3.28), and these days, I suggested, we would most of us naturally go on, 'black nor white, rich nor poor, Catholic nor Anglican, Orthodox nor Methodist, for all of you are one in Christ Jesus'. But back then it was not so obvious that we would add reference to those with disabilities, and I challenged them with what had happened. I had received an invitation which gave me not only a sense of privilege, but also of joy, because it provided an occasion when Arthur could join the worship of the community without a feeling of intrusion. This had been shattered, but this very shattering revealed the true meaning of his presence: it was a celebration of our wholeness together, and that celebration was essential to what I had to say. The trouble is wholeness is associated with perfection – we imagine a state in which all loss and brokenness, all sin and pain and failure is wafted away, and it is that which we think is perfection. Disability seems to undermine that wholeness. But our wholeness in Christ is a wholeness that can absorb and transfigure loss, brokenness, disability, failure, sin, hurt and death – we become whole when we can live with the cross at the centre of the community.

These two stories encapsulate the themes of this reflection. First, I want to consider the role of language in worship and the challenges presented by the person who is linguistically marginalized; then I turn to the question of what it means to participate in worship; and third I explore the importance of the incorporation of even those with the most profound disabilities for the Church to become the body of Christ, and for humanity to be restored to the image of God.

Wordless worship

It is difficult to know what Arthur takes in, given his lack of language. It makes one aware of how much language shapes our experience: after all we identify what we see or hear by naming each thing and so distinguishing it from other things in our vision or hearing. The process of naming differentiates, the significant is highlighted and other things recede into the background, often not noticed.

I once found myself contemplating the question of how exactly Arthur experiences the world without the possibility of such articulation. He certainly recognizes faces and places, and knows his regular routines. Sounds and music delight him, especially the human voice, as do patterns of light. The first word he attempted to copy was 'trees', and, like trees, pylons and suspended wires attract his attention as dark patterns against a light sky. He remains 'echolalic' (as his final school report put it), and perhaps associates 'car' with going out for a ride, and 'down' with being moved from his wheelchair to the beanbag. But since he sometimes just delights in articulating one or other of his limited range of 'words' at quite inappropriate moments, it is hard to know what he does understand – sometimes out in the car he will start repeating what we recognize as his attempt at 'bed-time'.

So what possible sense does he make of the average church service? Most obviously he responds to music, as my first story illustrates. The light of recognition comes into his face if I sing 'Away in a manger' or one of the nursery rhymes that he heard repeatedly as a baby. At home, I've watched his reactions change with the tempo and mood of the music on the radio, and in church you can see him listening. Human voices singing hymns certainly stimulate response in him. He also reacts to big open spaces, and especially anything patterned in light: I shall never forget the wonder on his face when we took him into Salisbury Cathedral and he gazed up at the vaults as the organ began to play. He seems to respond to atmosphere – though it is when the music stops that he thinks it is his turn to join in, and if the music has made him excited his noisy articulation precludes silence. Some congregations are capable of accepting that he is praising God in his own way, though one must admit that others find his presence distracting and disturbing, especially if it is a new experience.

My reflections on how he perceives the world are summed up in this poem:

Imagine a life with sound but no word –
A life full of music and buzzing and shouts
But no structure or form. Could meaning be there
At all, or would everything be absurd?

Imagine a life with sight but no sense –
A life full of colour and movement and shapes
But no objects or space. Wouldn't it seem
A random muddle, a jumble immense?

But patterns are there, and proportion discerned
In the slatted light of Venetian blinds,
In the fractals of trees or the web of a grill:
So some sense of beauty is learned.
Yet much blindness remains, and still there's a kind
Of incomprehension that shuts off the mind.

And expressions are there, and moods conveyed
In the tone of voices, in laughter, in tears:
In music's dynamics, its beat and its flow –
So some connection is made.
Yet much deafness remains, and still there's a kind
Of incomprehension that shuts off the mind.

Perception has limits. Our brain-damaged son
Lives a life full of colour and music and light,
A life full of loving and sharing and fun,
But really perception has only begun.
He has such limitations – yet still there's a kind
Of mysterious awareness enlarging the mind.

Perception has limits – our vision's too small.
As for loving and sharing, our failures appal.
We have such limitations – but still there's a kind
Of mysterious transcendence enlarging the mind.[3]

This poem shifts us on to consider the whole question of language in worship, for it suggests that what we have to do with in worship is quite beyond us, and that Arthur's limitations enable us to recognize our own.

Worship goes beyond words. Twentieth-century liturgical revisions, along with multiple updated translations of the Bible, seem to imply that we are supposed to understand. But if we think we can comprehend God, then God is reduced to the size of our own minds. This is a point made repeatedly by the early Fathers and theologians of the Church; indeed, Ephraim the Syrian, in his remarkable theological poetry, suggested that the incarnation of God's Word was not just in flesh, but in human language. God had to accommodate the divine self to our level, and speak to us in our terms. So God clothed the divine self in all kinds of metaphors and symbols. It was like someone trying to teach a parrot to speak, hiding her face behind a mirror so that the parrot thought it was speaking with one of its own kind.[4] The inadequacy of human language for the truth about God is fundamental to theology, and the attempt to put the whole truth into words conspires with attitudes to Scripture that reduce it to narrowly literal reference. There is a parable that does the rounds which invites us to imagine what sense a two-dimensional creature would make of our three-dimensional world, so as to stimulate us into appropriate humility – maybe there is a fourth dimension out there which is just as real but with our creaturely limitations we cannot perceive it. That same humility may be fostered by relationship in worship with someone like Arthur, by consciousness of the limitations in his perception of which we are aware and he is not, by deep identification with that reality of not being able to put the sacred into words or grasp it. Liturgy is in any case more than words – the words both point beyond themselves and are performative, so that the liturgy is an *act* of worship. Arthur reminds us that we are caught up in something bigger than ourselves – certainly bigger than our words, and bigger than our understanding.

I suggest that this may also have something to say about the propensity of those who lead worship to 'talk down' to people who have little theological sophistication, or to children or outsiders. If people sense a patronizing approach, they will be turned off, just as much as if things appear strange, foreign and incomprehensible. We might learn from the fact that no adaptation can get things down to Arthur's level. Far more important is the generation of the kind of atmosphere that makes people feel they are caught up in something totally beyond every one of us – a transcendent and healing mystery, which summons us out of our self-preoccupation and enables us to become incorporated into something bigger than ourselves.

Not all persons with learning disabilities are as incapacitated with language as Arthur is, but many operate with a very simple level of linguistic competence. I am impressed by the fact that in the worship at the L'Arche[5] community in Trosly-Breuil (the first place where people committed themselves to living in community with those who have profound learning disabilities) there is no compromise over the liturgy of the Mass. In their plain stone chapel, created out of an old barn, there are songs with guitars and simple sung responses, but also the long lections, a homily and intercessions that are usual everywhere. It is, of course, in the vernacular French, Latin having been superseded since Vatican II, but it is just as wordy as any other Mass or Eucharist. Few of those present are likely to follow all that much. Yet the sheer sense of habitude and familiarity, the togetherness and presence, creates an atmosphere to which the inarticulate sounds of those with profound disabilities seem to contribute, and some with a slightly higher level of competence, despite their considerable impairments, receive the immense sense of dignity and worth that comes from the privilege of serving at the altar. I remember, too, the worship in the chapel at the old Monyhull hospital, an institution for those with learning disabilities now closed because of changes in policy; in a service deliberately following liturgies used elsewhere in the Church, so that here too there was sharing in the one body of Christ, people with little or no language would rush to the altar rail to receive the sacrament with a simple 'thank you', somehow sensing the depth of what was happening.

The sense of sacred place, atmosphere and music may be more important than words for creating worship. That is not to say that words do not matter – for most of us they do, and for all of us the human voice is key to the sense of shared experience. But worship needs to transcend words, and praise may be expressed in 'Songs without Words'.

Participation in worship

I have spoken of being taken up into something bigger than ourselves. I would like to suggest that that is not a bad definition of worship. 'You have made us for yourself,' said Augustine of Hippo, 'and our heart is restless till it rests in you.'[6] Such an understanding implies that participation in worship is more to do with receptivity than with contributing.

In recent decades, there has been much drive to get more people to participate in worship by playing an active part, reading lessons, or offering intercessions. Does this really mean greater participation? Individuals who do these things may feel a greater sense of dignity and worth, and the congregation may feel they represent them in an important sense; but on the other hand, these individuals may feel nervous, and their performance may therefore not assist anybody, including themselves, to be caught up in something bigger. Participation in a concert or in the theatre does not mean going on stage yourself. It means responding to what is going on so as to be caught up into the action or the music, taken beyond in a way that leads to self-forgetfulness. Great preaching is like great acting, in the sense that it claims attention and moves people to respond, to see things differently, to change their attitudes, to live in a different imaginative world which provides a larger perspective within which to discover meaning and live out their day-to-day lives. Great music can lift the spirit to inner realms of wordless worship, even more effectively than singing oneself – though hymn-singing is for many the main experience of actual participation in corporate worship.

I want to suggest that the presence of Arthur in worship reinforces this point. How does Arthur participate? Mainly by his silence and the rapture on his face when the singing is lifting his spirit. Sometimes by echoing the intonation of the preacher's voice, or shouting his own name. Often by vigorous hand-clapping. Yes, he is less inhibited than most of us; but the point surely remains, even if our responses are internal and private rather than overt. Participation happens at all kinds of levels and in all kinds of ways. The sermon may not impact on Arthur in the same way as it does the elderly retired headmaster whose intellect is still engaged, and who needs some stimulating thoughts to feed his mind as well as his heart. The whole point about liturgy is that it stimulates participation and feeds people differently. The aim of worship is to generate the kind of participation that takes people out of themselves so that they become more truly themselves in the larger whole.

Arthur's contribution is small and potentially disruptive. That may in itself be a gift to the rest of us, jerking us out of habit into a new depth. But the question now is what does he receive – what is God doing in him in worship? It is impossible to know – a mystery of grace, which nevertheless has its signs in the responses I have described. He would not receive the communion elements even if offered – feeding him has never been straightforward! Sometimes he even resists a blessing – too many have forced their touch upon him in public settings. Yet somehow grace is mediated, and so being with him may help us to recognize that what we do matters less than being bathed, like him, in the music of voices and the smiles of presences, in a sense of abandonment to the sensations of sounds and sight, even bodily movement, as we receive grace through the mediation of the liturgical actions and through one another. What happens to any of us remains elusive – too often we invest too much in what we are conscious of – in 'feelings' of response. Arthur reminds us that often we may well receive grace without being fully aware of the fact and there is much more to receive than we can know.

Incorporation into the body of Christ

Worship is offered by the whole assembly of the body of Christ, and it is becoming part of that larger whole which is fundamental. It is 'a foretaste of the heavenly banquet prepared for all people'.[7] Challenged by someone about Arthur's eventual participation in the kingdom feast, I once wrote this poem:[8]

A party invitation! The heavenly feast!
Who'll be there?
Everyone's invited, even the least.
I've nothing to wear . . .
A special robe is provided, designed for you.
Look at my hair!
Don't worry – they'll give you a bath and a fine hair-do.
No gift to bear . . .
Just bring your musical instrument to play.
Arthur can't share.
Everyone will participate in some way.

98

Stuck in his chair?
Somehow he'll be fitted to play his role.
Will people stare?
No, no. He'll take his part in the joyful whole.
He'll be aware?
Everyone will respond and give of their best.
   Each has some flair.
   The conductor, you see, will be a special guest.
   Under his care
   The entire ensemble will play together as one.
That'll be rare.
That is how Christ will complete the work begun
   Suffering in prayer.
   There'll be music beyond any music heard on earth
   Throbbing the air.
   There'll be bread and wine. New life will be brought to birth.
   God will be there.
   You'll finally understand his infinite grace.
   There's plenty to spare.
Will we be able to see him face to face?
Look – if you dare!

So much for his ultimate participation (the point being that if in heaven he is 'cured' he will no longer be recognizably Arthur); what about now? As in my second opening story, I want to state quite categorically that here and now his participation is vital and essential for the body of Christ to be the body of Christ.

Translations of the Bible are usually to be read aloud in public, and therefore for reasons of respectability sometimes fail to reveal exactly what the words mean. There is a case in point in the famous passage about the body of Christ in 1 Corinthians 12. 'The members of the body that seem to be weaker are indispensable', reads the NRSV, 'and those members of the body that we think less honourable we clothe with greater honour, and our less respectable members are treated with greater respect' (12.22–23). The Greek shows that this passage is actually talking about the body bits we are ashamed of or embarrassed about, those we cover up. Persons with learning disabilities still provoke reactions of embarrassment, and they are the least powerful people in our society, usually dependent and lacking autonomy, with little control over their circumstances. But it is precisely such persons who need to be included if the body of Christ is to be whole. We must honour what we might be ashamed of: Paul is anxious to affirm that he is not ashamed of the cross – in his society it meant the shame of condemnation, and it would not be long before Christians were lampooned by graffiti of a crucified ass. We must affirm the weak: the body of Christ is a physical image, and the physical reality was that in his bodily existence Christ was abused, disabled and put to death. The resurrected Christ appeared with the marks of the nails.[9] Some aspects of God's image in Christ can only be reflected in the Church as the body of Christ by the full inclusion and honouring of those who have bodies that are likewise impaired.

This suggestion that the image of God can only be reflected in the body of Christ by the inclusion of damaged persons flies in the face of traditional presuppositions. In the history of Christian theology, the notion that humanity is made in the image of God has tended to have, first, an elitist and, second, an individualistic interpretation. My argument would be that the image of God is to be found fully only in Christ, and that its thrust is corporate.[10]

First, then: traditionally it has been assumed that the image of God is to be found in the human intellect. The mind or soul is in God's image, since the bodily (corporeal or physical) aspect of human nature can hardly represent the incorporeal, spiritual reality of the transcendent God. We should not underestimate the profound reaction against idolatry in early Christianity: no animal or human form should be taken to represent God who is invisible. By contrast, the perceived kinship between the human mind and God's Mind (or Logos), coupled with the analogy between the incarnation of God's Word (or Logos) in Christ and the embodiment of the soul/mind in the human person, encouraged a predominantly intellectual interpretation of how human beings are made in the image of God. This tendency may at times have permitted the positive acceptance of intelligent persons with physical disabilities: for example, Didymus the Blind (fourth century) was nicknamed Didymus the See-er because he saw more profoundly than those with physical sight. It has sometimes encouraged positive (if somewhat patronizing) responses to persons with profound mental disabilities on the grounds that 'you can see the soul peeping out through their eyes'. But is that really true? This approach is both inherently elitist and dualist in its understanding of human nature, and ultimately tends to exclude those, like Arthur, whose mental or physical incapacities significantly challenge the dualist viewpoint, since their physical being profoundly affects their entire personality and existence.

Second, in the more recent history of Christian theology, the notion that humanity is made in the image of God has tended to have an individualistic interpretation. It is taken to mean that each of us is made in the image of God, and therefore each of us deserves to be equally respected. It conspires with modern 'human rights' ideologies to encourage individuals to assert their right to a decent deal in society, and to recognition of each person's inherent dignity, no matter what their race, religion or impairment. This tendency has had positive impact in encouraging respect for those who are not white, male, able-bodied and intelligent. But it has also exacerbated the prejudice that we should all be perfect since we are made in God's image. Obvious failure to reach such notional perfection then becomes problematic. How can this person, who apparently has physical or mental defects, be made in God's image? The modernist rights approach may challenge the attitudes of some past traditional societies, but the success-oriented values of modern individualism encourage an interpretation of what it means to be in God's image which I would argue does not take account of core elements in Christian theology.

So let's reconsider what it means to be made in the image of God by returning to Scripture. The phrase occurs in the Genesis narrative of the creation of Adam. There are two important features to note. First, Adam represents the whole human race – the very name Adam means humanity in the generic sense, for the subsequent creation of Eve from his rib represents sexual differentiation in the human race. Second, Adam was indeed made in the image and likeness of God, but the story tells how this was marred by disobedience, classically known as the Fall. So glib theological talk about being made in God's image needs to be countered with a sensitivity to the corporate nature of that image, and the fact that all have fallen short of the glory (image) of God (Romans 3.23).

This reflection on Genesis 1 is confirmed by the New Testament. A reading of Paul's epistles soon shows that the dynamic of salvation depends upon the parallel between Adam and Christ. Adam is the 'old man', Christ the 'new man' (Romans 5.12; 2 Corinthians 5.17), and all of us (male and female) are in Adam and potentially in Christ (Romans 7; 1 Corinthians 15.22). Both are in some sense corporate figures. In Christ, we are a new creation, but as in Adam all die, so in Christ all will be made alive. In a sense Christ alone is the true image of God – the image of God in Adam (the old humanity) was marred. So we are only in God's image if we are in Christ, and it is by baptism that we are incorporated into him. It has always been of the greatest importance to me that Arthur was baptized as a baby – even though he cannot receive the sacrament or make a profession of the faith, he is held in God's grace and belongs to the body of Christ.

The body of Christ is essentially a corporate image – a body is made up of many members, all of whom bring different contributions to the whole (1 Corinthians 12; Romans 12). Indeed, as already noted, the weak limbs (members), and even those body bits we are ashamed of and cover up, are indispensable and are to be especially honoured; and because in his bodily existence Christ was abused, disabled and put to death, some aspects of God's image in Christ can only be reflected in the Church as the body of Christ by the full inclusion and honouring of those who have bodies that are likewise impaired. The founder of L'Arche, Jean Vanier, often speaks of brokenness. I once became fascinated by the fraction – the snapping – of the communion wafer. Perhaps the breaking of the body of Christ is necessary for the Church to be the Church. Only after the fraction can the broken pieces be gathered again into one loaf. As the Spirit of the living God breaks and moulds each of us, so the Church has to suffer the pain of brokenness so as to be humbled and ready to welcome those impaired. Christ had no form or comeliness – the broken crucified body was scarcely a pretty sight, hardly something to be welcomed. Those who have profound disabilities sometimes enable that shock to be felt. Maybe that is their prophetic vocation.

Conclusion

Someone once commented to me that 'Arthur's presence in church is gospel'. I believe that persons with even the most profound limitations have a vocation. They are a 'sign' in the biblical sense, pointing beyond themselves, in a number of ways. They are called to reveal to us, so-called 'normal' people, something about who we truly are: we are vulnerable creatures, and it is when our vulnerability shows up our dependence on one another that true community is discovered and the fruits of the Spirit can mature: love, joy, peace, patience, kindness, generosity, faithfulness, gentleness and self-control (Galatians 5.22). They summon us to true humility in the presence of the God who transcends all human language and conceptuality. They bear witness to the Christ who had 'no form or comeliness' (Isaiah 53.2), no beauty to attract us, but was despised and rejected, ensuring that that image is included as one facet of the body of Christ. They speak to us of a wholeness that incorporates our impairments, of a transcendence that does not negate the cross any more than the resurrection wafts it away with a magic wand, of an hour of glory in which all our darkness and 'gonewrongness' is embraced, entered and borne, and so transformed. And they show us that praise is most deeply to be found in 'Songs without Words'.

At one time, people imagined that the cosmic spheres created music, and so this heavenly harmony offered ceaseless praise of the Creator, presumably without words. The Psalms remind us that in worship we enter the wordless praise of the whole of creation:

Praise him, sun and moon;
    praise him, all you shining stars!
Praise him, you highest heavens . . .
Mountains and all hills,
    fruit trees and all cedars!
Wild animals and all cattle;
    creeping things and flying birds! . . .
Let them praise the name of the Lord,
    for his name alone is exalted;
his glory is above earth and heaven.
(Psalm 148.3, 4, 9, 10, 13)

Notes

1 Both stories have previously appeared, told in somewhat different words, in my book, *Face to Face. A Narrative Essay in the Theology of Suffering*, Peterborough, Epworth Press, 1985 and Edinburgh: T&T Clark, 1990.

2 Colin Hodgetts, *The Othona Psalms*, Bradwell-on-Sea: The Othona Community, 1976.

3 This is a revised version of a poem published earlier in *Face to Face*.

4 Sebastian Brock, *The Luminous Eye*, Rome: Centre for Indian and Inter-Religious Studies, 1985, pp. 44–5.

5 The L'Arche communities were founded by Jean Vanier and there are now 130 communities all over the world. Having begun in the Roman Catholic environment of Northern France, there are now ecumenical communities in Northern Europe and North America, and multifaith communities in India.

6 Henry Chadwick, *Saint Augustine's Confessions*, Oxford: Oxford University Press, 1992, p. 3.

7 *Methodist Worship Book*, Peterborough: Methodist Publishing House, 1999, p. 197.

8 Published formerly in *Face to Face*, Epworth version 1985, pp. 86–7; T&T Clark version 1990, p. 108.

9 Nancy Eisland, *The Disabled God: Towards a Liberation Theology of Disability*, Nashville, TN: Abingdon Press, 1994, explores this point.

10 The following paragraphs make use of material written for a WCC group preparing a statement on disability.

9

Blurring the Edges:
Finding Commonality by
Smudging our Differences

JANE E. WALLMAN-GIRDLESTONE

Blurring the edges

I am visually impaired. I exist permanently in a world where edges do
not exist visually for me. I live, what others inform me, is a blurred existence. Edges present a mixed and not always helpful addendum to the
busyness of my life. An edge can be potentially dangerous and debilitating, as the limbs I have fractured in the past will testify. An edge is only
imaginable to me through the sense of touch.

In my phenomenology, objects are defined by the often attractive,
abstract ways in which they smudge and mingle into each other. Edges,
on the other hand, are features to be physically negotiated with all
senses alert and with some trepidation. Edges represent an overture into
the unknown; a fuzzy, glossed-over visual blending that gives no clue as
to what is concealed or denoted. Edges are inherently hazardous, and do
not immediately reveal their full implications. I am instinctively nervous
of edges.

Developing a hermeneutic of suspicion as a disabled person

My life experience has made me a little suspicious of clusters of individuals claiming to have a unique take on what is in the best interests of
other people. The Church is one such organization. The medical model
of care dominated understandings of human value in society for many
generations.[1] A certain 'kill or cure' mentality prevails to this day in the
medical profession and amongst some individuals, particularly those
living uncomfortably with life-limiting conditions. This is manifest
increasingly in appeals to the legislature and the courts to give doctors

the power to make decisions involving the ending of life.[2] When possible a cure is offered or a 'normalizing' therapy; for example, blind children are often taught to smile. If such interventions have little impact or are rejected by the patient, the disabled person is discharged from medical provision.

More recently, despite a significant theological critique that challenges its perspective,[3] the social model has become a popular way of interpreting disability within our faith communities. This model emphasizes the assessment of disabled individuals in terms of their *ability* and with full recognition given to the ways in which society disables individuals through lack of access, prevailing assumptions and stigmatizing attitudes.

The Disability Discrimination Act has further encouraged churches to think in terms of enabling disabled people through access provisions. Of course this offers a valuable way of inclusifying Church, but it is a superficial exercise conveniently disguised as a task that can be completed.

It is from within this context that I am addressing the Church. I perceive the Church as both a theologically rooted ideal made manifest in the world as a witness to God and also as an organization profoundly influenced by the prevailing norms of society. In common with many, I have had, for much of my life, a yearning to belong – to something. For me, the Church has provided that space. God has provided the encounter and other people, the challenge and my means of personal accountability.

My scepticism of groups who have a highly developed shared agenda and conforming norms has become increasingly intense as I have grown older. I reflect on my attraction to (and at the same time repulsion from) some forms of organized religious expression. I am of the view that the Church spends so much of its time shoring up its diminishing power base that it has lost touch with its own dynamic history and heritage.[4] It has forgotten that one of its gifts in the past has been to be present in the broken, dislocated parts of society. It has been in these places that it has learnt the corporeal art of selflessness.

Choosing to be disabled – enabling uniqueness

The dominant influence in my spirituality is, unsurprisingly, a burning passion regarding social justice. I am currently exploring different 'pictures' of gathering and of expressing spirituality that are organically grown through the interaction of people who would consider themselves diverse in the first instance but, through engagement with each other, immersed in their common humanity. Many of these people have little engagement with traditional religious expression. Some consider themselves 'in recovery' after bad experiences as congregation members.

When I meditate, I sometimes envision that we have the potential as the body of Christ to be a collage, a living sculpture or a fantastical botanical garden of shared similarities. Differences are a given part of relationship; finding the commonality seems to be increasingly the challenge. The challenge is to identify a way of communicating symbolically and metaphorically through ritual and liturgy in ways that are not confined within the frame of a set of definitive values and carefully defined valid responses. More blurred edges and cloudy corners.

Finding commonality in Christian liturgy

Liturgical expression within the Christian tradition is fraught with conceptual and ideological difficulties for a practitioner committed to retaining a degree of ambiguity about attributed value and meaning. Cranmer understood this perfectly and is attributed with saying that whatever we speak and memorize, we will come to believe.

The Christian tradition demands that believers pledge intellectual, spiritual and social allegiance to a set of ideals. For some, these bear very little correlation with their actual life experience. Indeed there can be a distinct differentiation between the practice of religiosity and the lifestyle choices a person makes. Christianity characterizes this as an awareness of falling short of the ideals of the Christian life. A more therapeutic understanding of this might encourage less emphasis on the shamefulness of shortcoming[5] and more on the befriending of oneself.

Smudging liturgy or choosing not to mop up mess

It is not the *distinctiveness* of the gospel message but the *universalizable* nature of its themes and images that attract me. In other words, I am committed to using Christian imagery and ritual as a way of counterpointing the shared metanarrative of humanity. I see Christian liturgy as the 'touching places' or moments for potential *metanoia* (transformation) within the context of all human emotion.

Disabled Christians, by their very presence, are a physical reminder that not everything the Christian Church teaches 'takes'. They have not been healed. Some would even say they challenge the efficaciousness of Christ's teaching as they are manifestly not 'whole'. They represent an opportunity to explore where contrasting worlds can meet and share. I am not denying the considerable goodness that exists in the fabric and practice of the best of organized religious expression. It offers pastoral care, consideration and a value system to all its membership. However, our current, arguably life-limited, status as an institution is partly due to an unwillingness to reassess in the light of a constantly evolving world (not to mention our cosmos) what part Church and faith can play now – and how we can express this provisionality of perspective.

To give an illustration: I grew up in South London during the 1970s – a period of significant racial tension within some inner-city communities. I was a white girl in a racially mixed school with a high proportion of black and Asian children. I neither noticed nor was aware of the implications of this (beyond the obligatory Anti-Nazi League Badge we all wore). This was *normal* to me. I left home for college and entered an almost exclusively white environment. I thought something was seriously wrong. The few black or Asian students experienced discrimination and alienation from the predominant values. I converted to Christianity and saw it for some time as a 'catch all' – a value system which I felt provided the vocabulary not so much for answering the universal questions of human beings ('Why am I here?' and so on) but the means of articulating truth and the intended path for the whole of humanity. Jesus was the only Way, Truth and Life. The Bible said so; it must be true. I have been challenged concerning this position and wonder whether this was the arrogant hyperbole of a convert. It is actually extremely demeaning and abusive to those who do not share my system for making value judgements. I was abusive because I chose to cling on to what was distinctive and dominant. It was easy from a position of power to deny what was counter-cultural and hardly recognizable, the silenced voices of those whom my newly acquired values oppressed.

Then I discovered another, less comfortable life: a commitment to live alongside vulnerable people – children and adults with mental health issues. At the time I thought I was just becoming a mum; adopting children. It was an invitation to explore a new and even more complex phenomenology, way outside my experiential comfort zone. I saw acute poverty within the UK; the agony of disability without advocacy; the unjustness of discrimination and social ostracism; the cruelty of the social services; unimaginative education departments and the inadequacies of the criminal justice system; not to mention the invasive, judgemental and often counter-productive procedures that form our welfare state – I could go on. I found myself feeling like Cassandra[6] and wondering why, when so many people clearly recognize and acknowledge the injustices they encounter, they, we and I did so little about them.

Every now and then I would have a sneaking suspicion that my activities as an accredited minister were a skilled subterfuge. Despite teaching unconditional love, the practice of the Church is actually highly conditional and codified. The edges of who belongs, who is welcome, who gains power and influence and who is to be subjected to the Church's care and witness are well defined. I was discovering what it was like to become a blurred figure. I was a person of authority and even a little power as an authorized minister, but I had entered a hinterland where my power was irrelevant, my ability diminished, my faith irrelevant and even considered dubious and my personhood blurred almost to the point of invisibility.

Hughes, a psychologist specializing in supporting households offering care to young people who have had traumatic pasts, talks a great deal about the process that those who offer care to the most vulnerable undertake.[7] He describes it as a journey towards emotional maturity. In reality, to empathize with the most 'edgy' in every sense – those whose worldviews are radically altered by early abuse – is to allow access to our own vulnerabilities. There is nothing like the moment of revelation when an eight-year-old names your adult fear, pain or weakness. You have to develop a rooted spirituality, theology and sense of self-worth to sustain yourself and others.

'Smudging liturgy' is one way that we can begin to embrace and discover – even celebrate – something of the transient nature of life as we live it, to discover what it might mean to find commonality with each other, not only within the faith community, but with those of other faiths and none. It could be a way of inclusifying without patronizing and without too many assumptions.

I am not a great advocate of masses of experimental, homespun worship, not only because I am a dyed-in-the-wool Anglican, but also because it is so difficult to separate personal agenda from what is offered through worship to God. God, we all hope, has a loving preoccupation, at some level, with humanity's agenda; but in the context of public liturgy there is a necessity to protect the gathered community of faith from the particular agenda of the worship leader, at least to some degree. There is method in the madness of liturgical form. It makes us confront again and again through the familiar cadences of the prayers and narratives of our past, our shared communal story – some of which feels comfortless and barbaric or simplistic and naïve to a contemporary ear. It is from within this blurred extremity that we can effectively explore commonality. We can begin to risk smudging the edges in ways that make individuals feel safe, but gather some of God's favoured people into a sharing and celebration of our common good.

Healing services are an excellent example of the trouble we can inadvertently get ourselves into when attempting to create an authentic expression of inclusivity in our churches. It is no surprise that for some disabled Christians healing services are fraught with difficulties. Interestingly, I know of very few who would argue that the ministry of healing per se should be abandoned by the Church. No matter how inventive the hermeneutical cycle, we cannot escape, as Hull very aptly noted, the idea that disabled people are historically caricatured as 'miracle fodder'.[8] So how can we inclusively offer a healing intention?

I am indebted to the therapeutic practices I have engaged in as a foster parent and as a therapist. These have enabled me to explore how we merge contrasting, and at times conflicting, narratives, values and visions. One approach common in play therapy is to explore universalizable themes through non-verbal activities. One activity that I have translated into a worship context is 'the memory of love', described below. This has a number of variations but is essentially a highly inclusive healing liturgy. It recognizes the powerful place of unresolved experiences in life whilst recognizing that all of us, at some level, have experienced love from another or others.

The memory of love

This ritual works exceptionally well within the context of a baptism or as a healing act in a contemplative act of worship where healing has not been named. Alternative words can be drawn from the conventions used in your own tradition to name sorrow, distance from God, separation or emotional alienation from others or ourselves. If it is a dedication, naming ceremony, confirmation or reaffirmation and the person is comfortable taking a central role, this can be emotionally very powerful for them and those who affirm them by their presence.

I would personally resist any element of performance. I would encourage people to participate informally. It could be used with the closest chosen household members and friends before a more formal service. During the ceremony, those gathered are witnessing and celebrating the memories of love for the other – and getting in touch emotionally with their own experiences of love.

The process is as follows. A large box of assorted candles, different sizes and colours, some used, others brand new, some reflecting a particular season (for example, birthday candles), is provided. A sand tray or similar and matches and a taper are also required. The person is invited to take time choosing candles that represent for them people who have shown them love. They could select an unused candle and say that this will represent a named figure who was like a mother to them. Or a stubby candle that reminds them of a cuddly toy that has been with them through thick and thin. They can also decide whether the candle needs to be lit in due course.

The candles can be attributed out loud with the name of the person or affirmed silently in the person's heart. Or the *type* of love or kind of person can be noted: for example, 'This is the teacher who told me I was good at games'. In a small group, some enjoy saying a little more about why the person's love was important. 'This candle reminds me of my mum. She was dead strict, but I never doubted her love. Ever.'

Once the candle is securely placed in the tray the person can either light the candle to indicate the intensity of the love they experienced from the person or leave it unlit. They may feel that the love was important, but something stands in the way of their appreciating all that the person was, or limits a free flow of forgiveness occurring. In this case the candle remains unlit.

Children will often undertake this whole process intuitively and will have a very clear sense of which candles they want to light. Adults may need more time. There are no wrong or right answers. Reassurance, calm and attentive listening are the key factors. Sometimes just feeling the warmth on your hand, seeing the flicker of the flame, or being with attentive people is enough.

When such candles as are needed have been placed and those that need to be lit have been, the person is asked to put their hand gently above the flickering flames. They can feel the warmth of the memories of those who have cared for them and about them. They may wish others to join them – and feel the memories of warmth and love too.

This is a healing ritual and one which reminds the participants that they have experienced love even if in the current time they feel stressed as new parents, or recently bereaved, or dealing with day-to-day life. There are for all of us things to be thankful for and good memories in among other more challenging times. It is not a ritual that can be used as a means of conflict resolution. Sometimes people make choices in front of family and friends that surprise them. It is important that it is never used to facilitate the manipulation of others. It is essentially a method to access past, positive experiences; so it is important to check out that this is realistic for the person and the context. If in doubt use the following alternative.

All those present take as many candles as they wish and name their hopes and dreams for the person who is their focus. They can have as many goes as they want or they can simply light a candle or say the words of their hope silently in their heart. 'I hope you will be happy . . .' 'I give you my time . . .' 'I promise to do my best by you . . .' When all the candles are lit, the person then feels the warmth of the gathered community's love and affirmation.

Mingling experience

Most of us experience a significant sense of belonging when we believe our stories have been heard and honoured by others. The difficulty arises when we have a sense that we are being humoured (at worst) or 'being done good to' – a common experience among disabled people encountering the Church. The current emphasis on access issues in our church can contribute to an underlying script which implies that as the church has stumped up the cash to put in the ramp, buy the large-print hymn books, adapt the toilet and fit the induction loop, what more do 'they' want? The good news is that *they* want exactly what *you* long for; to feel acceptable and in community. Disabled people may come desperately seeking cure, comfort or consolation. Above all they are searching for a sense that they are as they are and you are as you are, and there is something to be gained from being in relationship with each other.

As I have identified, a key concept here is to seek ways of creating commonality rather than accentuating difference. Within disabilist theology, Eiesland reinterprets the body of Christ radically. Disabilist theologians bring to the table an encouragement to the Church to embrace a theology of limitation. It is through the acknowledgement of the liminal experience in each of us that we meet at a shared level of pain and need. Eiesland depicts the crucified Christ as a more appropriate image of the body of Christ and encourages the Church to convert to a theological perspective that values weakness.[9]

We can mingle experience and merge difference in numerous ways. The senses of touch and smell can be well used here, although all the correct checks and balances must be in place regarding the protection of children and vulnerable adults. Within the Anglican and Roman churches there is a strong tradition of anointing. This is a highly stylized way of representing the specialness of a person before God. It is used in both churches at formal confession; at moments of life transition; and before death.

In the retreat space I work in, we use anointing at our Gathering to Break Bread and Drink Wine service. After a simple prayer of confession, the authorized minister anoints each person in turn with scented oil with the words:

God forgives you.
Forgive God.
Forgive one another.
Forgive yourself.
In the name of the Creator, Redeemer and Sustainer, Amen.[10]

Interestingly this has had a very unifying impact on people who have come to stay, almost irrespective of their faith position. We find commonality in acknowledging our individual and corporate finitude.

Blending diversity into common cause: the fantastical botanical garden

Even the most severely disabled individuals are caught for a second by light, dark, sound, fragrance, colour, texture. Some of these sensory reactions may be obtuse or differently functioning but it is a wise liturgist who does not assume that because a person cannot see or hear, they cannot *experience* something of the journey, for example the audio translation of the picture being passed around the group. The key is to recognize that they may well *experience* and *express* differently and that, when possible, it can be profoundly life-enhancing for the *whole* worshipping community if the breadth of responses is fully explored and honoured.

It still amazes me that we share worship with God and each other with low expectations generally. Whether we are moved to the dizzy heights of awe or plummet to the depths of desolation, we are often uncritical about what has triggered this and why it might be important. We often put our dissatisfaction down to the choice of hymns, the quality of the homily or the worship style – even the minister leading it! We rarely share together what was and remains meaningful to us in terms of *God-talk* – talk to and about God. We stay on the safer ground of sharing thoughts about a biblical passage or remembering those who have sought our prayers.

In reality, we can learn a great deal from one another; how to tread gently around each other's sensitivities and not trample on newly emerging shoots, if we know where they are. We can be attentive in prayer and grow spiritually when we feel that our needs are being met – not just by some divine Supernanny in the sky, but in carefully constructed worship which affirms us and the authenticity of all we are trying to be and do.

Here is another ritual we have developed in our community, the creation of what we playfully name 'the fantastical botanical garden'. In a gathered worship community, the process can be offered on a number of levels, but the emphasis would be on encouraging people to work as collegially as possible, evolving safe and appropriate team work as they go. Strong, dominant people who claim knowledge should be placed in a team together – and not allowed to be the spiritual equivalent of bindweed. They must be celebrated in their context – which is among others who will enjoy their stimulating and energized engagement.

The 'fantastical botanical garden' can work as a flower and plant display for a special service – or it can be organized as a more permanent, organic reminder of belonging. In the latter example, an area of the grounds of the church can be set aside for planting up – and suitably prepared. Inclusivity demands that attention is paid to access and a variety of methods and styles of planting. Thought can also be given to aroma and texture. There may be an electronic link which provides a multimedia dimension, or natural sounds like running water. Lighting and music – live or recorded – would also enhance and transform atmosphere. Consideration should be given to ethical and ecological issues – should this be an edible garden? What about wildlife? Can we make use of any produce?

The fantastical botanical garden can be a virtual display; a multimedia triptych that reflects what members of the faith community hold dear. If it is multimedia it will be accessible on many levels. The idea can be worked in worship too by inviting contributions in small sharing groups. Perhaps a favourite thing is brought in and shown and then presented at the altar. In the case of people with severe disabilities it may be that the group enjoy in silence what the disabled person also delights in non-verbally, rather than hearing a preamble from a carer about the value of the item to the person.

Whatever form it takes, this is a doing, rather than a planning, exercise. As a garden or living organism display, individuals can donate and then be given a pack of seeds to grow at Harvest in the autumn and return with pots in the spring. It doesn't matter if it is a couple of large containers to go inside the church or a large bed in the grounds – the basic idea is the same. By what people contribute they will be saying something about what God or faith in God means for them. When possible they should say something about what the growing or the choice has meant in their imaginings of God. Introverts may like to write their comment on a weatherproof label and leave it with their plant. For people who don't like growing things, bringing a stone with a special thought or name on it works well. The aim is to find similarity in difference in a real sense.

For one person an enormous sunflower might represent the generosity and vibrancy of God. For another, a cluster of sweet peas speaks of hope. For a third, potatoes symbolize never being hungry. It is a very personal and very human series of gestures, a patchwork of a living testimony that God has called each of us by name to be and work together. It enables us to find what we have in common. In this case, quite literally we hold in common a commitment to prepare, plant and sustain the growth of this tiny part of creation: our triptych, our collage or our multimedia presentation or our small patch of earth.

With such a shared task it is possible to surprise everyone with the unexpected originality and beauty of what can be achieved. It can create a powerful sense of community identity and thanksgiving. It is a living symbol of a loving and caring Church.

Concluding reflections

Much of what I have been highlighting is concerned with finding pathways in liturgy that affirm commonality rather than accentuating difference. I have set this within the context of the Church's existing patterns of worship, prayer and ministry, but I have attempted to stretch the boundaries of practice. I have done this, not out of an irrevocable attachment to existing liturgical tradition, but because I believe rituals function most effectively as an affirming device within the context of what is familiar and has been sanctified by becoming second nature to us. If we constantly change the rhythm of liturgy we are encouraging people to shift in and out of their personal comfort zones and potentially remain hyper-vigilant in their engagement with each other and with God. The consequences are that engagement in a wide variety of liturgy all the time is either so profound that high-spot services make everything else pall into insignificance, or the quality of the liturgy is so superficial that it does not impact on the community's consciousness in truly transforming ways.

One of the inherent difficulties with much of the liturgical provision available for me as a disabled theologian is that it is neither inclusive nor inherently affirming of disability, ethnicity, gender or diversity of sexual orientation. Much of it is presented in the language and with the aspirations of the powerful in mind.

However, rather than dismiss much of our spiritual heritage as paternalistic and power-crazed, I would rather reclaim it and find within it what it can give to the commonality agenda I am presenting. We not only sanitize our religion if we edit out the parts of our liturgy which make us angry or uncomfortable, but we also run the risk of not remembering our past – a sometimes abusive and violent history of domination and destruction in the face of difference. So I would want to hear stories of a vengeful God told in church; not as a salutary reminder of Judgement Day (although for all I know I may one day have to eat my words and face just such a moment) but rather as an opportunity for the body of Christ to reflect together on the meaning of our past and how it has shaped our present faith and our future hopes. What does a vengeful God mean to a person now using a wheelchair following a car accident? What does forgiveness mean to a mother of three struggling on benefits? What does 'Peace be with you' mean in practice to an asylum seeker?

For me, our liturgy, whatever its form or its emphasis, must be sewn into the tapestry of life and experience – not just in this time and place, but for the whole of eternity. It's tempting to think the tiny stitches we will add here and there won't count or that much of what I seem to be about is unpicking the committed work of others. On the contrary, like embroidery, the liturgical and spiritual life of the Church develops resonance and depth with each overlay; each additional texture and colour; each hint that all is not quite as clear cut as it first seemed.

Notes

1 Simon Brisendon, 'Independent Living and the Medical Model of Disability', in T. Shakespeare, ed., *The Disability Reader: Social Science Perspectives*, London: Cassell, 1998, reprinted 1999, pp. 20–7; L. Barton, ed., *Disability and Society: Emerging Issues and Insights*, London: Longman, 1996.

2 'British woman denied the right to die', <http://news.bbc.co.uk/1/hi/talking_point/1880828.stm>.

3 R. McCloughry and Wayne Morris, *Making a World of Difference: Christian Reflections on Disability*, London: SPCK, 2002, chs 1 and 2.

4 John Spong, *Why Christianity Must Change or Die: A Bishop Speaks to Believers in Exile*, New Jersey: HarperCollins, 1998.

5 Stephen Pattison, *Shame: Theory, Therapy, Theology*, Cambridge: Cambridge University Press, 2000.

6 Cassandra was a Greek prophetess who was condemned to a life where her words of wisdom and insight would never be understood and acted upon by those around her.

7 Daniel Hughes, *Facilitating Developmental Attachment: The Road to Emotional Recovery and Behavioural Changes in Foster and Adopted Children*, Lanham, MD: Jason Aronson, 1997.

8 An expression of Professor John Hull, Professor of Practical Theology, The Queen's Foundation, Birmingham.

9 Nancy Eiesland, *The Disabled God: Towards a Liberatory Theology of Disability*, Nashville: Abingdon Press, 1994.

10 St Columba Chapel, *Alturlie Point Prayer Book*. Adapted from *A New Zealand Prayer Book: He Karakia Mihinare o Aotearoa*, Auckland: Collins, 1989.

10

'Lord, I was Deaf':
Images of Disability in the Hymn Books[1]

JOHN M. HULL

Introduction

In an earlier article, I studied some of the many references to blindness in hymns.[2] I concluded that when the blind condition is treated as a symbol of sin and unbelief, a largely unconscious prejudice against blind people is reinforced. I suggested that the continued uncritical use of such hymns contributes to the marginalization and disempowerment of blind people in church and society. I remarked that 'the situation regarding people who are hard of hearing is pretty much the same',[3] but I did not deal specifically with the imagery of deafness. In the present study, I will present some examples of the metaphor of deafness in hymns, and I will add further examples of the use of blindness, leading to a discussion about the theological and ethical significance of this usage.

Deafness in the hymn books

Let us start with the well-known hymn by William T. Matson (1833–99), the second and third verses of which go as follows:

Lord, I was deaf: I could not hear
The thrilling music of Thy voice;
But now I hear Thee and rejoice,
And all Thine uttered words are dear.

Lord, I was dumb: I could not speak
The grace and glory of Thy name;
But now, as touched with living flame,
My lips Thine eager praises wake.[4]

It is estimated that there are about 50,000 people in the United Kingdom whose first, preferred language is British Sign Language (BSL).[5] This has been recognized by the UK government since 2003 as a language. The UK, however, does not have any official languages but in New Zealand sign language is the third official language of the country following English and Maori. It was once widely believed that signed languages, of which there are probably thousands in the world, were crude, concrete replications of spoken languages but this view has long since been abandoned. It is now known that signed languages offer all the subtlety and variety of spoken language, both at the concrete, immediate level and at the most abstract and philosophical. In some respects, indeed, signed languages are superior to spoken ones. Speech is linear, and mainly confined to sound, whereas signed language makes sophisticated use of space, movement and sequence and the possibilities of simultaneity through the use of body and head movements as well as hands gives to signed language a remarkable richness which is indicated in the growing genre of signed poetry.[6] In addition to those whose preferred language is BSL, one must also recognize that about one person in seven in the UK has some degree of hardness of hearing, although retaining a preference for English as the medium of communication.

While Deaf[7] activists co-operate with other sections of the disabled community in campaigns for recognition and equality, many do not regard deafness as a disability but as a feature of a persecuted linguistic minority. There are cases, mostly in small or isolated communities with a large number of Deaf people, where some form of signing has become general throughout the community. In such situations attention is seldom drawn to the inability to hear or speak as a significant characteristic of someone.[8] Moreover, study of the spirituality, religious life and theology of Deaf communities has revealed distinct characteristics, often involving sophisticated perceptions and sensitivities that may not be present in speaking and hearing communities.[9]

However, there is little trace of this respect for Deaf culture in the hymn books. For example, no. 85 in *Hymns, Ancient and Modern* is a seventeenth-century hymn first published in English in 1839 and intended for use during evensong. It is a meditation on John 1.5 'The light shines in the darkness, and the darkness did not overcome it'. Sensory deprivation is used to illustrate a negative attitude towards Judaism.

Now heaven's growing light is manifest
Through Judah's land which in the darkness lies;

But they have steel'd their breast,
And closed their earth bound eyes.

Now signs of present Godhead teem around,
The dead are raised, feet to the lame are given,
The dumb a tongue hath found,
The blind man sees the heaven.

But Israel hath become blind, deaf and dead . . .[10]

Most of the references to deafness in hymns can be traced back to the influence of the Bible. This appears in three ways, the most important of which is the healing miracles of Jesus.

To Thee they went, the deaf, the dumb,
The palsied and the lame.
The beggar with his sightless eyes,
The sick with fevered frame.[11]

The second biblical influence is eschatological hope. When the kingdom of God comes in its fullness, there will be no more sicknesses and impairments, as is foretold in Isaiah 35.5, 6, 'Then the eyes of the blind shall be opened, and the ears of the deaf unstopped; then the lame shall leap like a deer, and the tongue of the speechless sing for joy.'

Surely he cometh and a thousand voices
Shout to the saints, and to the deaf are dumb;
Surely he cometh and the earth rejoices,
Glad in his coming who hath sworn: I come![12]

This presumably means that unbelievers, who are described as being deaf and dumb, will not be aware of the triumphant voices announcing the second coming of Christ. The well-known hymn by Graham Kendrick takes up a similar eschatological theme but more positively.

He comes the broken hearts to heal
The prisoners to free.
The deaf shall hear, the lame shall dance,
The blind shall see.
. . .
Make way! (Make way!)
And let his kingdom in.[13]

Whenever Jesus Christ is preached his earthly miracles are symbolically repeated, and at the announcement of the gospel disabilities flee away.

> Hear Him, ye deaf; His praise ye dumb
> Your loosen'd tongues employ
> Ye blind, behold your saviour come
> And leap, ye lame for joy![14]

The third biblical influence which can sometimes be detected is the God of the Bible depicted as a perfect human being with no trace of impairment.

> Lord, we are few, but Thou art near,
> Nor short Thine arm, nor deaf Thine ear;
> O rend the heav'ns, come quickly down,
> And make a thousand hearts Thine own.[15]

In many hymns, the reference is not so much to hearing impairment as to the refusal to listen on the part of people with hearing, a refusal for which they may be regarded as morally culpable. Many hymns also refer to hearing people as being unable to hear, or unable to hear clearly because of a spiritual incapacity for which they may or may not be responsible.

> May Thy dread voice around,
> Thou harbinger of light,
> On our dull ears still sound,
> Lest here we sleep in night.[16]

> Give us the tongues to speak,
> In every time and place,
> To rich and poor, to strong and weak,
> The word of love and grace.
> Enable us to hear
> the words that others bring,
> interpreting with open ear
> the special song they sing.[17]

The contrast between the literally deaf who are nevertheless open to religious experience and the literally hearing who nevertheless refuse to

respond to faith is made specific in John Keble's poem or hymn for the
Twelfth Sunday after Trinity:

> The deaf may hear the saviour's voice
> The fettered tongue its chain may break
> But the deaf heart, the dumb by choice,
> The laggard soul that waits
> The guilt that scorns to be forgiven,
> These baffle e'en the bells of heaven.[18]

In English, as in most languages, to hear is to pay attention, to listen
with understanding and receptivity. A parent might say to a disobedient
child, 'You are not to do that! Do you hear me?' and when a congregation prays 'O Lord, hear our prayer and let our cry come unto Thee' it
is a plea for the divine response. There is a sliding scale from explicit
references to members of the Deaf community although these are also
intended in a metaphorical sense, to such expressions as 'She was deaf
to my entreaty' where the reference is to a refusal to respond, and to
such expressions as Antony asking the Romans to lend him their ears
and the prayer 'O give me Samuel's ear'.[19] When Jesus said 'If you have
ears to hear then hear' there was no negative reference to deaf people.
But surely, in that case, we might reflect, no negative reference to the
literally deaf is intended in any of these hymns?

There may be unintended consequences of both speech and action,
and when these are realized by the speaker or the actor, the nature of the
consequences comes to the foreground of intention and demands
choice. That deaf people have been marginalized, patronized, excluded
and persecuted is a matter of history, and that history is not over yet.
Therefore we have to look for the causes or contributory factors that
have built up or sustained those attitudes. There can be no doubt that
the use of deafness as a metaphor for incomprehension and disobedience at least suggests a negative attitude on the part of society and to
some extent sustains it, whether consciously or not. After all, you might
as well say that those who speak and understand only French are inat-
tentive, stubborn and disobedient when given orders in English! It is
simply that they don't speak English, and neither do many of those
whose preferred life-long language is BSL. This says nothing about their
intelligence, their interpersonal skills or their religious sensitivity, and
the same is true, of course, of people who have lost part or most of their
hearing later in life, whether or not they use BSL. So when church tradition, whether in Scripture or in hymns, speaks of those who refuse to

pay attention to the Christian message or to respond to the appeal of Christ as being hard of hearing or deaf, a link is set up, whether asserted or merely taken for granted, between those attributes and people in the Deaf community.

The problem is complicated by the fact that one cannot voluntarily close one's ears. We have eyelids but not earflaps. We can close our eyes to a situation, meaning that we refuse to take note of it, but such a figure of speech would be inappropriate for the sense of hearing. We would not normally or naturally say that someone closed their ears to an appeal for help; we would say that the person had refused to listen or, to put it more poetically, was 'dull of hearing'. When we say 'he was deaf to their entreaties' we mean no more than that he failed to hear or respond to certain sounds just as a Deaf person might have done. To say that Deaf people do not respond to spoken language is, at one level, merely to remark that Deaf people have their own form of communication but on the other hand these expressions almost always carry with them a critical or negative meaning. We criticize someone for being deaf to an appeal because we believe that there should have been a response and that the person was responsible for not responding, but Deaf people are not responsible for not responding to spoken appeals.

We have now reached a position where we can establish a criterion for the unacceptable use of the metaphors taken from the sense of hearing. The question we must ask is whether the expression, intentionally or not, is pejorative. Are Deaf people, whether literally or metaphorically, being blamed or having moral, spiritual or character defects attributed to them, directly or by inference? In short, when John Keble writes

Come, Lord, come wisdom, love and power
Open our ears to hear.
Let us not miss the accepted hour
Save Lord, by love or fear.[20]

there is no disparaging reference to members of the Deaf community. When Charles Wesley, on the other hand, writes

Hear Him, ye deaf, His praise, ye dumb
Your loosen'd tongues employ.

there is clearly an implication that those who do not respond to the Christian message because of insensitivity or disobedience are like members of the Deaf community. To say this is not to criticize Charles

Wesley. He had no way of knowing about the sophistication of British Sign Language, and he probably had no idea that there is a spirituality and theology of Deaf people which might be as profound as that which is found in the speaking community. We today, however, do know or should know these things and should be able to remove those elements in our tradition that continue to collaborate with this ancient, ignorant prejudice.

Blindness in the hymn books

Let us now turn to the more frequent occurrence of visual metaphorical language. When J. M. Neale translates a hymn from the late evening service of the Orthodox Church, there is no hint of a disparaging attitude towards blind people.

> Lord, that in death I sleep not
> And lest my foe should say
> 'I have prevailed against him'
> Lighten mine eyes I pray.
> O, Jesu, keep me in thy sight
> And guard me through the coming night.[21]

Similarly, when Bishop James Russel Woodford (1820–85) speaks of 'our darkened sight' the context shows that he is thinking of the contrast between day and night or perhaps a sky overcast with heavy clouds and a clear sky. There is no hint of a negative allusion to blind people.

> 'Til from our darkened sight
> The cloud shall pass away.
> And on the cleansed soul shall burst
> The everlasting day.[22]

References to 'dim eyes' are more ambiguous. Here the reference is not to the weather, or to the rotation of the earth, but to people with poor sight:

> Yet when Thine Easter news was spread
> Mid all its light, his eyes were dim.[23]

The reference is to St Thomas and although the Gospel of John describes him as a stout unbeliever who demands visual and tactile proof of the resurrection, there is nothing in the story to suggest that he had any problems with his eyesight. 'Dim eyes' has become a metaphor for his lack of faith.

Another ambiguous example comes from the well-known hymn 'Holy, Holy, Holy'. Verse three reads

Holy! Holy! Holy! Though the darkness hide thee
Though the eye of sinful man Thy glory may not see.[24]

It is one thing to say that God dwells in darkness but it is another thing to claim that it is because of sin one cannot see. No doubt it is sin that prevents human beings from becoming aware of the divine glory, but as one who on many occasions has been asked about the alleged sin which brought about my blindness, I cannot be comfortable with this line.[25]

I have a similar sense of slight discomfort with the words in the well-known hymn 'Break thou the bread of life'. The third verse goes:

O send Thy spirit, Lord,
Now unto me,
That he may touch my eyes,
And make me see:
Show me the truth concealed
within Thy word,
and in Thy book revealed
I see Thee, Lord.[26]

This is a prayer for understanding based upon the sense of sight. The reference to being made to see by the touching of the eyes brings the metaphor close to the idea of blindness, reminiscent as it is of the miracle of the man born blind in John 9.

There are many cases, however, where the metaphor of blindness is used less ambiguously to describe sinful, unbelieving or unresponsive people.

Thou knowest what we are, how frail and blind,
Thou still rememb'rest that we are but dust
Like as a Father pitieth, Thou art kind.[27]

In a hymn written in 1899 for the war in South Africa blindness is identified with careless living. This is odd, since one of the most obvious features of living as a blind person is that one has to be so careful about everything.

Spare us, good Lord! If just the strife
Yet still from guilt we are not free.
Forgive our blind and careless life
Our oft forgetfulness of Thee.[28]

As with deafness, many references to blindness in the hymn books are influenced by the miracles of Jesus.

Pass me not, O mighty Spirit!
Thou canst make the blind to see;
Witnesser of Jesu's merit
Speak the word of power to me,
Even me.[29]

Another example is the hymn by Tommy Walker from 1995:

Only you are the Author of life
Only you can bring the blind their sight
Only you are called prince of Peace.[30]

Other hymns are influenced by the sermon preached by Jesus at Nazareth. An example is the popular and beautiful hymn from the Iona community.

Will you let the blinded see
If I but call your name?
Will you set the prisoners free
And never be the same?[31]

The same influence is probably to be seen in the hymn by C. A. Callington (1872–1955) although there are also traces of the commission given to Paul following his brief loss of sight.

Tell the praise of him who called you
Out of darkness into light.
Broke the fetters that enthralled you
Gave you freedom, peace and sight.[32]

Another influence is Revelation 3.17.

> We are wretched, cold and naked,
> Needing all things, poor and blind;
> Thou hast raiment, riches, healing,
> Meet for body, soul and mind.[33]

Most descriptions of blindness in the hymns refer to personal conversion or to the transforming power of Christian faith.

> I was once in darkness, now my eyes can see,
> I was lost but Jesus sought and found me.[34]

> Once I was blind,
> Yet believed I saw everything
> Proud in my ways
> Yet a fool in my part.[35]

In the light of Matthew 23.17, where Jesus is described as having spoken of blind fools, the connection in this hymn between blindness and foolishness is regrettable.

Perhaps the most striking cases are when the metaphor of blindness is used not to describe one's own shortcomings but those of others. So, in 1936, Percy Dearmer wrote

> O, free the world from blindness,
> and fill the world with kindness,
> Give sinners resurrection,
> bring striving to perfection.[36]

In a similar vein, Chris Cartwright, in 1991, writes

> Interceding for a nation
> That is dying, lost and blind,
> Let us see them with the eyes of Christ.[37]

In 1996, Lex Loizides sings

> Our hearts were turned away,
> But then the light of Christ broke in
> And made us live again.

> And if you can heal our blindness,
> You can save our nation too.[38]

Occasionally the hymn writers show an awareness that it may be religion itself that will be the problem. 'Let not our worship blind us to the claims of love'.[39]

Further thoughts about the criterion

Before we began to refer to the metaphor of sight and blindness we had arrived at a discriminating criterion. This was to ask ourselves if the metaphor suggested a disparaging comparison with groups of disabled people. I would now like to suggest a more searching rationale for this. If sighted and hearing people use the imagery of light and sound to express their experiences in the world they inhabit that is natural and inevitable. However, if able-bodied people make disparaging allusions to people who have very different experiences this may not only betray ignorance of those ways of life and is discourteous, but may reinforce a prejudice against disabled people that will in turn give credibility to the view that Christian faith does not offer answers to the search for equal opportunities: it may actually be part of the problem. In other words, when we consider the sliding scale of metaphors from those that refer explicitly to various impaired states through to those which merely use the various ideas of light and sound, sight and speech, we should distinguish between those that speak to our own world, the one we know and experience, and those that refer negatively to other people's worlds of which we have no first-hand experience.

In saying this, I do not overlook the fact that there may be hymn writers who are themselves blind yet continue to use disparaging metaphors of their own condition. This is to be explained by the combination of a piety that does not adopt a critical stance towards the tradition, and immersion in the assumptions of a society in which the inferiority and the marginalization of disabled people were simply taken for granted.

In the light of our new principle it is possible to comment on the situation of people with other impairments such as those who use wheelchairs for mobility. Biblical precedent such as the eschatological hope expressed in Isaiah 35.5 and some of the miracles in the Gospels do encourage the hymn writers to refer to lame people. Lameness can be used as a disparaging metaphor for sin. Such expressions are as unacceptable as the explicitly pejorative references to blind and deaf people. Merely referring to standing up, however, comes into the category of speaking of the body's symbolism which is natural to those who have legs and can use them. A wheelchair user should no more object to 'stand up and bless the Lord, ye people of His choice' than I as a blind person have any right to object to 'the Lord is my light, my strength and my salvation'. True, the Lord is not my light, because I have no light sensation, and wheelchair users cannot respond to the invitation to stand up in the presence of the Lord.[40] However, just as able-bodied people should not thrust the demands of their experience upon others, so people with impairments should not demand that able-bodied worlds should conform to theirs. The principle is to rejoice in your own world without making disparaging remarks or setting unreasonable limits upon the natural life-worlds of others.

A limited range of disabilities are referred to in the hymn books. These are usually those that find a symbolic place within the vocabulary of the Bible: blindness, deafness, being lame or having leprosy. We referred earlier to the hymn 'Thine arm, O Lord, in days of old', quoting the line 'the beggar with his sightless eyes'. This replaced the line, found in the older version, 'the leper with his tainted life' which has not reappeared in that particular hymn since about 1950. References to diseases such as AIDS and cancer are rarely if ever found in hymns, partly because they are regarded as contemporary conditions, and partly because they are not referred to in the Bible.

Bodily metaphors

This discussion raises questions about the whole use of metaphors based upon the human body. Such language is inevitable, depending upon the kind of body you are born with, and without it language would become very colourless. We could not speak at all without metaphor and most of our metaphors are based upon very early body experience.[41] When we say such things as, 'I can't quite follow you', 'we seem to have gone about as far as we can with this discussion', 'at this point our thought encounters an obstacle' and so on we are using language that originates in bodily life in the world. Rooted in our earliest infancy, such expressions not only make language more meaningful but become more or less invisible as metaphors. If we were spirits, unconscious of pain, obstacles, hunger or death and if we communicated by spiritual intuition without the use of hands, lips and tongues, we might be able to manage without such metaphors, but then we would no longer be human. The bodily experience of most human beings takes place in a world in which there is light and darkness, sound and silence, arms and legs, mobility and music, but modern understandings of human rights demand that the plurality of human worlds should be recognized. This demand bites deeply (another body metaphor) into a tradition that has not found it easy to recognize plurality. The very idea that some day in the future the diversity of human persons will converge upon the experience of the majority illustrates this difficulty. The concept of a homogeneous perfection against which diversity is considered to be imperfect encourages the marginalization of minority groups. Perhaps it will be said that able-bodied people, who are in the majority, are fully justified in speaking negatively of blindness and deafness. After all, it might be said, would not the deaf prefer to hear and the blind to see?

In the first place, Deaf culture is becoming increasingly autonomous. It cannot be assumed that Deaf people would prefer to hear; the assumption would be considered by many in the Deaf world as part of the arrogance typical of a powerful majority. In the case of blind people, with their greater loss of independent movement, and the loss of so much visual beauty, it might be more unusual to find blind people who would not prefer to see.[42] Be this as it may, it does not justify the assumption or the claim being made by sighted people. The situation is rather similar to the relationship between the rich and the poor. It may be that the poor are blessed, but it is not the place of the rich to say so. Moreover, sometimes the disparagement of presumably less desirable states leaves an uneasy feeling (another body metaphor) that it springs from a nervousness about the loss of a normality. Anyone can lose sight or hearing at almost any time. Normality is as temporary and as fragile as blindness and deafness appear to be undesirable. So let not the strong people glory in their strength, nor the normal in their normality nor the wise in their wisdom, but let the one who glories, glory in the Lord. Certainly, there are many Christian disabled people whose experience testifies that whether they live or die, whether they see or not, whether in wheelchairs or not, they live in the hands of God and that is another bodily metaphor.

Conclusions

Negative metaphors of various disabilities are not only found in the hymn books and the Bible, but are common in the media and in everyday speech. Perhaps they will become less common in a more enlightened community. We will always have to face the fact that much of the classical literature of the world embodies such negativity. What are we to say, for example, of the use of literal blindness as a metaphor in Shakespeare's *King Lear*? It seems reasonable to hope that just as the presence of anti-Semitism in *The Merchant of Venice* and of misogynist views in *The Taming of the Shrew* present problems for contemporary producers, so references to *The Hunchback of Notre Dame* and the blindness of Gloucester will increasingly be regarded as traces of archaic prejudice. Will the same thing happen to the Bible or will enough Christians be inspired by its generally redemptive message to distance themselves and others from its lesser negative motifs? The greatness of Shakespeare will survive realization of the presence of some less acceptable attitudes and the same is true of the spiritual majesty of the Bible.

In view of the fact that Christian faith has so much potential for human liberation it is sad and puzzling to see that the realization and implementation of this has taken many centuries. Although the biblical doctrines of creation and redemption surely imply that no human being should own another one as his or her property, parts of the Bible are fairly complacent towards the institution of slavery. For centuries it was in the interests of the wealthy and powerful to collaborate with the convenience of slavery, and this is still the case in some respects today. Similarly, the equal creation of men and women and the equality of their calling in the Christian community should have enabled those who were newly created in the image of Christ to overcome the patriarchal prejudice which is found in so much of the Bible, but it did not always do so. The recognition that disabled people are not subhuman and that much of what we call disability is caused not by their impairment as such but by the attitudes and environment of the surrounding society has also been very slow to mature. The miracles of Jesus, which might perhaps have encouraged the inclusion of disabled people in the community, have seldom been interpreted in this way.[43] The miracles certainly encouraged a mission of healing but this often took the form of isolation and exclusion. Taken literally, the miracles have encouraged the view that there is no real place for disabled people among the disciples of Jesus;[44] taken symbolically they have led to the negativity which we have been discussing. The liberation offered by Jesus in his death and resurrection was not enough to overcome the negative imagery of the Bible.

These are sad reflections, but not hopeless ones. To use two more bodily metaphors, the night is far spent but the morning is at hand. Many contemporary hymn books have been careful to remove traces of imperialism and patriarchy. Sensitivity towards the negative images of disabled people has hardly begun, but it is not impossible that this will be the next wave of reform. Let us conclude with one final example, perhaps the best-known and loved hymn in which a negative image of blindness is conveyed.

Amazing grace, how sweet the sound
That saved a wretch like me;
I once was lost but now am found,
Was blind but now I see.[45]

I would like to suggest a slightly altered version.

Amazing grace that set me free
And brought me to the light;
I once was blind but now I see,
Was black but now I'm white.

Most people today would, I imagine, find the last line objectionable. So why not the second last line?

Notes

1 I would like to express my thanks to the Allan and Nesta Ferguson Charitable Trust whose grant made this essay possible, and to my research assistant Jonathan Taylor.

2 John M. Hull, '"Sight to the Inly Blind"? Attitudes to Blindness in the Hymn-books', *Theology*, vol. CV, no. 827 (2002), pp. 333–41. <http://www.johnmhull.biz/Sight%20to%20the%20inly%20blind%2022%20October.htm>

3 Hull, '"Sight to the Inly Blind"?', p. 339.

4 'Lord, I was blind: I could not see', *Congregational Praise*, London: Independent Press, 1951, no. 378, p. 413.

5 The Royal Association for Deaf People, <http://www.royaldeaf.org.uk/page.php?id=100177>

6 R. Sutton-Spence, 'Aspects of BSL Poetry: A Social and Linguistic Analysis of The Poetry of Dorothy Miles', *Sign Language and Linguistics*, 3:1 (2000), pp. 79–100. <http://www.ingentaconnect.com/content/jbp/sll/2000/00000003/00000001/art00004>.

7 In the disability literature, Deaf with a capital often refers to people whose pre-ferred communication is Sign Language while deaf with a lower case refers to hearing loss in general.

8 Nora Ellen Groce, *Everyone here spoke sign language: hereditary deafness on Martha's Vineyard*, London: Harvard University Press, 1985.

9 Wayne Morris, 'Theology Without Words: A Critical Examination of Theology

in the Deaf Community', Unpublished PhD Thesis, University of Birmingham, 2004.

10 *Hymns, Ancient and Modern: Historical Edition*, London: William Clowes, 1909, p. 115.

11 E. H. Plumptre (1821–91) 'Thine Arm, O Lord, in days of old', in *Common Praise*, Norwich: Canterbury Press, 2000, no. 347.

12 F. W. H. Myers (1843–1901), 'Hark What a Sound and Too Divine for Hearing', in *Common Praise*, no. 28, p. 57, verse 2.

13 Graham Kendrick (1950–), 'Make Way! Make Way!', in *Songs of Fellowship*, Eastbourne: Kingsway Music, 1998, no. 384.

14 Charles Wesley (1707–88), 'O for a Thousand Tongues to sing!', in *Common Praise*, no. 534, verse 5.

15 William Cowper (1731–1800), 'Jesus, where'er thy people meet', in *Common Praise*, no. 492, verse 5. The reference is to Isaiah 59.1 and on the question of God as a normal or supernormal human being see my article, 'Blindness and the Face of God: Toward a Theology of Disability', in Hans-Georg Ziebertz et al., eds, *The Human Image of God* [Johannes A. Van Der Ven Festschrift] Brill, 2000, pp. 215–29. <http://www.johnmhull.biz/Blindness%20and%20the%20Face%20of%20God.html>

16 C. Coffin (1676–1749), tr. I. Williams in 1839 'Lo! from the desert homes', in *Hymns, Ancient and Modern*, no. 234, p. 332, verse 4.

17 Michael Forster (1946–), 'Come, Holy Spirit, Come!', in *Common Praise*, no. 179, verse 4.

18 John Keble, *The Christian Year*, London: J. Parker, 1827.

19 James Drummond Burns (1823–64), 'Hush'd was the evening hymn', in *Hymns, Ancient and Modern*, no. 584, p. 728.

20 John Keble (1792–1866), 'When God of old came down from heaven', in *Common Praise*, no. 199, p. 424, verse 7.

21 tr. Dr J. M. Neale 'The day is past and over', in *Hymns Ancient and Modern*, no. 19, p. 26, verse 4.

22 James Russel Woodford (1820–85), 'Within the Father's house', in *Hymns, Ancient and Modern*, no. 87, p. 116, verse 6.

23 William Bright (1824–1901) 'How oft O Lord, Thy face has shone', in *Hymns, Ancient and Modern*, no. 226, p. 324, verse 2.

24 Reginald Heber (1783–1826), 'Holy, holy, holy! Lord God Almighty!', in *Common Praise*, no. 202, p. 431, verse 3.

25 For examples, see my *In the Beginning There Was Darkness*, London: SCM Press, 2001, pp. 49–52.

26 Mary Lathbury (1841–1913) and Alexander Groves (1842–1909), 'Break thou the bread of life', in *Common Praise*, no. 286, p. 613, verse 3.

27 Ernest Edward Dugmore (1843–1925), 'Almighty Father, Unoriginate', in *Hymns, Ancient and Modern*, no. 334, p. 455, verse 5.

28 Somerset Corry Lowry (1855–1932), 'Lord, while afar our brothers fight', in *Hymns, Ancient and Modern*, no. 519, p. 660, verse 4.

29 Elizabeth Codner (1824–1919), 'Lord, I hear of showers of blessing', in *Hymns, Ancient and Modern*, no. 593, p. 736, verse 4.

30 Tommy Walker, 'I will give you Praise', in *Songs of Fellowship*, no. 270.

31 John Bell (1949–) and Graham Maule (1958–), 'Will you come and follow me if I but call your name?', in *Common Praise*, no. 622, p. 1338, verse 3.

32 C. A. Callington (1872–1955), 'Ye that know the Lord is gracious', in *Common Praise*, no. 628, p. 1351, verse 3.

33 August Blair Donaldson (1841–1903), 'Glory to the first-begotten', in *Hymns, Ancient and Modern*, no. 629, p. 780, verse 12.

34 Joan Parsons, 'I once was in darkness', in *Songs of Fellowship*, no. 263.

35 Stuart Townend, 'I will sing of the lamb', in *Songs of Fellowship*, no. 856, verse 3.

36 Percy Dearmer (1867–1936), 'A brighter dawn is breaking', in *Common Praise*, no. 135, p. 291, verse 3.

37 Chris Cartwright, 'From your throne, O Lord', in *Songs of Fellowship*, no. 725.

38 Lex Loizides, 'We stand together before our saviour', in *Songs of Fellowship*, no. 1103.

39 George B. Caird, 'Almighty Father, who for us thy Son didst give', in *Common Praise*, no. 374, p. 799, verse 4.

40 I am referring to the words of hymns not to the conduct of public worship. There is a growing awareness of diversity in congregations, and increasingly leaders of worship are using such expressions as 'If you normally stand then please stand now' or 'If you would like to stand please do so', which respect the varieties of physical posture which may be convenient for the worshippers.

41 Mark Johnson, *The Body in the Mind: The Bodily Basis of Meaning, Imagination and Reason*, Chicago: University of Chicago Press, 1990.

42 Unusual, but not unknown. Oliver Sacks describes the case of Virgil, a blind man from Kentucky who was deeply disorientated and depressed when sight was restored to him. There are other reports of such cases. Oliver Sacks, *An Anthropologist on Mars*, London: Picador, 1995, pp. 102–44.

43 Graham W. Monteith, *Deconstructing Miracles: From Thoughtless Indifference to Honouring Disabled People*, Glasgow: Covenanters Press, 2005.

44 John M. Hull, 'Could a Blind Person have been a Disciple of Jesus?', in *Ministerial Formation* [World Council of Churches Education and Ecumenical Formation], no. 92 (2001), pp. 20–1. <http://www.johnmhull.biz/Could%20a%20blind%20person.html>

45 John Newton (1725–1807), 'Amazing grace', in *Common Praise*, no. 375, verse 1.

Brokenness, Love and Embrace:
Eating Disorders and the Eucharist

CLAIRE CARSON AND NICOLA SLEE

Introduction

In this essay, we seek to offer some reflections on the complex relation
between eating disorders and the theology and practice of public liturgy
in the Church, especially the celebration of the Eucharist. We begin by
locating ourselves within the concerns of the piece, explaining why the
issue of food and its symbolic meanings is important to us; then go on to
set the discussion within a wider theological and historical framework,
in particular referring to feminist analysis of women's eating practices,
before discussing some of the problematic aspects of eucharistic and
food symbolism for believers suffering from eating disorders; finally we
offer some liturgical resources which are not intended to be limited to
use with those with eating disorders but which attempt to redress an
unthinking use of food imagery, where food and drink symbols are only
permitted to have positive, rather than more nuanced, significance. Our
intention throughout is to find ways in which Christian liturgy (especially, but not only, eucharistic liturgies) can be as radically inclusive
and positively affirmative of human bodies – in all their glorious
ambivalence, woundedness and beauty – as possible.

Contextualizing the discussion

This essay takes its inspiration from Claire's research into appropriate
pastoral responses to those with eating disorders conducted during the
late 1990s. Claire's motivation in conducting this research stemmed
from her own experience and personal struggles of being anorexic and
part of a church community. During her training for ordination at
Queen's, she decided to reflect on her previous experience and to see if

it might be of benefit to other people with eating disorders, as well as those with pastoral care for them. The aim of the research was to explore some of the possible theological, spiritual and pastoral issues that people with eating disorders might face if they were part of a Christian community, or had some Christian faith connection. Claire interviewed a number of people who had experience of eating disorders, particularly anorexia nervosa, and who also had some link with a church. She was interested in exploring both the positive and negative aspects of Christian practices, liturgical, pastoral and social. Through her research, she wanted to raise awareness of eating disorders in the Christian context and to develop appropriate and sensitive pastoral responses. The research was never seen as only of relevance to those with eating disorders, however; it has much wider implications for the Church, as it is about deconstructing the messages given to people about their bodies, their sense of worth and value, in and through its liturgy and public teaching.

As Claire's supervisor at the time, Nicola recognized the significance of this research, since there has been very little contemporary study of eating disorders from a theological or liturgical perspective (in contrast to more historical studies by Bynum and others). At a more personal level, Claire's research has challenged Nicola to re-evaluate her own assumptions about, attitudes towards and symbolic appropriations of food – and, in particular, to recognize the ways in which food practices and imagery can be a much more painful and ambivalent arena for others than it has been for her. Growing up in a large farming family where food was always abundant and mealtimes were at the heart of daily life, Nicola's associations with food are overwhelmingly positive. Throughout both childhood and adult life, the preparation and sharing of food have always been sources of pleasure and delight. Food symbolism features fairly frequently in her poetry and liturgical writings as a symbol of generosity, sensual pleasure, communion with the divine and with others,[1] although occasionally food takes on more fraught meanings.[2] At the same time, Nicola's own experience of ill health has given her a different context from which to explore the frailty and woundedness of the body, and to connect this to the ecclesial reality of the fragile body of Christ.

Out of these very different experiences of food and the ways in which food can carry deeper symbolic meanings, we have dialogued together about the need for theologians, liturgists and pastoral workers to be far more aware of the diverse ways in which food and eating symbolism will be appropriated by different members of the Christian community;

and, in particular, to become aware of the ways in which the centrality of food symbolism in the Eucharist can be a source of deep pain and exclusion for many who struggle, in different ways, with eating disorders.

The body, food and liturgy in theological and historical context

The imagery of food and the practice of eating – as well as refraining from eating – are central to all religious traditions, and Christianity is no exception. The Scriptures are full of eating imagery: from the creation of the garden in which food is given for human sustenance, through the narrative of the so-called 'Fall' in which food becomes a symbol of temptation (but perhaps, too, of wisdom); through Israel's wilderness wanderings in which God provides manna and quail; into the prophetic literature in which the image of the heavenly banquet of fine wine and abundant food capture the vision of the messianic age; in the Wisdom literature where Wisdom invites all who hunger to her table; in the Gospels, where Jesus' parties are legendary, and where he uses images of bread and wine to speak of the most intimate offering of himself to his disciples; in Paul, whose theology of incorporation into the body of Christ is reflected in his call to honour the body in the way in which eucharistic liturgy is celebrated. One might claim that of all religions, Christianity is most inescapably committed to the body and to the sacramental significance of eating and drinking as the way in which the individual body of the believer is incorporated into the mystic and ecclesial body of Christ. It is not simply the eucharistic liturgy as such that recalls the presence of Christ most profoundly, but, arguably, any table fellowship at which food is shared and the stranger is welcomed become the place where Christ is re-presented and the gospel re-enacted. The Christian tradition of saying grace before and after meals testifies to the honouring of the meal table as one of the chief places within daily life where God's grace and goodness are routinely received and recognized.

Food, then, takes on a richly freighted significance within Christian theology, liturgy and pastoral practice. And food is never neutral within Christian self-understanding. As the gift of the Creator, food is respected and honoured and demands to be handled with reverence; but, more, there is a strong scriptural concern for the right sharing of bread with the hungry, so that the way in which food is distributed becomes a measure of the holiness of the community. God's bread is for all, and therefore whatever provision God's people enjoy is to be shared with others. Even more, as the core symbol of Christ's body, the ritual sharing of bread and wine demands to be conducted with reverence and attention to the bodily needs and condition of all who partake of the love-feast. The liturgical consumption of food must be all of a piece with the community's behaviour when not gathered in the liturgical assembly. Or, to put this conversely, the ritual consumption of food is always more than mere biological activity; eating and drinking both mirror and perform wider social, ecclesial and spiritual meanings.

Social, gendered and sexualized meanings of food

The meanings of food and its relation to both public and private prayer and spirituality are, therefore, highly complex, nuanced and multi-layered in Christian tradition. They are also strongly contextualized in particular historical periods, social and culture milieux, including gendered settings. The meanings of food can and have changed dramatically in different eras and settings. The availability and variety of food supplies, the ability to store food, the culinary skill and traditions of a community, the health and hygiene traditions of a culture concerning the preparation and consumption of food; the different taboos around food and the penalties for the violation of those taboos – all these factors and others will influence and shape the ways in which food is perceived and the variety of symbolic meanings it can carry for a society and for a religious community.

Within Christian tradition, food has certainly been strongly gendered in its social and theological meanings. Women have been mainly responsible for the routine preparation and serving of food in the domestic sphere, while men have been those permitted to offer food ritually and sacramentally in the liturgy, as priests. At the same time, as Bynum and others[3] show, women mystics and religious in the Middle Ages found ways of imbuing food with their own highly particularized meanings, and their practices of abstinence, on the one hand, and of adoration of Christ in the sacrament on the other, can be read as highly developed means of exercising a kind of 'control' over their bodies which was denied them in a more overt, religious and political sense. Women's regulation of food continued to be one arena in which they could exercise power, both in the domestic sphere of food preparation but also in the spiritual and ritual sphere of their own prayer, public as well as private. This is not only an ancient phenomenon, as modern mystics such as Simone Weil and many other 'holy anorexics' demonstrate. Physical asceticism, including the renunciation of food as well as of sexuality, has always been an attractive – if highly dangerous – spiritual path for women, as Ann Loades explains:

> Getting control of her body for a girl or woman retrieves her from the sense of helplessness and unbearable inadequacy that she experiences in society and Church by virtue of being female. By means of her asceticism she commands attention; she commands in herself at least at times tremendous energy, and may find what she believes to be communion with God. So she develops techniques to control a self-induced and self-perpetuating system of rewards, and she can then by-pass the religious controls of priests and confessors, those who seem to deny her autonomy.[4]

Hilary Mantel, in a review of a number of historical studies of adolescent girls' ascetic practices, agrees, regarding anorexia, both in the past and in contemporary society, as 'an accommodation, a strategy for survival', a way of 'wanting out', of 'buying time' as the young girl moves towards adolescence and is confronted with the realities of what it means to take on social expectations of femaleness.

> Anorexia . . . seems like mad behaviour, but I don't think it is madness. It is a way of shrinking back, of reserving, preserving the self, fighting free of sexual and emotional entanglements. It says, like Christ, 'noli me tangere'. Touch me not and take yourself off. For a year or two, it may be a valid strategy; to be greensick, to be out of the game; to die just a little; to nourish the inner being while starving the outer being; to buy time.[5]

For women, then, as Carroll Saussy suggests, 'food is not only a matter of survival; it is a psychosocial issue deeply connected to identity, self-esteem, intimacy, health, community, and celebration'.[6] If food has so many potential meanings, so, then, does abstinence from food. As Catherine Garrett suggests, 'An eating disorder is itself an extreme form of desire: a spiritual craving expressed through the body'.[7] And Joanne Woolway Grenfell puts it vividly: 'eating disorders symbolically reflect social relations; the anorexic is refusing to take in other people's visions of who she is; the bulimic is vomiting out the intrusions of others, and the compulsive eater is attempting to control the world by taking it into herself'.[8] Carol Lakey Hess makes the same point when she describes

American anorexic teenage girls as 'prophetic sign-bearers' 'calling our culture to repentance'.[9] Grenfell suggests that young women in particular play out the tensions within the religious community around body and sexual identity, authority and social cohesion, and specifically around the changing roles of women in the home and workplace. While these tensions belong to the community as a whole, they are picked up, so to speak, and

> played out on the bodies of those who are particularly susceptible to anxiety about their physical selves, those who are already struggling with the tension between their identity as subjects of their own lives and as objects of the community's contested identity and fears about its future, and those who are grappling with their own issues of belonging in relation to group expectations.[10]

While feminist and pastoral theologians have begun to address the complex issue of eating disorders and their psychological, theological and spiritual meanings – both positive and negative – for women and girls particularly (though not exclusively),[11] little attention has been given to the liturgy as a site of difficulty or possibility with regard to eating disorders. To this we now turn.

The Eucharist as an experience of exclusion

The Eucharist, which is at the centre of Christian worship and spirituality, should be an encounter of radical inclusivity, if it is truly to mirror and represent the radical welcome and inclusivity of Jesus' own table fellowship. Yet, in practice, the Eucharist is often experienced as a place and a ritual of exclusion – and in very many different ways. For people who suffer from an eating disorder, the Eucharist can be experienced as a place of painful contradiction and exclusion in quite specific ways that centre on the food symbolism of the ritual. Rather than being experienced as a rite of healing and reconciliation, it can become an experience more akin to nightmare: a time of panic and anxiety as participants attempt to find ways to avoid receiving the bread and the wine and yet at the same time to be included in this rite.

For people with eating disorders, the thoughts and feelings which arise during a service of Holy Communion will vary enormously, evoking different responses to the language of prayers, but likely including the terror of touch at the peace and a strong sense of exclusion from the symbolism and action of eating and drinking the body and blood of Christ around the table with others. Such strong emotional and psychological reactions to eucharistic imagery and practice only make sense if we consider, as Woolway Grenfell and others suggest, that eating disorders focus and mirror a whole series of tensions and contradictions within the religious community, as well as within the body of the individual, around physical, sexual and religious identity.

For people with eating disorders, as well as the centrality of images of food and sharing, the language of some of the prayers can reinforce their sense of guilt, shame and unworthiness. In many Anglican rites of Holy Communion, the idea that 'we are not worthy' is reinforced over and over again. Even though we are assured of God's forgiveness near the beginning of the service, we still go on to say later on that we are not worthy. The 'Prayer of humble access' emphasizes that our bodies are sinful and need to be made clean, a message which tends to overshadow that of God's mercy. For people who are already feeling a sense of shame about their bodies and a sense of unworthiness at being at the table, these messages can create and reinforce an overwhelming sense of guilt.

Speaking from her own experience, Claire comments:

For me, receiving communion became impossible. In the beginning, I would still attend eucharistic services as I had always done. But I longed to escape the images of food, and especially the sharing of food. First the problem had centred around sharing food socially in the church, but then the Eucharist started to be a problem. One day when I was at a Eucharist I noticed that there was real bread on the altar. I was absolutely terrified. As the time for communion came closer I kept thinking, 'will I receive, won't I receive? Will people notice if I don't? Will people be offended if I don't? What does this service mean to me if I don't?' The questions buzzed around my head relentlessly, but the overwhelming sense was of sheer terror at the thought of letting real bread touch my lips, still less actually pass through my throat into my stomach. I felt utterly guilty and ashamed of how I was thinking, but I couldn't possibly tell anyone.

As the Eucharist had always been central to my Christian life, I was at a complete loss as to what to do when I found it so difficult. The Eucharist had been a time for me to bring everything I was before God, alongside others in that community, but suddenly I found it impossible to offer even a tiny part of myself, let alone to receive anything from anyone, especially God. I struggled with wanting to be alone and hide from the world and from God, but at the same time I longed for some sort of intimacy. I felt that there was nothing in the church practices, in prayers and liturgy that was helpful to me. There seemed to be nothing that affirmed my body and helped me to truly value myself.

For some people with eating disorders the reception of communion may not be a problem, but, for others, receiving communion may feel difficult if not impossible. Some anorectics feel that communion is the only 'food' they can eat. While they may see most foods as bad and unclean, polluting their body, they believe that the bread and the wine which are the body and blood of Jesus will cleanse them. For others, the Eucharist can be very traumatic. They may not like eating in front of others in everyday life; therefore to gather round the table with others in church may be very uncomfortable. They feel watched and on show. Whether the minister is using real bread or wafers might be very significant. Many people with anorexia never allow a piece of real bread to pass their lips in months or even years. The experience of being confronted with the offer of bread and wine can cause much pain and tension within them, resulting in an extreme sense of guilt and shame that they cannot participate in this central act of worship. This may lead to deep feelings of isolation and marginalization or even self-exclusion from the community.

It is essential that those in public ministry who have responsibility for the preparation and celebration of eucharistic rites take time to think through the liturgies they use from the perspective of those with eating disorders, and indeed from the perspective of many with a low self-image. For those experiencing a sense of alienation from their own bodies – whether because of eating disorders, or other issues – the language of prayers and the symbolism and actions of the liturgy can have a profound impact, either reinforcing negative self-image and a sense of unworthiness or blame, or finding ways to affirm the fragile identities of those who long to be present, but perhaps need to be present at the edge of the liturgy, rather than participating in the same way as others for whom the consumption of food is non-problematic.

As Christians our food is vitally important in its material substance; it fulfils a symbolic role in the Eucharist, but its symbolism is dependent on it maintaining its connection to the very real body of the crucified Christ and to the broken bodies of those who receive it. So both the practice of the Eucharist and the interpretation of scripture need to stress that Christianity is not about perfect bodies – of communities, or of individuals – but about human reality and flaws.[12]

Rethinking food symbolism: alternative liturgical resources

In this final section of our essay, we offer some liturgical resources that we have developed out of our own different experiences of eating disorder and of illness, in which eating takes on a variety of meanings contrasting with those likely to be assumed in much mainstream, authorized liturgy. These are not to be seen as definitive liturgical texts, but as occasional, experimental rites, in which we have been seeking to 'write the body' – our own bodies, the bodies of those we care about, the larger body of Christ, both ecclesial and mystical – in ways that are authentic and truthful to our own experiences of woundedness, longing and hope. The intention of offering these resources is not so that they will be copied or reproduced (although we are happy for them to be used) so much as that they may arouse an awareness in others of the multiple ways in which liturgy can either exclude or include, and provoke others to try their own experimentation in their own settings.

The Eucharist needs, above all, to be made more 'spacious', with room for all, in ways that can be healing and life-giving for all, both those who feel able to receive the elements and also those who do not, without excluding the latter from participation. This requires those in ministerial roles to exercise a careful awareness of who is present and what their needs might be, and also an openness to developing alternative liturgical practices – for example, making it possible for those who are not receiving to hold the bread and wine, to allow the presence of Christ to come as close as is comfortable, without any pressure to consume being exerted.

Alternative liturgies need to be created, acknowledging the difficulties and the struggles of people with eating disorders, where their voices can be heard, their anger and their pain expressed. There needs to be space within liturgy and worship for developing and using alternative symbols, stories and practices, which affirm bodies – the bodies of all people, not only those with eating disorders, but all of those – and isn't this all of *us*? – who, in different ways, know ourselves to be incomplete, needy, broken, dysfunctional, yet also created, called and loved into being by the One who sees in us the image of God.

There are two kinds of material below: first, some shorter liturgical 'fragments', which can be used in a variety of contexts, formal or informal, inserted into larger liturgies or used, as appropriate, in pastoral situations. Two longer pieces follow: a more developed litany and, finally, a larger quasi-eucharistic liturgy which centres on the sharing, but not the consumption, of bread and wine.

Prayers for people with eating disorders[13]

These prayers were written out of our own different experiences of eating disorders and of illness, and out of our common desire to bring these different body experiences into both personal and public prayer and to allow such experiences to shape the prayer of the whole ecclesial body. While they emerge out of quite specific bodily experiences – eating disorders, migraine and chronic fatigue – they are more generally concerned with the struggle to affirm and acknowledge the body's hungers and needs, its goodness and its imperfection, as the only site for discipleship and worship. As such, their meaning and use is not limited to those with eating disorders or the specific bodily experiences from which they emerged.

You created me

Loving God,
You created me in my mother's womb,
and you love me just as I am.

Loving God,
help me to love myself –
all that I am and all that I have to offer.

Loving God,
help me to value myself –
all that I am and all that I have to offer.

Loving God,
help me to believe in myself
and find a place and a sense of worth in this world.
Amen.

Help me to respond to my body's needs and hungers

Loving God,
help me to respond to my body's needs and hungers.

Help me to look after myself,
free from guilt and fear
in the knowledge that I am worthy. Amen.

Help me to know when I am hungry

Help me to know when I am hungry and when I am full.
Help me to know what I should do.
Help me to deny myself
as some people have taught me to do.
Help me to accept what is rightfully mine. Amen.

A grace after sickness[14]

After vomiting, I rise and eat again.
The food that I could not stomach yesterday
tastes of earth and heaven.
I chew bread slowly.
I sip water.
I marvel that I am upright.
It is enough.

A litany for messy eaters

Nicola writes: 'I wrote this piece to explore and express something of the diversity of meanings food might have for those gathered at a eucharistic celebration. It could be used as a form of intercessory prayer, or as a litany before communion.'

For Catherine, who can't eat the bread because it will make her sick;
For Desmond, who won't touch the wine because he's an alcoholic;
For Rachel, on an enforced liquid diet of chemicals because her bowel is packing up;
For Grace, who must eat little and often because she's diabetic;
For Michael, who's lost all his teeth to jaw cancer and must be fed like a baby;
For Redge, on a low-fat diet to prevent the recurrence of heart attack:

**We are all one body
Because we all partake of the one bread.**

For Justin, who buys only from Waitrose and uses the finest recipes;
For Audrey, who swears by her microwave and buys bargains past their
sell-by date;
For Jonas, cooking curry for twenty and inviting in all the neighbours;
For Sidney, who eats always alone, and feeds the leftovers to the cat;
For the brothers at Glasshampton, eating in ritual silence;
For families catching up on the day's gossip over the supper table:

We are all one body
Because we all partake of the one bread.

For farmers who can't get the price of a decent meal for their livestock;
For fruit pickers, tea-pickers, cockle pickers doing slave labour;
For fisherfolk whose stocks have been shrunk by over fishing;
For people whose livelihood on the land has been devastated by flood or
drought;
For others uprooted from land by war and famine;
For all who work for policies of fair trade and ethical land use.

We are all one body
Because we all partake of the one bread.

For we who stand around this communion table;
For those who are too anxious or fearful to come;
For those who have walked out in anger, hating our hypocritical rheto-
ric;
For those who would come but have not heard an invitation;
For people of other faiths sharing ritual food with other meanings;
For all who long to be included at the welcome table:

We are all one body
Because we all partake of the one bread.

Cherishing fragments

Claire writes: 'I created this liturgy for use during Eating Disorders
Awareness Week to remember those with eating disorders and the pain,
exclusion and isolation they can feel. I wanted to create a liturgy that
acknowledged these feelings as well as creating a space for people to
participate in communion without consuming.'

A table in the centre of the room is covered with green and purple cloths (colours of the ribbon raising awareness of eating disorders). Bread and wine are placed on the table. Written prayers for those with eating disorders are placed around the space. Quiet music is played as people gather.

Greeting

All are welcome here around this table.
No masks are needed.
God's love is for all.

Rest in the stillness.
in the loving presence of God.

Peace be with you
and also with you.

Music is played or an appropriate song sung.

Let us keep space and silence together.

Confession

We remember that God is a God of forgiveness
and a God who loves unconditionally.

Silent reflection

Forgive us, loving God,
Forgive us, loving God.

Loving and forgiving God,
you give us a dream for our lives,
but sometimes it seems too much for us,
and we become afraid and tired.

Silence

Sometimes we feel so guilty that we can't grasp the wonder of your love
and the freedom of your forgiveness.

Sometimes all we want is to be held in the palm of your hand,
yet we are afraid of closeness,
we are afraid of being touched,
we are afraid that you will not accept us we are,
we are afraid that you will judge us.

Loving and forgiving God,
although we may push you away and long to escape from your presence
do not leave us when we need you most.

We ask for you to be a quiet presence which is interwoven in our lives,
both at times of despair and in times of joy.

**God, help us know that we are forgiven and that we are loved uncondi-
tionally.**

Acknowledging the difficulties, we say together,
We are forgiven,
Thanks be to God!

Reflection

Poetry and stories from people with eating disorders can be shared

Intercessions

We pray for all people with their many needs and longings . . .

We offer prayers for those with eating disorders . . .
Let us light a candle for each fragile cause,
for each vulnerable person we know,
who needs to be carried to safety,
and cherished in the arms of a loving, forgiving God.

We pray for their families and friends,
for nurses, therapists, doctors caring for them . . .
For support groups, the Eating Disorders Association and others who
seek to provide support . . .

We remember those who accompany people with eating disorders on
their painful journey of recovery.

We pray that you will give them strength, courage and patience when times are difficult, when their loved one seems to be taking two steps back rather than moving forward.

God, be with them in their despair and in their grief
for the person they feel they have lost as a result of an eating disorder.
Help them believe in a future hope for recovery . . .
Although the path is long and unclear, may they know that you, dear God, are always with them.

Silence is kept in which we give thanks for support received and given.

Thanks be to God for good and faithful friends.

The sharing of the bread and wine

Although it may be painful for us to eat this bread,
yet we are still part of the body,
united with Christ in his suffering body.

Bread is passed around but not consumed.

Participants are invited to remember those with eating disorders by holding a piece of bread in their hands. After a period of silence, reflective music is played, during which people are invited to place their unconsumed piece of bread back in a basket on the table.

Reflective music is played.

Loving and compassionate God
we place into your hands all of our prayers spoken and unspoken.

Loving God,
Receive all of our prayers. Amen.

Prayer of affirmation

God you created us in your image
Help us to love ourselves as you love us

God you created us in your image
Help us to make space for people to be themselves

God you created us in your image
Help us to affirm and value one another

God you created us in your image
**Help us
to listen,
to love,
to cherish,
to affirm,
to accept,
to include
all people for who they are and who you have made them to be.
Amen.**

Blessing

Compassionate God,
embrace us with your love and peace,
and the blessing of God,
the Creator,
the Liberator,
and the Sustainer,
be among you and remain with you
this day and always. **Amen.**

Notes

1 See, for example, 'Banquet', 'Word' and the series of Graces in Nicola Slee, *Praying Like A Woman*, London: SPCK, 2004, pp. 98, 113, 117, 120.

2 As in, for example, 'Morning sickness', *Praying Like A Woman*, p. 13.

3 See, for example, Caroline Walker Bynum, *Holy Feast and Holy Fast: The Religious Significance of Food to Medieval Women*, Berkeley: University of California Press, 1987; Rudoph M. Bell, *Holy Anorexia*, Chicago: University of Chicago Press, 1985; Walter Vandereycken and Ron van Deth, *From Fasting Saints to Anorexic Girls: The History of Self-Starvation*, London: Athlone Press, 1994.

4 Ann Loades, 'Christ also suffered' in *Searching for Lost Coins: Explorations in Christianity and Feminism*, London: SPCK, 1987, p. 44.

5 Hilary Mantel, 'Some girls want out', *London Review of Books*, 26:5 (4 March 2004), at <http://www.lrb.co.uk/v26/no5>, p. 10.

6 Carroll Saussy, 'Food, glorious food?' in Jeanne Stevenson-Moessner, ed., *In Her Own Time: Women and Developmental Issues in Pastoral Care*, Minneapolis: Fortress Press, 2000, p. 296.

7 Catherine Garrett, *Beyond Anorexia: Narrative, Spirituality, and Recovery*, Cambridge: Cambridge University Press, 1998, p. xiii.

8 Joanne Woolway Grenfell, 'Religion and eating disorders: towards understanding a neglected perspective', *Feminist Theology*, 14:3 (2006), p. 373.

9 Carol Lakey Hess, *Caretakers of Our Common House: Women's Development in Communities of Faith*, Nashville: Abingdon Press, 1997, p. 132.

10 'Religion and eating disorders', p. 369.

11 See, for example, Jane Dasher, 'Mana in the desert: eating disorders and pastoral care' in Jeanne Stevenson-Moessner, ed., *Through the Eyes of Women: Insights for Pastoral Care*, Minneapolis, Fortress Press, 1996, pp. 171–91; Carol Lakey Hess, *Caretakers of Our Common House*, chapter 4; Garrett, *Beyond Anorexia*, and Saussy, 'Food, glorious food?'

12 Woolway Grenfell, 'Religion and eating disorders', p. 384.

13 The following three prayers are by Claire. Two of them appeared originally in Neil Paynter, ed., *Blessed Be Our Table: Graces for Mealtimes and Reflections on Food*, Glasgow: Wild Goose, 2003, pp. 216–17.

14 This grace is by Nicola and appeared originally in *Blessed Be Our Table*, p. 261 and subsequently in *Praying Like A Woman*, p. 98.

Part 4

Gender and Sexuality

Introduction

If liturgy always takes place among embodied persons within the body of Christ, then attention to questions of gender and sexuality within the liturgical setting becomes imperative. The bodies which constitute the gathered assembly are gendered in specific ways and are sexual bodies, constituted at least in part by their particular gendered and sexual histories, longings and wounds. Of course, what it means to be gendered, sexual selves always interacts with other contextual factors, particularly cultural ones, so that sharply differing accounts can be given of the meaning of gender and sexuality in diverse cultural settings. Liturgy needs to engage with such cultural variation in sensitive ways.

Feminist liturgical studies is one of the more established discourses upon which this book has been able to draw, and, to a lesser extent, there exists a growing body of liturgical studies from gay, lesbian and queer-identified theologians. This is reflected in the essays in Part 4, all of which assume some kind of at least general familiarity with core issues which have been addressed within this literature over several decades, relating to the range of ways in which gendered language, symbolism and imagery function in liturgy, for example, the heteronormativity of worship in all the mainstream churches and the search for a more expansive, inclusive space in which unthinking assumptions about gender and sexual identity are not made.

The essays in Part 4 take forward feminist and LGBT/Q liturgical studies in new and significant ways, and demonstrate the vibrancy of the ongoing debates. The first two essays describe and reflect on the development of intentionally experimental whole liturgies, inspired by feminist theology, liturgy and poetry in particular, although in two different settings. Alastair Barrett discusses the development of a liturgy for Holy Week in a small post-industrial urban parish, focused on the anonymous woman of Mark 14.3 who anoints Jesus for his burial. Relating the marginalized, forgotten woman in Mark's Gospel to Melissa

Raphael's work which unearths the forgotten experience of women in the Holocaust, Barrett weaves a rich and original reading of Jesus' passion, both decentring Good Friday as it is traditionally located in theology and liturgy, and recentring it via the experience of a neglected community of care. Rachel Mann describes and reflects on an experimental and self-consciously feminist liturgy developed at Queen's with a group of fellow-students for Women's World Day of Prayer and employing novel images from the poetry of Adrienne Rich and Audre Lorde, as a way of 'digging into the silt of language for fresh ways to make the transcendent available for ourselves'. The following two essays offer a detailed commentary on smaller liturgical texts which might form part of a larger liturgy. Nicola Slee reflects on one of her liturgical texts, 'Litany to a dark God', suggesting ways in which this text both subverts patriarchal and heterosexist liturgical norms and holds a tension between apophatic and kataphatic approaches to the naming of God, allowing neither full dominance but preserving the sense of both the mystery of the divine and the real knowability of God within the forms of human discourse and knowing. Deryn Guest offers a detailed commentary on one of the psalms of lament, Psalm 42, as a way of reflecting on, and ritualizing, her own experience as a lesbian who has come out of a Christian congregation and feels in exile from her religious past, as well as that of other lesbians who experience profound dissonance between their sense of themselves as lesbians and their longing for God and for belonging to a community of worshippers. Liturgy that can speak to the deep pain and unresolved tension of such people 'needs strong language and imagery, it needs to be open to expressions of dismay and despair, to permit the acknowledgment that God can send weal and woe, light *and* darkness (Isaiah 45.7), and to give voice to protest'. The psalms of lament can provide such a language. Finally, Alistair Ross offers a rather different kind of reflection which engages with issues of gender and sexuality from a different perspective. Writing as a pastoral theologian, as a therapist and as a Baptist minister, Ross explores some Jungian archetypes – those of the stag and the doe – for their potential to express 'neglected fragments of the self' as well as different aspects of the Spirit's activity in the person. Tracing the significance of these symbols in Scripture, later tradition and contemporary fiction, Ross suggests that, as archetypes, the stag and the doe avoid traditional gender stereotypes, and that 'each has their own strength and each invites the person into the life of the Godhead through the Spirit'. While some feminists will remain critical of the Jungian notion of the archetypes, Ross's thesis is a suggestive one that repays attention.

12

'You Have Anointed Us':
De-centring Good Friday from the Edges of Holy Week

ALASTAIR BARRETT

Introduction: un/earthing a buried story

'Wherever the good news is proclaimed in the whole world, what she has done will be told in remembrance of her' (Mark 14.9). Jesus' powerful affirmation of the actions of an anonymous woman who anoints his body 'beforehand for its burial' (v. 8) stands in starkly ironic contrast to the woman's marginalization – perhaps even burial! – within the institutional churches' storytelling. In a small Anglican church, in an insignificant corner of the West Midlands, we 'remembered' her, on the Wednesday of Holy Week 2005.

Here, I reflect on that liturgical experiment, tracing my own theological journey of its un/earthing back, through an 'off-centre' take on Good Friday, to the unsung stories of Jewish women in the death camps of the Holocaust. What emerges, I hope, is the beginning of a conversation: between liturgy and theology; between buried texts, and dark and differing contexts; between wordless actions and spoken interpretations. First and foremost, I seek to open up some 'betweens' within Holy Week itself – disrupting, de-centring and subverting its familiar focuses, flows and theological frameworks – and dare to suggest that the anonymous anointing woman incarnates ('makes flesh') the love of God, in ways which abide through Good Friday and beyond, and which we might realistically inhabit (liturgically and practically) ourselves.

De-centring Good Friday

'My God, my God, why have you forsaken me?'(Mark 15.34)

If the anointing woman has been consigned to the edges of the Church's passion story, is God keeping her company there? In Mark's and Matthew's crucifixion narratives at least, the cry from centre-stage is one of god-forsakenness. As a centring cry, it has much gravity, echoing as it does in the cries of the abandoned and the suffering, the outcast and the oppressed, across time and space – cries which demand some kind of response from *us*, as well as from God. Where *is* God at the cross? I find myself growing less and less comfortable with answers that place God, simply, 'in' the abandoned, suffering one(s), as if that is somehow enough. Where is God *with* the god-forsaken?

Where was God in Auschwitz?

The cries and the questions of Good Friday find a particular resonance with those of Jews who suffered, and Jews who have since reflected on, the genocidal dehumanization, terror and destruction of the Holocaust. As Jewish feminist theologian Melissa Raphael observes, the mainstream of Jewish post-Holocaust theology has shied away from finding any 'place' for God in Auschwitz: a turn against the dominant tradition in biblical and rabbinic Judaism which 'saw suffering as the divine punishment for Israel's transgression or disobedience', but a deeper renunciation too, of attempts to accept or justify any kind of link between God and innocent suffering.[1] Instead, theologians have preferred to speak in various ways of the 'hiddenness' of God in Auschwitz: as a divine mystery; as a deferral to human freedom – 'That man may be, God must absent himself';[2] or, most radically, as morally complicit by 'turning a blind eye to Jewry's abuse'.[3] God did not protect or save his people, so God either 'turned his face away' from Auschwitz or (as in Elie Wiesel's best-known work[4]) God *died* there.

From the edges of this tradition, however, Raphael tells a different theological story of the Holocaust, and one which, for me as a Christian theologian, challenges me with the opportunity to 'speak Holy Week differently' too. Her critique of post-Holocaust theology, first, is that it has been patriarchal through and through, not least in assuming 'that (masculine) free will is the essence of human personhood', and in being 'markedly androcentric in its model of God and its historical focus'. Even radical 'protest theologies' have concentrated on 'God's failure to be patriarchal *enough*': 'the classical attribute[s] of omnipotence and mercy [are] still predicated of God and the protester is angry that God chose to refrain from its exercise'. As Raphael argues, in 'evidence-driven' modernity especially, the 'dissonance' in a story of a God 'who promises protection and then, empirically, fails to deliver it' leads to one conclusion: 'God can no longer be trusted'. If, as in Psalm 22, God is 'one who abandons us and is silent in the face of our suffering,'[5] says Raphael, then 'there can be little to experientially distinguish this God's silence from his non-existence'. So it is with the '*Who?*', much more than the '*Where?*', of God in Auschwitz that Raphael is concerned: 'what is to be distrusted is not God but a particular model or figure of God'; 'God's silence in Auschwitz was the silence of an omnipotent God-king who was never there in the first place, but was one who reigned in the minds of those who required divine sanction for their own hierarchical rule'.[6]

Wiping the face of God

Into the silence left behind with the disappearance of this patriarchal 'god', Raphael painstakingly retrieves echoes of a 'counter-tradition' from within Judaism, and a 'counter-testimony' from Auschwitz. In contrast to an 'interventionist' God, with power over life and death, who, for some reason, absents himself from Auschwitz, Raphael seeks to uncover a God who is first and foremost *present*. 'Presence, a keeping watch, is a function of love. A present God paces back and forth, circling the object of her concern; an absent God seems to have walked away.' Judaism has traditionally named the immanence of God 'Shekhinah' – and this is the name Raphael seeks to rediscover as being most faithful to the God who did not forsake the Jews of Auschwitz: Shekhinah is 'the real presence of a suffering God' – not, as in Christian tradition, incarnate in a human individual, but with, among, even *as* the assembled community of Jewish men and women. The 'power' of God in Auschwitz, Raphael argues, was not in God's ability to *stop* the destruction of relationship – what a theology of 'covenant' affirms, however, is 'the infinite flow of God's power' to *renew* relationship. Furthermore, it is *in the embodied relationships* of the people of Israel that this 'transformatory power' of love 'makes itself felt in the world' – paradigmatically in the act of *welcome*, 'the one seeing and opening to the other'.[7]

Raphael retrieves and uncovers, however, not just a largely over-looked theological tradition, but also the largely overlooked stories of courageous, persistent physical care by women and among women in the camps of Auschwitz. The Holocaust attempted – so often successfully – to isolate human beings from each other, and desecrate their personhood to the point of erasing it, through the destruction of the gas chambers and the mud and filth of the camps. One woman, Olga Lengyel, recalled the 'struggle to overcome the disgust we felt for our companions, and for ourselves'. But struggle they did: with defiance, longing for liberation, love and the most basic practicality, the testimonies of many women in Auschwitz describe how moments of touch, wiping and washing – even the barest, most ineffective gestures towards genuine washing – became moments of restoration of relationship and personhood, whether for the living, the dying or the dead.[8]

Drawing on Buber's theology of God's radiant presence attaining its 'full brightness' not *within* human beings but only where 'immediacy is established' in the 'seemingly empty space' *between* them,[9] and on Levinas's more developed ethics/theology of 'the summons of the face of the other',[10] Raphael is now able, almost poetically, to illuminate her answer to the question, 'Where was God in Auschwitz?' In that place where Jewish women's personhood 'was getting ever less perceptible', so too, consequently, was the presence of God. 'Shekhinah did not hide her face,' rather, it was hidden by 'the holocaustal assault' itself; when human faces were hidden behind 'the accretion of filth', so too was God 'de-faced'. And yet, in the similarly barely perceptible – because not powerfully dramatic or explicitly 'religious' – 'ordinary' actions of women, in the midst of the 'wholly non-ordinary' conditions of Auschwitz – in the simple, emblematic action of 'wiping filth from a face' – God's face too was made visible to those with eyes to see it:[11]

when a woman lifted up her cast down face to the summons of her mother, daughter, sister, or friend it caught the reflected light of the Shekhinah on its upturned surface, reflecting the glory or *kavod* of God's face back into the world – even a world which was, for them, over, and a world which, become Auschwitz, had turned God away at the gates . . . Rabbinic midrash compares the Shekhinah or divine presence to light, to what shines. 'Washed' by ersatz coffee, urine, brackish water or love alone, the reflective face lit God's way into, through and out of, Auschwitz.[12]

Where was God at the cross?

Melissa Raphael is doing Jewish, not Christian, theology; her focus is Auschwitz, not Golgotha. I find myself wanting to share her reflections and her un/earthed stories primarily for their own sake, wary of repeating, in even a small way, Auschwitz's evil of turning human beings into 'functionaries' rather than 'subjects', 'means' rather than 'ends'.[13] But reading Raphael as a Christian has been revelatory for me: the testimonies of the Jewish women of Auschwitz shed new light on the face of the God we share; their stories open up the possibility of recognizing God's presence where God is seemingly nowhere to be seen. When those around me are singing of the Father who 'turns his face away' unable to look at the one who bears 'my sin upon His shoulders',[14] from my guts I agree with Raphael's verdict: *this* God – and the theologies that make so much of both his omnipotent 'power to protect' and human 'free will' – 'can no longer be trusted'.

Even Jürgen Moltmann, who takes with utter seriousness both the horrors of Auschwitz and Jesus' cry of god-forsakenness, fails, for me, to escape Raphael's critique of patriarchal theology. In a now classic piece of theological poetry, Moltmann describes Jesus' experience of abandonment as an event that takes place, ultimately, 'within God himself': 'the cross of the Son divides God from God to the utmost degree of enmity and distinction', and into that event, somehow, are taken up 'all the depths and abysses of human history'. The cross is, in some sense, God's holding God's breath: the answer to Jesus' cry comes not immediately, but two days later. It is only with 'the resurrection of the Son abandoned by God' that God is reunited with God 'in the most intimate fellowship', 'only with the [final] resurrection of the dead, the murdered and the gassed'[15] that both the cross and Auschwitz might, eventually, be redeemed. Christians have always believed – or, at least, have sometimes remembered to believe – in a God not of protection but of resurrection. But where is God in the meantime? Where is the God of resurrection in the silence of Golgotha? Was the silence following Jesus' cry of god-forsakenness 'the silence of an omnipotent God-king who was never there in the first place'? Or might we, if we look into the shadowy edges of Good Friday, uncover some trace of a God who is not absent but *present*?

Keeping watch over God

'The New Testament story of the cross has two sides. On the one hand is the story of the guilt of the disciples who fled. On the other is story of the solidarity of the women who remained under the cross.'[16] If the dominant story of Matthew's and Mark's Gospels, as we commonly hear them, is that Jesus at his death was abandoned by both God and his human companions, then the stories of the women of Auschwitz urge us to seek out a similar 'counter-testimony' at the edges of Good Friday. 'There were also women looking on from a distance', says Mark, women followers (including Mary Magdalene) who had accompanied him all the way from Galilee to Jerusalem (Mark 15.40–41); there was also Joseph of Arimathea, who takes down Jesus' body from the cross, wraps it in a linen cloth, and lays it in a tomb (15.42–46) – the tomb to which the women also came, and to which they will return, with spices to anoint the body (15.47—16.1).[17] The journey of the body of Jesus from cross to tomb is *not* a solitary one: barely perceptible they may be, but there are women – and men – who stay with him, watch over him, hold him, carry him, lay him to rest.

Melissa Raphael dares us to perceive the 'crucial link between God's being made present and the seeing and touching of faces and bodies that have been made unseeable and untouchable'; she challenges us to read 'the religio-ethical response' of 'staying by the side of the other', as *itself* 'the essence of presence'.[18] Might we also dare to imagine that, in the small, faithful fragment of loving community that accompanies the body of Christ from cross to tomb – a community of women and men who embody their love in purposeful, socially dangerous, physical care – there is incarnated the abiding presence of God? I find myself pushed to the edges of Christian orthodoxy with such a question, but I am convinced that it is to the edges that Jesus' cry of god-forsakenness takes us. Is it remotely conceivable that the silence of God at Golgotha is not that of absence, nor of 'chosen or enforced inactivity', but of a 'keeping watch' at the edges, an attentive, listening presence that 'hears [Jesus] to speech' here, and will do so again, before too long, in the Easter garden?[19] Is it imaginable that, even in the thick darkness of Good Friday, something of the radiant presence of God shines in that 'seemingly empty space' between the dead body of Jesus and those who responsibly, carefully, lovingly touch it, who seek to restore to it something of the personhood erased by the institutional desecration of crucifixion?

'In remembrance of her'

The small community of loving, bodily care that surrounds the dying and dead Jesus is pushed to the very edges of the passion story by the evangelists' fascination with the crucifixion itself. At those edges, however, we rediscover that unnamed woman who, Jesus says, 'has anointed my body beforehand for its burial' (Mark 14.8). Although her 'labour of love' takes place in a Bethany home a few days before Good Friday, for me she has become emblematic of the 'Good Friday community'.[20] What she has, by her anointing, 'written on Jesus' body' (to borrow Jeanette Winterson's phrase[21]) bears a multiplicity and depth of overlaid meanings, and will not, as Jesus' own interpretation of it indicates, be quickly or easily erased. Furthermore, although the evangelists' spotlight rarely strays from Jesus, what this woman has done will, says Jesus – in striking, almost eucharistic language – be told 'in remembrance of *her*' (14.9).

A tangle of texts

Her story is, however, less well told by the Christian Church than Jesus' affirmation suggests, and this is surely to do, in large part, with the careless history of 'tangled texts' in which she is caught up. If you belong to a church that uses a version of the *Revised Common Lectionary*, she will be remembered, if you are lucky, once every three years: at the beginning of the long Passion Reading on Palm Sunday (Year B). Even then, however, if you are a little strapped for time, you can opt to ignore her:[22] what might be a prophetic heralding, opening the passion narrative, is, in practice, deemed an unnecessary 'edge' to the 'central' story. There is another, parallel, story that cannot be so easily ignored: Mary of Bethany – Jesus' friend and disciple who, in an act of gracious, abundant hospitality, anoints his feet (John 12.1–8) – turns up at the Eucharist on the Monday of Holy Week (in places where such a thing happens), and also gets a Sunday to herself (Lent 5 / Passion Sunday in Year C)! There is yet a third Gospel story of an anointing woman – in Luke 7.36–50, recounted on a Sunday in Ordinary Time in Year C (Proper 6) – who although anonymous, seems to be the best known: this woman's reputation as a 'sinner', propagated by Simon the Pharisee and then Luke in his turn, has been enthusiastically taken up and imaginatively extended by countless commentators (professional and otherwise) who have followed them over the centuries. The casual weaving together of these three quite distinct anointing stories, along with that of

Mary Magdalene – who the Gospels tell of, quite separately, as a disciple, a woman from whom seven demons had been cast out, and the primary witness to the cross and resurrection – has all but obscured the profound significance of the anointings in Mark and Matthew (and indeed in John); the startling 'good news' has been buried in a tangle of texts.

Interpreting an action (i): Mark and Matthew's story

If we let Mark's and Matthew's account speak, then, disentangled from its associations with its siblings, what *is* it that the woman has done here? She bursts into the story without introduction, anoints Jesus' head without explanation, and, after Jesus' words, disappears from the narrative without any further mention. It is Jesus who explains 'what she has done', defending and affirming her against the angry criticisms of his fellow dinner-guests; but even his 'explanation' is far from clear. Putting words, unbidden, into a woman's mouth is a common patriarchal temptation.[23] Any 'explanation' of the woman's action risks 'fixing' and 'limiting' the scope and power of its meaning, but Jesus' mysterious words do, at the very least, leave us with a question: what *does* it mean to anoint a body 'beforehand for its burial'?

'What she has done' would have been, in itself, by no means unfamiliar to first-century Palestinian Jews. Anointing with oil had a variety of uses: for healing wounds; honouring guests at a banquet; signifying wealth, royal status or 'consecration'; and embalming dead bodies at their interment.[24] But there was something about the excessiveness, and perhaps 'out-of-place-ness', of this anointing, that so disturbed those who witnessed it. They speak of 'waste', but perhaps their anger also expresses other discomforts: being 'upstaged' in discipleship and hospitality by a stranger (this is explicitly the sense in Luke's version of the story – see Luke 7.44–47); the intimations of death; and, just possibly, the 'prophetic' or 'priestly' resonances of the woman's action. For Mark and Matthew, the anointing truly does mark the beginning of Jesus' passion. Judas' decision to betray Jesus follows immediately after the story of the anointing, and is quite possibly precipitated by it. Might we discern, implicit in the narrative, the faintest of hints that this anointing really *is* a consecration: a commissioning of a king, even the Messiah himself, by a prophet or priest of YHWH?[25]

Interpreting an action (ii): John's story

At the risk of re-tangling two disentangled threads, the Johannine anointing adds further 'body' to the embryonic 'Good Friday community'. For John, the woman has a name – she is Mary (the sister of Martha and Lazarus) and she is no stranger, but a close and constant friend. For John, the excessiveness of the anointing is such that 'the house was filled with the fragrance of the perfume' (John 12.3) – sounding somewhat like the smoke-filled Temple where the prophet Isaiah encounters God (Isaiah 6.1–5): thus, an ordinary home is made a holy place.[26] John's anointing is not, however, a prophetic or priestly anointing of the head, but rather a 'wiping' of feet. And what is that? The humble work of a servant? The intimate touch of a lover? Or both and more – the anticipation, even initiation, of the sacrament of 'loving one's friends to the end' which Jesus himself will shortly demonstrate to his disciples and command them to imitate (John 13.1–17)?

Weaving a story of God at work

To weave together two, similar but different, stories for a piece of liturgically embodied theology is to risk confusion, but also to embrace paradox – and paradox, when daring to speak of incarnation, allows space for a certain humility: are we speaking of human flesh, or of God ... ? Both ... Just possibly ...

The woman who anoints Jesus is, because of what she does, anticipating, founding, even embodying the 'Good Friday community'. The love with which she anoints Jesus' body, 'beforehand for its burial', is a 'love which *stays*', which 'abides' with Jesus; a love, as Melissa Raphael said of the 'staying-there' of the women of Auschwitz, 'infused with a mysterious energy that was, in the circumstances, miraculous'; a love which sanctifies the unholiest of places; a love which embodies the '*hesed*' (faithful, gracious love) of God.[27] Is this simply what it means to be a faithful disciple of Jesus – in stark contrast to the betrayal, denial and abandonment by Judas and the other male disciples, who are so angered by her actions? Is this woman 'the paradigm for the true disciple'[28] – or something more? In her costly love, her self-sacrificial service, the conflict she provokes, and her silence in the face of her accusers, is she anticipating Jesus' own passion?

She is Mary; she is unnamed. She is friend; she is stranger. She is prophet; she is servant. She is priest; she is lover. In her we see true discipleship. In her we see God-in-the-flesh.

Un/earthing 'Holy Wednesday'

Whispering a suggestion that takes us right over the edge of Christian orthodoxy, in the liturgical context of a Holy Week Eucharist in Oldbury – a traditionally white, working-class, but now increasingly ethnically and culturally diverse, area of the post-industrial Black Country – is, by necessity, to offer what Gordon Lathrop calls a 'broken symbol', to tell a story with holes in it, gaps, spaces, in which and through which we might just possibly encounter God.[29] In attempting some kind of – inevitably non-identical, hopefully faithful – repetition of the woman's anointing, with necessarily limited explanation and interpretation, the 'invention', or 'discovery', of 'Holy Wednesday' was to invite an unsuspecting congregation into an unfamiliar and quite possibly disorientating context, to meet with an unfamiliar and quite possibly disorientating stranger.

Expectation: 'Come among us and touch us with your love'

The very first words of the liturgy, not unusually, encourage the congregation's *expectation* that here they will encounter God:

Generous God, extravagant Giver
come among us
and touch us with your love

Passionate God, suffering Servant
come among us
and touch us with your love

Surprising God, unexpected Stranger
come among us
and touch us with your love

These opening responses also sketch out some of the characteristic 'marks' of this God – again, not unusually. The 'marks' chosen, however, deliberately prepare us to encounter God in an 'unexpected stranger' – in a much more specific sense than the language of a 'God of surprises' often suggests. We come expecting to meet God in Jesus, and so we shall; but we are being prepared to meet God elsewhere too.

Resistance: 'Forgive us when we suspect your extravagance'

Those around the anointing woman were angered simply by what she did. For someone on the edges of the narrative to be so affirmed as she is by Jesus, let alone to be associated so intimately with God's incarnate presence, is disorientating and discomforting for many present-day onlookers too. But are the anger at 'waste', and the discomfort 'that God could be like *that*', in fact symptoms of that in-built resistance to God that we often call 'sin'? Our prayers of penitence seek to address this resistance in us, and 'bring us back' to the possibility of encountering God here:

Trusting in God's abundant love,
and seeing before us the road to the cross,
let us confess our fears and failures,
and seek God's healing and forgiveness.

Generous God,
you lavish your love on us;
forgive us when we suspect your extravagance.
Lord, have mercy.
Lord, have mercy.

Passionate God,
you lay down your life for us;
forgive us when we fear your vulnerability.
Christ, have mercy.
Christ, have mercy.

Surprising God,
you come to us when we least expect you;
forgive us when we turn you away.
Lord, have mercy.
Lord, have mercy.

Holy God,
holy and strange,
holy and intimate,
have mercy on us.

May the God of love
bring us back to himself,

forgive us our sins,
and assure us of his eternal love
in Jesus Christ our Lord. **Amen.**[30]

Connections: 'You have anointed my head with oil'

The liturgy then moves on into the work of 'making connections', within Scripture and outside it – each link adding a little strength to a 'cat's cradle' which might just support the weight of the central story/act of anointing. In both the Old Testament reading (Isaiah 61.1–11, 'The Spirit of the Lord has anointed me . . . '), and Psalm 23 ('you have anointed my head with oil . . . '), it is clearly *God* who anoints. Turning then to the Gospel reading (Mark 14.3–9), we are invited, implicitly at least, to ask ourselves: who is it who anoints *here*? At the same time, who it is who is *being* anointed is also an open question: Isaiah's 'me' is inescapably taken on by Jesus (in Luke 4.16–21), but is it now extended to us, his disciples (see, for example, Luke 9.2)? We are used, these days, to reading Psalm 23's 'valley of the shadow of death' as being ours, through which God accompanies us; but, in the light of the story of cross and resurrection, is it also Jesus'? Might he have prayed both the twenty-second and the twenty-third Psalms from the cross?

As well as the scriptural 'grammar' of anointing, connecting Jesus' with our own, there is also the web of associations with some of the profoundest moments of physical contact in the Christian vocabulary. Making the sign of the cross, with oil, on the forehead, seeks to evoke a common memory of the anointing of baptism (our deepest, shared 'commissioning'), the (rather more recent) 'ashing' of Ash Wednesday (with its call to 'be faithful to Christ') and, for some at least, experiences of being anointed when ill or when ordained, and of the anointing of the dying. While following the Markan–Matthean action of anointing the *head*, my sermon that evening in Oldbury drew also on the Johannine parallel, with its 'breaking', 'pouring' and 'wiping' of feet, which point to this moment as a 'first Last Supper'. Using 'Love' and 'God' somewhat interchangeably (we sang 'O Love that wilt not let me go' as our first hymn), I suggested that there, in that service, we were being anointed *with* Love (anointed alongside Jesus); *for* Love (commissioned for the way of passion and compassion); and *by* Love (touched by the divine power that can bring life even out of death).

Commitment: 'to stay close to our brother Jesus'

And so to the anointing itself, introduced with these words:

> Remembering Mary's costly gift,
> and our baptism's costly calling,
> let us commit ourselves not to flee in fear,
> but to stay close to our brother Jesus
> in the days and nights before us,
> and to follow his way of loving-kindness
> wherever it may lead us.

Amid the layers and intricate webs of meanings and associations in the liturgy, one key thing is brought to the foreground here: we are committing ourselves to stay with Jesus, to join what I have called 'the Good Friday community'. For those who did return to church on Good Friday, this commitment was reinforced then, with a 'Dismissal' that is less a command to 'Go' as a desire to *stay*:

> Lord Jesus, beloved friend:
> with the women who watched with you in your agony,
> with the men who cradled your body,
> with the women and men
>   who brought love and spices to your tomb,
> give us the courage
>   to stay,
>   to wait,
>   to love,
>   to return,
> that, being steadfast in the face of death,
> we may be ready to embrace the shock of resurrection.
> **Amen.**[31]

Identification (i): 'Walk humbly the way of Christ'

The 'Good Friday community' were, I suggest, Jesus' most faithful disciples. Staying with Jesus meant – and still means – following in his way. Only in that context dare we talk of the faithful community 'incarnating' God in our places and in our time. The words of anointing, drawing on Micah 6.8, were these:

Walk humbly the way of Christ:
do justice, love tenderly, and do not be afraid.

When all who wished to had been anointed, we turned to our prayers
of intercession:

As God has reached out and touched us,
so let us remember those others, near and far,
who need the touch of God's love
through our prayers, our passion, or our presence.

As today's successors of the 'Good Friday community', being 'anointed
with Jesus', 'staying' with him, and 'walking' his 'way', mean that our
focus is re-oriented so that we continue his God-anointed labour of love
among the oppressed, broken-hearted, imprisoned and mourning of *our*
world. At the end of the prayers, this continuity between our anointing
and Jesus' is re-visited and re-emphasized:

Living, loving God:

As Mary anointed Jesus
for the way of extravagant giving,
call us to your work.

As Mary anointed Jesus
for the soothing of his wounds,
touch us with your healing.

As Mary anointed Jesus
for his dying and burial,
pour upon us your compassion.

As Mary anointed Jesus
with the love stronger than death,
drench us in your resurrection life.

Identification (ii): 'You have anointed us'

Similar themes are echoed again in the concluding responses and blessing, returning us to the threefold expectation of God of the liturgy's
beginning:

Generous God, extravagant Giver,
you have lavished your love on us:
Make us overflowing
with your generosity.

Passionate God, suffering Servant,
with arms open wide you have embraced our world:
Keep us steadfast
as we walk with you the way of the cross.

Surprising God, unexpected Stranger,
you have anointed us with courage and strength:
Touch our hearts with your passion
fiercer than the grave.

And may the blessing of God almighty,
the Father, the Son and the Holy Spirit,
go with us as we journey
through this Holy Week, and into the day of resurrection. **Amen.**

With 'you have anointed us', we are returned also to the question implicit in the connections between the Scripture readings: *who* is it who anoints? Might we recognize the 'extravagant giver', the 'suffering servant', the 'unexpected stranger' who anoints Jesus, as 'God touching God'? Might the 'Good Friday community' be the faithful and persistent, yet silent and barely perceptible, answer to Jesus' cry, 'My God, my God, why have you forsaken me?'? Might we too, anointed by God in ambiguous and disorienting contexts, and occasionally faithful in often quiet and barely perceptible ways, participate in the ongoing incarnation of God, here and now?

An ongoing conversation?

It was more than a year after that first 'Holy Wednesday experiment' when I began to commit these reflections to writing, but the two most theologically and liturgically literate women attending the service that night could still recall their dominant feelings and reactions to it. In short, between them it left them 'cold', 'puzzled' and 'horribly uncomfortable' – but it also left them with questions. 'Too much oil', 'unfamiliarity with this use of oil' and too much 'touch' in two days, were complaints, perhaps not entirely unconnected with the Gospel story itself. Finding herself in something of a 'scriptural muddle', one woman went away to re-read the stories. Both women, aware of its more familiar uses within Christian tradition, requested some kind of 'theological teaching on anointing'. For both, what seemed to be most needed was more 'explanation', 'justification', or perhaps simply *preparation*: 'for the anointing of "Holy Wednesday" truly, boldly and simply to "speak" to us,' they seemed to be saying, 'we need to come to it better equipped to "place" it within the bigger story'.

How much *can* symbolic actions be 'explained'? How prepared can we ever be for encounters with God the 'unexpected stranger'? If the events of 'Holy Wednesday' are inherently disorientating, might they also be the beginning of a 'new orientation'[32] which takes us into Good Friday more prepared to recognize God, and wait with God, at the shadowy edges of Golgotha, and in all the places of our world where God is seemingly nowhere to be seen? I am left, at this point, with as many questions as ever. Might the liturgy itself be made more *'questioning'*, to better reflect the mood of the theology behind it? How might questioning and conversation be *continued* from their liturgical beginnings? Might the gathering together of 'the Good Friday community' be a theme more explicitly followed through Holy Week, even through conversations and workshops outside the week's key liturgical moments? Might there then perhaps be space within which to tell of the women of Auschwitz, and to encourage others gathered to speak of places where they have glimpsed the faithful, abiding – if unexpected, unfamiliar and often barely perceptible – face of God?

Notes

1 Melissa Raphael, *The Female Face of God in Auschwitz: A Jewish Feminist Theology of the Holocaust*, London: Routledge, 2003, p. 27.

2 Eliezer Berkovits, quoted in Raphael, *Female Face of God*, p. 45.

3 Raphael, *Female Face of God*, p. 47.

4 'Where is he? He is here. He is hanging there on the gallows . . . ' Elie Wiesel, *Night*, quoted in Jürgen Moltmann, *The Crucified God: The Cross of Christ as the Foundation and Criticism of Christian Theology*, London: SCM Press, 1974, pp. 273–4.

5 'O my God, I cry by day, but you do not answer; and by night, but find no rest.' (Psalm 22.2)

6 Raphael, *Female Face of God*, pp. 28, 35, 52, 54, 49, 52.

7 Raphael, *Female Face of God*, pp. 47, 54–5, 41.

8 Raphael, *Female Face of God*, pp. 66–70.

9 Martin Buber, *On Judaism*, ed. N. N. Glazter, New York: Schocken Books, 1967, pp. 109–10, 113.

10 See, for example, E. Levinas in S. Hand, ed., *The Levinas Reader*, Oxford: Blackwell, 1989, p. 83.

11 Raphael, *Female Face of God*, pp. 100–1, 54–5.

12 Raphael, *Female Face of God*, pp. 105–6.

13 See Alistair McFadyen, *Bound to Sin: Abuse, Holocaust and the Christian Doctrine of Sin*, Cambridge: Cambridge University Press, 2000, pp. 80–104.

14 Stuart Townend, 'How deep the Father's love for us' © 1995 Thankyou Music.

15 Moltmann, *Crucified God*, pp. 152, 246, 152, 278.

16 Elisabeth Moltmann-Wendel, 'Is there a feminist theology of the cross?', in Yacob Tesfai, ed., *The Scandal of a Crucified World: Perspectives on the Cross and Suffering*, Maryknoll, NY: Orbis, 1994, pp. 87–98, 95.

17 In John's account (19.38–42), Nicodemus, who seems again to approach Jesus only in semi-darkness, helps Joseph bury the body, and brings the 'myrrh and aloes' for anointing it – a role given to the women in Mark (16.1) and Luke (23.56—24.1).

18 Raphael, *Female Face of God*, pp. 105, 100.

19 Rachel Muers, *Keeping God's Silence: Towards a Theological Ethics of Communication*, Oxford: Blackwell, 2004, p. 47.

20 Here (and elsewhere) I find myself shoulder to shoulder with Rita Nakashima Brock, in her description of the anointing woman as 'representative of the Christa/Community that would survive Jesus' death and witness his resurrection'. Brock, *Journeys by Heart: A Christology of Erotic Power*, New York: Crossroad, 1988, p. 97.

21 Jeanette Winterson, *Written on the Body*, London: Vintage, 1993.

22 The Church of England's *Common Worship Lectionary* gives the options of Mark 14.1—15.47 or Mark 15.1–39 [40–47]. ECUSA's version of the *RCL* offers Mark 14.3–9 as an optional alternative (to John 12.1–11) for a Eucharist on the Monday of Holy Week. Matthew's version (26.6–13) does not appear anywhere in the *RCL* and its variants.

23 Luce Irigaray's work in particular explores the ways in which female subjectivity is silenced: 'it may be the insertion of another voice, another tongue, into her (my) mouth; it may also be a noisiness through which her (my) voice cannot be heard; it may be an inability to see, hear, recognize our voice(s) – our "I" – *as* voice, as "I" (except when we merely mimic man's).' Lucy Gardner, 'Touching upon the Soul: The Interiority of Transcendence after Luce Irigaray', in Susan F. Parsons, ed., *Challenging Women's Orthodoxies in the Context of Faith*, Aldershot: Ashgate, 2000, pp. 135–53, 143.

24 Dorothy Lee, *Flesh and Glory: Symbolism, Gender and Theology in the Gospel of John*, New York: Crossroad, 2002, pp. 202–3.

25 Margaret Hebblethwaite makes much of this prophetic role in her re-telling of 'The Story of Mary of Bethany', in *Six New Gospels: New Testament Women Tell Their Stories*, Boston, MA: Cowley, 1994, pp. 94–114.

26 Significantly, Hebblethwaite comments that here the Markan–Matthean version is even stronger in its 'dramatic . . . reversal of sacred space': the anointing 'sanctifies' not simply 'the ordinary secular space of a normal home (John)', but 'the polluted space of a leper's house', a sanctifying that will continue with Golgotha (Hebblethwaite, *Six New Gospels*, pp. 103–4, n.17) and, as Raphael argues, Auschwitz.

27 Raphael, *Female Face of God*, p. 100.

28 Elisabeth Schüssler-Fiorenza, *In Memory of Her: A Feminist Theological*

Reconstruction of Christian Origins, 2nd ed., London: SCM Press, 1995, p. xliv.

29 Gordon W. Lathrop, *Holy Ground: A Liturgical Cosmology*, Minneapolis, MN: Fortress Press, pp. 25ff.

30 'Holy God . . .' is taken from Janet Morley's 'Good Friday Reproaches', in *All Desires Known*, 2nd ed., London: SPCK, 1992, pp. 43–5. The absolution is found in The Archbishops' Council, *Common Worship: New Patterns for Worship*, London: Church House Publishing, 2002, p. 95. One of the tensions for this Anglican priest doing this kind of work is the occasional unavoidable interruption into carefully crafted experimental liturgy of 'authorized' liturgical moments: here, the absolution, to be consistent with the theological flow, might perhaps be rather better expressed using female personal pronouns, and omitting the final 'in Jesus Christ our Lord'. As it is, the tension – helpfully, I suggest – refuses to allow us unambiguously to 'fix' God's presence in 'Mary' any more than in Jesus, keeping open Buber's 'space *between*' as the location of divine encounter.

31 This Dismissal evolved from Janet Morley's Collect for Good Friday, in *All Desires Known*, p. 13.

32 See Walter Brueggemann, *The Message of the Psalms: A Theological Commentary*, Minneapolis: Augsburg, 1984.

13

Liturgical Poetry/Poetic Liturgy:
An Adventure with the Kaleidoscope God

RACHEL MANN

Authentic liturgy . . . requires a lot of energy. This means it takes considerable time both to prepare it and also to assimilate it afterwards. Liturgy means lifting up a particular human moment and making it paradigmatic of all moments . . . we should properly be both exhilarated and exhausted when we have truly worshipped. The fact that most people experience liturgy as dead is a terrible testimony to the way it has been both routinized and transformed into a tool of alienation and domination.[1]

Introduction: breathing the mystery

The following liturgical texts were created for an act of worship at the Queen's Foundation, Birmingham, inspired by Women's World Day of Prayer 2004. The texts are self-consciously feminist in nature. That is, they emerge out of a critical reflection on the structural injustice which profoundly skews relations between the sexes and, thereby, implies a radical evaluation of what it means to be 'female' and 'male'.[2] They seek to embody a commitment to gender justice and employs expansive language in an attempt to reclaim and create richer visions of the Divine. They do this in an attempt to open up more satisfying ways for all – male and female, black and white, straight, gay, lesbian, bisexual and transgendered – to worship God. That is to say, the texts here take seriously the understanding of liturgy as 'the people's work', and 'people' means all the people:

It is the nature of the liturgy to be done by the people. It is not done to people. It is not done for people. It is not done in the presence of the people. People do it and the plural is correct because it is as a Church assembled that people do liturgy.[3]

Therefore, it is a living process making claims of truth: 'To be precise, the liturgy claims that when its work is being done, participants are engaging in a dialogue with God.'[4] Yet this process when engaged in as an expansive project (as it must if all are to be welcome) has both joys and attendant dangers:

> The Christian Church has said yes to Father, Son, Spirit. Some Christians have said yes to Sovereign, Lover, Mother, Wisdom and Way. Most would say no to Witch and Wigwam. I say yes and no to each. I will consider each new proposal, weighing its insight against the tradition. Each might capture something of mystery; yet it can become a black-robed male if it stands alone. The gem has many facets, and light must reflect off each for the jewel to shine.[5]

Diann Neu[6] suggests a number of markers or elements which may be found in feminist liturgy.[7] First it involves speaking out of silence, and thus entails finding a voice.[8] Second, it involves reclaiming traditional prayer forms.[9] The significance of this lies in the desire of feminists to express faith in a universal call to holiness. Third, Neu suggests that feminist liturgy seeks to be inclusive. Feminism thus offers opportunities for both women and men to discover richer conceptions of human being.[10] I wish to add one further marker: expansiveness.[11] In seeking to expand the liturgical community's vocabulary for speaking about God one is not seeking simply to 'add in words' where words were not before. Expansiveness seeks to take seriously the reality of God as eluding and exhausting all of our literary designations and yet, at the same time, because of her intimate involvement with us, she allows herself to be clothed, at least for a moment, in those frail designations. Feminist liturgical expression is likely to be expansive in nature precisely because it entails speaking out of silence and thus involves finding language for what has previously been excluded and repressed. In digging into the silt of language for fresh ways to make the transcendent available for ourselves, we begin to come to terms with our invitation to be co-creators with God: for I sense the liturgist signifies the people's calling to be poets. As Tomlinson notes, 'Scots are used to calling poets "makars", those who form new bodies of imaginative response, co-creators with Him who is Maker of all.'[12] Liturgy itself qua people's work seeks to help others find the transcendent in their lives and, like poetry, enables the people to see the gaps between words, discourses and situations, in order that we may encounter the beyond in the mundane midst. What Sara Maitland desires for theology is equally applicable in liturgy: 'We need jugglers and high-wire artists – sequinned, sparkling and dancing on the void – if theology is to measure up at all to the magnificent God whose gambling habits and sleights of hand boggle our simple minds.'[13]

Furthermore, expansive liturgy is deeply prophetic, bringing about God's 'new reality': 'For from such radical associations will come a re-imagining of the status quo, the evoking of alternative perceptions and subversive possibilities of the Kingdom . . . pointing to the new future given by God, urging people to work for its coming on earth.'[14] Thus, rather than imagination becoming a flight from reality, it energizes social and political change: like Jesus, the poetic minister will refuse to 'absolutize the present'.[15]

Learning to speak: context and the text's story

I want to say something about the text's story; about the silence out of which it emerged. I can only do that by saying a little about my story. For these texts, like so many feminist texts, are grounded in an embodied, specific story.

The story of these texts is, in essence, the story of my becoming a poet. It is therefore a story about finding a voice and learning to speak. It is a wrestling with the question: how shall I break the silence? Both as a woman, and as someone who identifies herself within what has become known as the Lesbian, Gay, Bisexual and Transgendered/Queer Community, I've experienced being silenced and excluded. Elizabeth Stuart notes, 'depriving people of language with which to make sense of their experience is a particularly effective way of keeping them silent and disempowered'.[16] During my late teens and twenties, I was educated and initiated into the Western academic tradition, studying for and ultimately teaching university-level philosophy. One might imagine that this experience was precisely a process of empowerment and liberation. Yet this enculturation into academia, which I had sought as a way of escape from limited social opportunities and as a way of expressing myself, eventually became stifling. Rather than discovering my voice, I learnt a useful style, which to a lesser or greater degree I adopt in writing the commentary for this chapter. However, I could not 'find' or 'locate' myself in the midst of the praxis of academic philosophy. Its obsession with particular forms of expression, with an almost reified conception of 'reason' and linear logic instead of becoming a place where I could increasingly locate my life, seemed to add another layer of silence.[17] Much has been written about the male bias in academia in general and philosophy in particular;[18] some of this may be overstated, but in any case I found myself increasingly at odds with the male-dominated world of 1990s' philosophy. I left academia and became involved in church-related community work in a poor urban environment; in order to flourish there I found I needed to discover and explore new ways of going on, of speaking and relating, listening and being. As both a user of language and someone for whom 'language' is my medium of being, I had to find new forms of expression. The language of philosophy, even of traditional theology, became like an idling cog. When I then became desperately and chronically ill, 'who I was' – in particular, who I was as someone who lives language – had to be reformed and rediscovered. Adrienne Rich, writing about her experience of a lesbian relationship, claims:

we're out in a country that has no language
no laws . . .
the maps they gave us were out of date
by years . . . [19]

Though writing about a relationship, her picture of pioneers needing to discover a whole new language and explore beyond the bounds captures much of my experience. Rich famously wrote a poem called 'Diving into the Wreck' and it is no accident that in the following liturgy I appropriate that image. For post-academia, post-cosy middle class life, post-good health, the second-hand, inherited stories and myths I'd relied upon were no longer plausible or good enough. I needed to find, perhaps invent, a new language, to dive into the wreck of myself for new ways of going on. I needed poetry. To put it another way: I had entered into a process that was about discovering my own voice, a process in which I continue to engage now. It is a process which, as Eavan Boland so aptly puts it, is 'a forceful engagement between a life and a language'.[20]

This process of voice finding, of poetry, 'witnesses to the transcendent, to the beyond in our midst, to the "more than" that beckons human beings beyond the immediate, the functional needs of the moment'.[21] It is almost too obvious to say it, but it does this through the very precise use of words; it is slightly less obvious to note that, equally, it does its 'work' through what it doesn't or refuses to say: that is, through its silences. Poetry is a 'kind of speaking' (or, a kind of writing[22]):

create

174

language that not only speaks *about* some thing . . . but mysteriously effects that of which it speaks, causing the hearer not only to think new thoughts, but to feel passions and aspirations and to sense a reality of which they might previously have been unaware.[23]

As David Constantine succinctly puts it, poetry is 'a widening of consciousness, an extension of humanity'.[24] In seeking to bring a poetic sensibility into the context of liturgy I have, in my own small way, attempted to offer language which arrests the participant and invites her to engage with a larger vision of the ground of our being.

Finally, I wish to note one troubling aspect of genesis of these texts: they were written as a result of a desire on the part of a group of predominantly women ordinands both to honour Women's World Day of Prayer yet also to have something which challenged and reflected the life of the theological community of which we were part. They were written, then, as substitutes for the original texts for Women's World Day of Prayer produced by women in Panama. It may sound precious to dwell on this point, but I was acutely aware that what I and my colleagues had agreed to do could be read as classic, if rather obscure, white middle-class women's imperialism. While we did and still can offer reasons for our decision to ditch the Panama material, I continue to sit uncomfortably with this question. For in so far as I was finding my voice, it might be argued that it involved, at one level, a silencing of others. I hope, however, that if these texts have any substance, they thereby can speak outside the narrow confines of a single enactment of them on a very special day in March 2004.

A Kaleidoscope God: Prayers for a Women's World Day of Prayer Service

Prayers of approach

Holy God, chuckling wise woman, tender and strange, we bless you.
Bless us, trouble us, bewitch us into delight in your love, mercy and
  grace.

Christ our Sister, unite us in your holy bleeding.
As you took spit and dust for healing,
take our hands, cracked and huge as washerwomen's, for God's work.
Take our sacred bodies for the healing of the world.

Birth-Spirit, as you coursed in intimacy through the veins
of Eve and Adam, Hagar and Abraham, Deborah and Lappidoth,
   Naomi and Ruth,
be the pulse of our lives. Desire us with your desire.

Prayer of adoration

God our Fox-Mother, nuzzle us.
Let us feel your pelt musky against moonlight,
blood damp from briars and running and running.
Allow us to caress your flesh, receive milk from your nipples,
and lick your wounds as you lick ours.

Prayers of thanksgiving

Lover-God, thanks be to you for kissing the day to life,
for caressing us with your Spirit through the cold-sweat,
wide-awake troubles of the night.
Joy and praise be to you, Lover-God

Delighter-God, thanks be to you for joy and laughter,
for welcoming all at the party for outcasts.
May our delight clink out like wine glasses at a wedding feast.
Joy and praise be to you, Delighter-God

Wildfire-God, thanks be to you for your passion,
your berserk fire that will not be contained,
inspiring strange love among women and men from everlasting to
   everlasting.
Joy and praise be to you, Wildfire-God

Tangling-God, thanks be to you for causing us to stutter in our
   certainties,
for seducing us into your sustaining web of truths.
Enmesh our delusions and self-harm.
Make us web-weavers, free to spin our identities according to your love.
Joy and praise be to you, Tangling-God

Prayers of confession

Christa, water-troubler,
we lay open our self-neglect before you.
We admit we have too often accepted roles
imposed on us by others.
Give us the oxygen to dive into the wreck,
dig out the pearl of our true selves
and return to the surface with identities
bought at great price.

Sister have mercy
Sister have mercy

Christa, Wound-mender,
We lay open our woundedness before you;
the fractures wrought by the slaps
and strokes of this world.
Anoint our scars. Unbreak our bones.
Ready us to struggle against violence and brutality.

Sister have mercy
Sister have mercy

Christa, world-liberator,
We lay open our injuring before you:
our violations of nature; our complicity in injustice;
our inheritance of a system that has labelled
women as witches or virgins, hysterical or mad.
We admit to the savage dog within
we too readily unleash on others;
we admit to the steel shutter we hide behind
hoping to keep the world out.
Free us to openness; free us to challenge injustice.

Sister have mercy
Sister have mercy

Christa, word-wave,
we lay open before you the meanness
of our images for you and for ourselves.

We admit the panic that makes us take refuge
in safe words and visions. Crumble the harbour-walls
of our imaginations that we may be awash
with your sea of sound connecting you with us,
and ourselves with the echo of the creative storm
pounding at your heart.

Sister have mercy
Sister have mercy

Prayers of intercession

Let us find space within ourselves
to hear God speak; that her prayer
for the world may be ours.

So we pray:

With the woman beaten for daring to try to find her own story . . .
With the perpetrator of the beating . . .

Breath of the Voiceless
Breathe your prayer through us

With the lesbian or gay man in the closet for fear of rejection . . .
With the person who confidently tells them they love the person, but
    hate the sin . . .

Breath of the Voiceless
Breathe your prayer through us

With the woman spat at or abused or excluded because she wears
    hijab . . .
With the racist who insults or attacks or ignores . . .

Breath of the Voiceless
Breathe your prayer through us

With the person angry at the slow rate of change in the Church . . .
With the person who'd rather there was no change at all . . .

Breath of the Voiceless
Breathe your prayer through us

With the woman running for her life from a relationship she can't
stand . . .
With the person planning an honour killing because they feel their
family has been shamed . . .

Breath of the Voiceless
Breathe your prayer through us

With those people whose position in the church and society is so
precarious they seek refuge in deep caves of silence . . .
With those whose position is so secure they get anxious at the slightest
challenge to their comfort . . .

Breath of the voiceless
Breathe your prayer through us

God of bread and wine,
lift up the soul of the world,
uneven as old flagstones,
and reveal the joyous pinpoint
on which it may balance its toppling spin.

Blessing

May the God of anger and mercy
stir that beautiful, boisterous black angel
growling within you, causing you
to cherish who you are
and who you will be.
And may you find in the electric storm
of your life that eye of calm
crackling with energy enough
for you to resist
being stripped of hope, faith and love.
And the blessing of God,
Wise-woman, wound-mender, wildfire
Be with you/us all
this night and always. **Amen.**

Commentary: Enriching 'the tradition'?

While being bold in its use of imagery, the liturgical text offered above is refracted through certain well-established liturgical practices. Thus, as previously noted, it adopts a recognizable liturgical shape, one which reflects commonly used practice in ecumenical and other church settings. It is, then, at a basic level 'traditioned'. There are important reasons for noting this at the outset of this commentary, not least because one of the questions posed by 'expansive language' is: 'doesn't such language potentially disable rather than enable worship?' In being 'traditioned' the text seeks to enable 'full, conscious and active participation in liturgical celebrations'.[25] Equally, liturgy may be 'traditioning' – that is, it may enable people to participate in worship in fresh ways that open them to different ways of worshipping and make fresh contributions to a tradition. Thus, I suggest that the liturgical texts above, while emerging out of and dependent upon the work of many others, invite the worship participant to be stretched deeper in the feminist liturgical tradition.[26]

There are, I sense, many comment-worthy aspects of the text. My comments will focus primarily on what I take to be a key area – the opportunities and challenges of expansive language.

Why name these texts 'A Kaleidoscope God'? On a surface level the word 'kaleidoscope', understood as a constantly changing group of bright or interesting objects, connects with the variety and richness of the language used. But at another level, the word understood in its basic Greek terms as 'looking at/giving attention to beautiful form/ideas' has helpful theological resonances; for in so far as the text enables worship it does so by drawing the people into a beautiful mystery. The reference to 'form' may be considered problematic because it suggests a Platonic formalism, rather than a concrete engagement with the world; this is a danger and yet I suggest that the images on offer in the text actually draw us into earthy, bodily form. The images in both prayers of approach and adoration are, in the best sense, earthy – referring to washerwomen and foxes, for example. Such images are feminist partly because they involve reclaiming body and nature as fit places of celebration and spiritual expression.

The prayers of approach self-consciously take a Trinitarian form. The desire here is to set the prayer firmly in Christian tradition while simultaneously being playful with it. This serious play tries to subvert some of the patriarchal assumptions regarding, for example, the exclusion of Hagar from the dominant stories of the tradition while reshaping that tradition. Thus, Abraham is not excluded, but his pre-eminence is decentred by placing him subordinate to Hagar. In using the image of Fox-mother, the prayer of adoration raises a number of issues. The prayer itself was inspired by American feminist Adrienne Rich's poem 'Fox'.[27] This difficult poem, ostensibly about the poet's longing to be close to a vixen yet digging deep into women's experience of pain and abuse, has the power to hook into a deep subspace in women's experience. As Marjorie Procter-Smith notes, it was Rich who, in talking about language and art, troubled over how humanly created forms translate 'violence into patterns so powerful and pure/we continually fail to ask are they true for us'.[28] In using Rich's image of fox I seek to find a beautiful form that doesn't disguise the violence done especially to women and thereby speaks a language true for women.[29]

Of course, some people may be anxious about using an image that seems so self-consciously to depart from apparent biblical tradition. And this is a reasonable concern which highlights the riskiness of expansive liturgy.[30] It strikes me as almost unavoidably the case that some people will feel either alienated or disabled in worship through such texts. Is that reason for suggesting the limited value of expansive approaches to liturgy? My answer is no, for the very experience of alienation may be a liturgical moment, that is, a point of revelation for that alienated person of the nature and shape of their presuppositions about God and worship. Marjorie Procter-Smith has noted that women, among other groups, have been forced by patriarchal liturgy to learn to 'pray between the lines changing liturgy as they go'.[31] Through the experience of liturgical alienation and exclusion, those people who have been served by patriarchal language may come to a new encounter of the God who stands with the outsiders.

The concern over the use of non-biblical images for God raises an important consideration about the extent to which a liturgy can be embraced by the people as the 'people's work'. But balanced against this is the importance, in some contexts, of making rhetorical impact. This is not about creating images for the sake of creating or being controversial for the sake of controversy; it is about bringing to birth images that allow voices, traditionally silenced, to be heard. As Brita-Austern notes, 'for persons who have lived under structures of inequality, domination and control [like gay people] the experience of feeling silenced is a common phenomenon'.[32] In losing voice, subjectivity is lost and, thus, lives become de-legitimated. Feminist liturgy, thus, must be voice enabling.

It is appropriate, given this context when I'm discussing 'dangerous words', to examine my use of colour and gender imagery. First, colour. The blessing refers to God 'stirr[ing] the beautiful, boisterous black angel growling within'. This image takes its inspiration from the African American poet Audre Lorde's piece 'For Each of You'.[33] I follow Lorde in seeking to reclaim the word 'black' as a word of resonant positivity, and thereby seek to locate my text in a tradition not only feminist in nature, but shaped by the insights of womanist thinking. The use of colour imagery reveals how expansive liturgy must achieve the precision of poetry – for words are readily misunderstood, especially when using reclaimed colour language. Thus, in order to emphasize the affirmation around the word 'black', I added 'beautiful' into a draft text which excluded it. When using this liturgical text, I suggest using a projected image of a black angel during the blessing in order to underscore the positive interpretation of the colour.

The use of female gender language, especially in reference to Jesus/ Christ, raises further issues. For while many congregations may be groaning towards a recognition that our talk of God as 'father' is symbolic and metaphorical (thus enabling us to refer to 'him' as 'her' and 'father' as 'mother'), Jesus, because of his earthly existence, may seem to be immune to such play. His physical masculinity may appear to act as what philosophers sometimes refer to as a 'rigid designator'. This is not the place to engage in theological debates about the difference between the earthly Jesus or the risen Christ. What I want to say is best expressed by Don Saliers when talking about the symbolic in liturgy:

> The liturgy is not a static system or structure to which we bring our life experience; rather it is a crucible for meanings that, if entered into with our whole humanity, make experience possible . . . liturgical participation is itself symbolic and parabolic . . . enacting the liturgy together is participation in the mystery of being Church.[34]

What Saliers says here about liturgy as 'crucible of meanings', making experience possible, seems utterly appropriate to expansive language about Jesus/Christ. It is in participating in expansive liturgy as a crucible of meanings *in excelsis* that the worshipping community begins to both speak and discover fresh experiential possibilities. Richer conceptions of humanity and God become available. As Kavanagh notes, 'liturgy is about nothing less than ultimate, rather than immediate survival. It is about life forever by grace and promise.'[35] It is to such a conception of liturgy, in resistance to liturgy as a tool of domination and alienation, that the feminist texts on offer here seek to speak.

Postscript: Wasted breath . . . a pointless exercise in preciousness?

Some notes from my journal, Tuesday, 9 March 2004:

> What a night! I feel proud of the liturgy I wrote for the service tonight. Tonight felt like a taste of heaven. I was practically in tears as I delivered the blessing. I was so nervous prior to the worship, expecting extreme reactions from the more conservative members of the community. They seem to be left either grumbling or confused. I've no doubt some will think it was a stunt, an orchestrated prank. Very few people seem to feel that they were unable to participate in the liturgy in any way. Tonight I see that worship can be a real anticipation of the Kingdom. I shall sleep soundlessly tonight. Tonight has been a profound encounter with an outrageous and strange God. It will take me a long time to come to terms with what's happened.

So (rather breathlessly) it was back in 2004. What can I say about 'The Kaleidoscope God' several years on? My main anxiety is this: that it was precisely the kind of service and liturgy which reek of a kind of liberal preciousness one might expect from ordinands wishing to display their 'talent' and 'radicalness' in the rarefied world of theological education! That is to say, the liturgy, for all ordinary parochial purposes, is useless. However, when I think that, I ask myself, from whose perspective and with whose voice am I speaking? And my answer gives me the clue as to why I should resist dwelling on such cynical conclusions. For though I have made only limited use of these texts in a parochial context,[36] to imagine that this fact somehow abnegates their value is to be 'parochial' in the meanest sense. The power of 'The Kaleidoscope God' in the context of theological education reveals the contextual nature of liturgy: in a theological community willing to explore ambitiously beyond the established tradition, my texts could – and can – stretch and feed, as well as be troubling. This context is a legitimate place for liturgy to be enacted. More than that, I remain convinced of the prophetic power (in Brueggemann's sense) of such texts. They allow us to see beyond the tyranny of the present, a tyranny which so often undermines vision and imagination. And though it may be some time before many of us are bold or crazy enough to risk worship as queer or expansive as 'The Kaleidoscope God', I trust that the time may come for just such holy tomfoolery. For what has been once said, makes available the space for it to be said again.

Notes

1 Rosemary Radford Ruether, *Women-Church: Theology and Practice*, San Francisco, CA: Harper and Row, 1985, p. 107.

2 See Nicola Slee, *Women's Faith Development: Patterns and Processes*, Aldershot: Ashgate, 2004, pp. 11–12.

3 Gabe Huck, 'The Very Nature of the Liturgy', in Kathleen Hughes, ed., *Finding Voice to Give God Praise: Essays in the many Languages of Liturgy*, Collegeville, MN: Liturgical Press, 1998, p. 299.

4 Marjorie Procter-Smith, *In Her Own Rite*, Nashville, TN: Abingdon Press, 1990, p. 13.

5 Gail Ramshaw, *Under the Tree of Life: The Religion of a Feminist Christian*, New York: Continuum, 1998, p. 65.

6 Diann Neu, 'Our Name is Church: Catholic Feminist Liturgies' in Elisabeth Schüssler Fiorenza, ed., *The Power of Naming*, London: SCM Press, 1996, pp. 259ff.

7 My markers of liturgy are all text and word focused. Liturgy, thankfully, cannot be reduced to words. As Aidan Kavanagh puts it, 'liturgy only happens in the rough and tumbled landscape of spaces and times which people discover' (cited in Gabe Huck, ed., *A Sourcebook about Liturgy*, Chicago, IL: LTP, 1994, p. 41). Full, conscious and active participation are predicated on numerous aspects of the liturgical experience – sight, sound, place, taste, etc., as well as words. Unfortunately there is insufficient space in this contribution to deal with non-textual matters.

8 So, for example, a number of the liturgical texts seek to name areas of experience (and particularly women's experience) like self-harm, which are typically excluded from liturgy. Brita Gill-Austern notes the significance of the concept of 'voice coach' in feminist pastoral and educative praxis, in Bonnie J. Miller-McLemore and Brita L. Gill-Austern, eds, *Feminist and Womanist Pastoral Theology*, Nashville, TN: Abingdon Press, 1999, pp. 149–69.

9 Thus, I self-consciously follow classical prayer forms – e.g. confession, blessing, etc.

10 So, although God is typically referred to by female pronouns and words, at various points I refer to both women and men (e.g. during the prayers of thanksgiving). The hope of the text is to open up fresh language for God and humanity that both women and men might come to use.

11 See Marjorie Procter-Smith's comments on 'emancipatory' language in *In Her Own Rite*, pp. 63, 66–7 and Gail Ramshaw's comments on expansive language quoted above.

12 Anne L. Tomlinson, *Training God's Spies: Developing the Imagination in Theological Formation*, Edinburgh: Contact Pastoral Monographs 2001, No. 11, p. 18.

13 Sara Maitland, *A Big Enough God: Artful Theology*, London: Mowbray, 1995, p. 145.

14 Tomlinson, *Training God's Spies*, p. 19.

15 Walter Brueggemann, *The Prophetic Imagination*, Philadelphia, PA: Fortress Press, 1978, p. 119.

16 Elizabeth Stuart, *Daring To Speak God's Name*, London: Hamish Hamilton, 1992, p. 10.

17 It might be suggested that I'd put far too much store in the 'goods' which philosophy had on offer; that's probably correct. In my defence, one can appropriately argue that I was only showing the enthusiasm of the young.

18 The literature is extensive. See, for example, Lilli Alanen and Charlotte Witt, eds, *Feminist Reflections on the History of Philosophy*, Dordrecht: Kluwer, 2004; Sandra Harding and Merrill Hintikka, eds, *Discovering Reality*, Dordrecht: D. Reidel, 1983; Louise Antony and Charlotte Witt, eds, '*A Mind of One's Own': Feminist Essays on Reason and Objectivity*, Oxford/Boulder: Westview, 1993; Judith Butler, *Gender Trouble*, London: Routledge, 1992.

19 Adrienne Rich, *The Fact of a Doorframe, Collected Poems 1950–1984*, New York: Norton, 1984, p. 242.

20 Eavan Boland, *Collected Poems*, Manchester: Carcanet, 1995, p. xii. I take Boland's words a little out of context (which refer to her wrestling with her Irish/cultural inheritance and her life story), but they speak powerfully into my life.

21 Nicola Slee, *The Public Use of Poetry*, Audenshaw Papers 215, 2005, Hinksey Network, p. 1.

22 I have no wish here to engage in the post-structuralist debate, inspired by Jacques Derrida, about the relationship between 'speech' and 'writing'.

23 Slee, *Public Use of Poetry*, p. 2.

24 Cited in Neil Astley, ed., *Staying Alive: Real Poems for Unreal Times*, Tarset: Bloodaxe Books, 2002, p. 18.

25 Austin Flannery, ed., *Vatican Council II: Conciliar and Post-Conciliar Documents*, New York: Costello, 1977, p. 14. A further factor worth considering when wishing to enable participation is the judicious use of humour. When this liturgy was enacted for Women's World Day of Prayer, a very funny, but astute, sketch about the relationships between men and women was used immediately after the prayers of approach. It was noticeable how many of the people who had obviously been shocked by those prayers visibly relaxed after the sketch.

26 The 'feminist liturgical tradition' includes, among many others, Radford Ruether's ground-breaking work, Diann Neu, Janet Morley and Nicola Slee.

27 Adrienne Rich, 'Fox', in *Poems 1998–2000*, New York: Norton, 2001, p. 25.

28 Procter-Smith, *In Her Own Rite*, p. 1.

29 I make further creative use of Rich's work during the confession when I refer to 'diving into the wreck of our selves'. The image of the wreck within feminist discourse was shaped crucially by Rich's famous 1973 poem 'Diving into the Wreck' (Adrienne Rich, *The Fact of a Doorframe*, p. 162). Thus I seek to fold my text into and honour the tradition.

30 The inclusion of the prayer of adoration was the one section of the liturgy on which I was directly challenged, primarily I believe on the grounds that it departed so thoroughly from biblical conceptions of God. I appreciated the force of the criticism, yet remain convinced of the value of including it. Yes, the picture of God as 'fox-mother' was and is a difficult, left-field image and yet I know it drew a number of people further into the liturgical action of our worship. I wish as much could be said for many of our regular, common-coin pictures of God.

31 Marjorie Procter-Smith, *Praying with our Eyes Open: Engendering Feminist Liturgical Prayer*, Nashville, TN: Abingdon Press, 1995, p. 31.

32 Brita Gill-Austern, 'Pedagogy under the Influence of Feminism and Womanism', in Miller-McLemore and Gill-Austern, eds, *Feminist and Womanist Pastoral Theology*, p. 153.

33 Audre Lorde, *The Collected Poems of Audre Lorde*, New York: Norton, 2000, pp. 59–60.

34 Don E. Saliers, 'Symbol in Liturgy, Liturgy as Symbol: The Domestication of Liturgical Experience', in Lawrence J. Madden, ed., *The Awakening Church: Twenty*

Five Years of Liturgical Renewal, Collegeville, MN: Liturgical Press, 1992, pp. 74 and 76.

35 Aidan Kavanagh, *On Liturgical Theology*, Collegeville, MN: Liturgical Press, 1984, p. 153.

36 I have used the intercessory prayers and blessing on a number of occasions, and, considering that I am currently based in a rather formal, middle-of-the-road Anglican church, they have been well received.

14

Writing the (Feminine) Divine:
Reflections on the Practice of
Contemporary Feminist Liturgy

NICOLA SLEE

Introduction

In this chapter, I want to offer a commentary on a liturgical text of my own, 'Litany to a dark god' (a text which has been quite widely used in a range of liturgical settings and the occasion of some controversy),[1] as a way of reflecting on what it is I think I am about in writing feminist liturgical texts which address God as the divine feminine. I hope that this does not seem unduly self-referential; and, if it does, readers must forgive me. Actually, it is a novel experience for me to reflect in writing in a sustained way on one of my own prayer texts. In writing poetry or liturgy, my level of conscious awareness of intentionality, significance or practical usability can vary widely, but frequently the writing is of an intuitive nature where considerations of this kind are not to the fore. It is only later that one stands back and sees the piece whole. It is perhaps later again, after the piece has been prayed and lived in over a matter of time – both privately and publicly – that one can begin to discern some of the layers of meaning. I am sure this is a common experience for writers, particularly poets. So I am grateful for an opportunity to stand back and reflect on a piece I wrote some years ago, and, in doing so, to raise wider questions about the variety of strategies feminist liturgists have used and may use in reworking gendered spiritual traditions in liberating ways.

I see my writing as part of that larger enterprise of feminist liturgical and poetic discourse which has flourished for the past three or more decades out of a wide range of grassroots and experiential contexts of Womenchurch[2] and other ritual gatherings both within and on the edges of the institutional churches. While there is huge diversity within this movement, one can identify common features, or what Marjorie Procter-Smith prefers to term 'values', which she names as contextuality, commitment to process, 'experimentality', rejection of hierarchical forms of liturgical leadership and a commitment to shared leadership, and the relativization of denominational, confessional and traditional divisions.[3] Most of my own liturgical writing has been occasioned by particular community contexts and needs, and has been shaped by the women and men who have formed these communities. (I think particularly of the Women in Theology and Movement for the Ordination of Women networks, now disbanded, which were highly significant for me in the late 1970s and 1980s in forming my own feminist theological identity and helping me to find a new way of praying, as well as the experimental St Hilda Community and an unnamed community meeting at St Mark's, Wimbledon over a number of years and, over more recent years, the Catholic Women's Network and, on a broader scale, the European Women's Synod movement.[4] Communities of theological education in which I have worked have also been significant places in encouraging and provoking liturgical and poetic creativity: the Southwark Ordination Course, the Aston Training Scheme and, for the past eight years, the Queen's Foundation in Birmingham.) I see myself as both speaking with my own particular voice when I write liturgical texts, but also – and without denying the differences that are always as significant in any community as the connecting threads – attempting to speak out of and for the particular community or communities to which I belong and to whom I owe allegiance; and, more widely still, stretching beyond the particularities of any one setting towards all those women and men who identify themselves with the quest for fresh emancipatory liturgical discourse. I have been both influenced by, and see myself as sharing a solidarity with, other creative liturgists working in the UK such as Janet Morley, Jim Cotter, Kathy Galloway, Jan Berry and hymn writers such as June Boyce-Tillman, Janet Wootton, Brian Wren and Doug Constable,[5] as well as being shaped by wider liturgical movements such as those represented by the Iona community[6] and the various feminist networks and communities I have already mentioned. Beyond specifically liturgical contexts, I also situate my own work within the field of revisionary feminist poetry, and have been strongly influenced by the writings of many contemporary women poets, including Elizabeth Jennings, Kathleen Raine, U. A. Fanthorpe, Carol Ann Duffy and Eavan Boland from this side of the Atlantic, and Anne Sexton, Adrienne Rich, Audre Lorde, Marge Piercy, Denise Levertov and Mary Oliver from the other.[7]

The writing of liturgical texts is, of course, only one dimension of liturgical creation. The text forms merely the written script or suggestive rubrics which must then be brought alive in the assembly of the people, or in the personal prayer of the individual. Marjorie Procter-Smith speaks of at least three kinds of emancipatory discourse or language that are brought into play in any act of liturgy: verbal language must be accompanied by visual and physical symbols, gestures and patterns,[8] and it is the interaction of the whole that makes for living ritual. Indeed, words themselves may not be necessary: I have attended eucharistic rites in which the entire liturgy was performed in silence, using movement and physical gesture without words.[9] Nevertheless, in most liturgies, spoken words and texts do form a central part of the action, providing a framework and a focus for the visual and the physical discourse. And even where words themselves are not spoken, they form the essential linguistic framework of intention and understanding without which the symbolic gestures themselves would have little meaning. We are linguistic animals, and language forms our thoughts, our intentions and our desires.

Naming the (feminine) divine

A or perhaps *the* central issue in feminist liturgy, as in feminist theology, has been, and continues to be, the naming of the divine. In liturgy, this question is, as Procter-Smith suggests, 'primary and urgent',[10] because liturgy assumes an encounter with the divine and, in a real sense, cannot happen unless such an address is actualized. Liturgy cannot wait on the deliberations of the theologians but happens, day in, day out, week by week, as the people of God cry out to God – a God whose presence we may doubt and whose activity we may query but to whom we nevertheless offer our prayer. Liturgy and prayer are the places, then, where persons and communities learn to encounter and name the divine, are the places of primary theology – as theologians have always known. Feminist liturgies offer a plethora of new and recovered images of God while critiquing and destabilizing patriarchal ones. In my own writing, I have played with a variety of ways of naming God: God as stroppy middle-aged mother, as hiker, spinster, quester, jester; as dark lover or as mysterious, unnamed presence in darkness and winter, as the One encountered in every human worker, neighbour, stranger, fool and friend. I have used, as other writers use, a range of literary and theological strategies for naming and addressing the divine: sometimes using non-gender specific terms, at other times, gendered ones (both male and female, or only female); at other times again, moving beyond the human realm to draw on natural images of sea, wind or darkness; sometimes using images in tension and contradiction, at other times staying with one image and developing it in a range of different directions; sometimes deliberately employing rhetorical excess, at other times seeking to hone down language to a bare minimum, emphasizing the spaces between words and the silence beyond every image.[11] Every poem or liturgical text is partial, provisional, incomplete. It cannot do everything; perhaps it can do something. And it is highly contextual; it can only do whatever it does in the context of the persons and settings in which it is used. The poem or liturgy does not mean in abstraction or isolation; it takes on meaning in context, and may mean differently as it is spoken and inhabited by different persons and communities bringing different questions, experiences and insights to the written text. This is a way of insisting upon reader-response in the context of liturgy; or perhaps, better, pray-er-response!

Litany to a dark god

Having acknowledged the provisionality and contextuality of all liturgical speech, I turn now to an examination of my 'litany to a dark god'.

I hear her voice in the night shadows
but I do not see her face
I feel her breath on the cold night air
but I cannot touch her flesh
Near to me as breathing
intimate as touching
in the darkness she eludes my grasp
she evades my touch
All her ways are strange to me
and all her paths are hidden

She is speaking to me in the darkness
but I do not comprehend what she is saying
She is leading me in the darkness
but I cannot tell where she is moving
She is pursuing me in the darkness
but I cannot discover her purpose

Under the velvet cover of night she seduces me
and I cannot resist her advances
Under the blanket of stars she gazes at me
and I cannot refuse her glances
Drawn to her darkness
I come in under the belly of her shadow
Entranced by her obscurity
I enter in where knowledge is no more

Here I must stay under the dark gaze of her loving
Here I must rest under the fragrance of her silence
Here I must wait under the shadow of her wooing
while she speaks to me
and she sings to me
and she cradles me
and croons to me
in words no other may utter
in a language unknown to any other lover

And so she will charm me and bind me
She will pierce me and bless me
She will fill me and empty me
She will rouse me and quiet me
She will wound me and heal me
She will quicken me and deaden me
in her deep and unyielding darkness
which no tongue may name nor finger trace
no searching plumb nor mind guess

And I will enter into this darkness
where I have never walked before
And I will submit into this darkness
to a terror never dared before
And I will yield into this darkness
to a loving never ventured before

And of her darkness I must know and I must know nothing
And in this darkness I must be made and I must be unmade
And of her darkness I must be possessed and dispossessed of all
    things

The piece takes at least part of its inspiration from the evocative image of the dark female lover in the first song of the Song of Solomon, in which the woman speaks:

> I am black and beautiful,
>   O daughters of Jerusalem,
> like the tents of Kedar,
>   like the curtains of Solomon.
> Do not gaze at me because I am dark,
>   because the sun has gazed on me.
> (Song of Solomon 1.5–6a)

This text has occasioned much critical comment which need not concern us here,[12] except to note that the identity of the Shulamite woman remains obscure – in itself, a poignant symbol of the obscurity of women and particularly black women in biblical and theological traditions. The image of the black and beautiful lover was highly suggestive to me at a time when my own experience had pushed me beyond previously workable names and understandings of the divine towards a far more mysterious and apophatic sense of God as dark yet desirable stranger. While I do not consider the autobiographical context out of which the poem was written to limit its range of associations or meanings, it may be helpful to know that it was written out of a liminal time of change and grief, marked by prolonged ill-health, loss of job and home, major surgery and the loss of the capacity to bear children – a time in which previous conceptions of the meaning and direction of my life were breaking apart and before new ones had been birthed to take their place. While the sense of God remained intensely real for me, the identity and purposes of God had become mysterious and unknown; or, if known, known in an entirely instinctual and bodily kind of way that had more to do with unknowing than knowing. In a very real sense, I wrote this piece to discover who God might be for me and who I was in relation to the divine. Is not this the impulse for all authentic prayer? We do not know the one to whom we pray, even less do we know our own nature or names, but seek a connecting and salvific relation with the mysterious source of our life.

Formally, the poem employs many of the characteristic features of biblical and liturgical language, drawing on the psalms and the Song of Solomon, in particular. Repetition, parallelism of various kinds and rhetorical paradox and contradiction are used throughout.[13] The use of the first person singular places the piece in the tradition of the psalms of personal lament, witness and prayer, rather than in the more generalized first person plural voice of much liturgical discourse (the typical 'we' of prayers of approach, confession and many credal statements). By deliberately employing the cadences, rhythms and formal features of archaic biblical and liturgical language, the litany implicitly claims the authority and dignity of scriptural speech for a contemporary, feminist community, thereby both subverting and reclaiming patriarchal religious discourse.

Reclamation and subversion are at work in this piece in other, more complex ways. In particular, the poem draws extensively on two ancient religious traditions or ways of speaking of God: first, the use of the model of romantic and erotic love as a way of imaging the relation between God and the believer, and second, the negative or apophatic mystical tradition in which God is named in terms of darkness, unknowability, negation and paradox. These traditions, rich, varied and complex as they both are in their historical trajectories and expressions, have been gendered in powerful ways (the first more obviously than the second, but the second too), reflecting and reinscribing dominant gender relations, with ambiguous if not harmful effects for women believers. Praying in and through these traditions is by no means unproblematic for women believers or for any who challenge the implicit gender relations underlying them. By reworking, re-gendering and combining these two traditions, my poem attempts to subvert their patriarchal power and to offer suggestive strategies for addressing the divine.

First, then, the poem draws on the tradition of romantic and erotic love used to image the relationship between the divine and the human. This tradition, in which God is imaged as the passionate lover of the soul, is found in all major religious traditions and is frequently employed in the Hebrew scriptures,[14] finding its most intense form in the Song of Solomon. It was developed extensively in Christian mystical tradition from the patristic period onwards, drawing on the New Testament bridal imagery for the relation between Christ and the Church,[15] with a particular flourishing in the medieval period,[16] continuing in every period up to the modern era, and still to be found in much contemporary hymnody, prayer and spirituality,[17] though significantly less visible in officially sanctioned Christian liturgy. In its biblical and traditional forms, of course, this tradition is a highly gendered and patriarchal one – though there have always been voices which disrupt and subvert the dominant masculinist one, including in Scripture itself.[18] Despite the apparent mutuality and non-hierarchical nature of the romantic relationship to modern consciousness, in its biblical and traditional forms this is not a relationship of equality or mutuality. God is the sovereign, male lover, who is ruling patriarch as well as suitor, maker of heaven and earth as well as questing lover, husband to a wife who has no legal rights to land, possessions or control over her own body. It is a relationship of dominance and hierarchical control: God the divine lover has all the power, initiative and subjectivity, while the female beloved is largely passive in the face of the divine quest and gaze. Her salvation lies in being sought and won by her divine lover, and in submitting to the ecstasy of divine love. For all the eroticism of this tradition in its original biblical and later expressions, in practice this was a highly spiritualized conception of erotic love, finding its most intense expression in monastic settings of sexual renunciation and clerical celibacy. It often coexisted with denigration of the body and sexuality, and of the female body and sexuality in particular. Its effects have therefore been highly ambiguous for women: while allowing a certain degree of spiritual freedom to women to cultivate the life of the soul and of prayer, and permitting a channelling of celibate women's sexual longings into their spiritual lives, this has been at the cost of a dualistic spirituality in which women's bodies and minds have been under the control of male hierarchy and which has had little positive effect on women's real relationships with male lovers and partners.[19]

Recent official liturgies of the mainstream institutional churches have largely eschewed this romantic and erotic tradition; not, we may suppose, out of an awareness of its problematic gendered status so much as an instinctual (and unconscious?) avoidance of sexualized language in public liturgy. Feminists, as well as gay, lesbian and queer theologians, have been noted for their reclamation of the language of the erotic as one expression of the intention to speak and think from the body and to foreground sexuality in the human relation to the divine. When the patriarchal and heterosexist discourse of romantic, erotic love is reclaimed and subverted by women to name their own desires and longings, its dualistic and controlling effects may be undercut. I am by no means the first feminist liturgist to attempt such a reversal of the tradition; in the USA, Carter Heyward has employed the language of the erotic in striking ways both in her prose theological works and in a number of liturgical texts;[20] in the UK, Janet Morley has employed this strategy to particularly powerful effect in a number of the pieces in her classic collection of prayers, *All Desires Known*, as have many contemporary feminist poets.[21]

In my 'litany to a dark god', as in a number of Morley's pieces, the divine lover is posited as female and takes on the power (but also the powerlessness), the initiative and subjectivity (but also the kenosis and vulnerability), of One who desires, seeks, pursues and waits upon the human beloved, with passionate longing yet without controlling dominance or threat of violence. God becomes the passionate female lover, and in this regendering of the tradition, its patriarchal dualism and rejection of the body and sexuality are undercut, as is the implicit power relationship between male and female, divine and human. When a sexual language of passionate desire is claimed by the divine female, in pursuance of the human beloved, this gives the strongest possible theological legitimization to female bodily and sexual desire. Women's bodies and erotic desires are projected onto the deity and thereby imaged as not only good but as explicitly sacred, holy, godly. In my poem, the dark god is imaged repeatedly in concrete bodiliness, even in voluptuous sensuality: the poem is full of references to her body parts and gestures ('face', 'flesh', 'touch', 'glances', 'belly', 'gaze', 'fragrance') as well as to her erotic advances and intentions (she 'seduces' and 'woos' and 'cradles' and 'croons'). In such ways, the regendering of the tradition of erotic divine love provides a powerful avenue for reclaiming female bodiliness and sexuality. But in my poem it is not only the divine lover who is imaged as female. When the human beloved is also positioned as female, the heterosexist assumptions of the traditional model are also challenged and subverted, and a lesbian erotic is brought into play. God the female lover desires and searches out the human beloved who has now become the woman of her choice. Here the patriarchal image of the sovereign male lord wooing the subservient female disciple is done away with entirely. There is no room at all for dominant male power in my poem, simply because there is no space given to male desire at all. (Of course, when the reader or speaker is male, a heterosexual erotic is resumed, but another reversal then takes place; because the poem gives the initiative to the female divine lover, a patriarchal power dynamic is, once again, subverted, and the male believer is invited into a relation of kenotic self-emptying and vulnerability.)

It is clear that, in the poem, the relationship between the divine lover and the female beloved is not an entirely equal or mutual one. The divine lover is still the active, initiating pursuer, over and against the (female) speaker who is pursued. There is a vulnerability, a self-yielding and surrender in the poem (on the part of the speaker) which is essential to the lived experience out of which it was written. Yet I want to insist that this is not a coerced surrender to the patriarchal God of dominant power, but a willing self-yielding to a God beyond patriarchy, who is both like and unlike the female beloved, both known and unknown, yet whose desire is not for domination but for the intimacy of knowledge, loving and holding. Yet there is fearfulness and risk in the self-surrender, because this is a 'dark god', who is as hidden as she is revealed. Here the poem draws on and combines with another ancient spiritual tradition, that of apophatic encounter, a tradition which both deepens and subverts the certainties of the erotic encounter with the divine.

The second biblical and mystical tradition which my poem draws upon, regenders and attempts to subvert, is the apophatic tradition of prayer and spirituality in which, in contrast to the kataphatic way, God is approached by means of a via negativa, by way of silence, negation and paradox in which all our prayer and theology stutters 'not this, not that', and every positive image must be cancelled out by its opposite. This tradition, with deep biblical roots in the Hebrew injunctions against idolatry, the unpronouncability of the divine name and the mysteriousness of the divine 'I am', has been a powerful one in Christianity, though sidelined and repressed by Protestantism in its elevation of the Word and its dogmatic confidence.[22] On the face of it, the apophatic tradition, like the tradition of erotic divine love, appears to offer potential for an inclusive and emancipatory form of feminist discourse – and I believe it does, with its iconoclastic tendencies and its invitation to limitless creativity. Yet it too, in its historical expressions, has been a gendered and patriarchal tradition. Even within the openness of the apophatic way, in which any and every positive identity of God was contradicted and cancelled out, the masculinity of the deity was not questioned. God may have been imaged (or not imaged) by Pseudo-Dionysius as 'not greatness, not smallness, not living, not life, not king, not wisdom, not sonhood, not fatherhood'[23] and even by Meister Eckhart as 'nonGod',[24] but God's femininity, motherhood or sisterliness was never negated because never postulated in the first instance. The apophatic way was parasitic on the kataphatic and, to that extent, was limited by the patriarchal and dualistic assumptions of every positive affirmation about God.

Nevertheless, there is much to be said positively for this negative way! Its elusive, paradoxical and fluid speech about the divine, self-consciously provisional and aware of its own metaphoric nature, offers a potentially expansive and emancipatory strategy for contemporary feminists. Its positive valuing of darkness and unknowing as the underside of rational faith provides a discourse for affirming black as beautiful, the wisdom of intuition and imagination and the knowledge of the body as over against white as right, the dominance of rationality and the will to control. A number of contemporary theologians and spiritual practitioners have reclaimed this tradition in interesting ways to reaffirm the body, the imagination, darkness and blackness, surrender and unknowing in faith experience. Matthew Fox speaks of the via negativa as one of the essential four paths in creation spirituality, while many black, postcolonial and womanist theologians have reclaimed the language of darkness to speak positively of black experience; Janet Morley has drawn extensively on imagery of darkness in her prayers and poems to evoke the mystery and unknowing of encounter with the divine. In my 'litany to a dark god', I am glad to stand in such company.

In drawing on apophatic tradition and combining it with the language of the (lesbian) erotic, I am attempting a number of things. First, I am trying to find a specifically feminine gendered language for those experiences of liminality, unknowing, paradox and contradiction which have been central to my own faith journey as a woman and are also, I contend, highly significant to many other women. I am wanting to suggest, perhaps, that there are specifically gendered experiences of not-knowing which demand their own forms of discourse; this is certainly so in the arena of prayer, where women have experienced themselves as silenced and undesired by God. My research into women's faith development has highlighted for me the number of women for whom apophatic ways of faithing are the only ones possible: women for whom it is not possible to positively describe or affirm the nature of faith or of God but for whom denunciation and contradiction are the only avenues of prayer and spirituality. Thus in my poem, what is affirmed about God – the constant repetition of the divine 'she' against the continued dominance of 'he' in almost all mainstream liturgical settings, the affirmation of her passionate searching love, her bodily nearness and intimacy, her manifold and diverse acts of loving – is in tension throughout with the divine otherness, elusiveness and mystery. The dark god evoked in the poem is, in a very real sense, nameless and faceless, and her namelessness and facelessness are also, paradoxically, revelatory: revelatory and, strangely, a source of power. (As Procter-Smith writes, 'Even a God who is nameless has that namelessness in common with countless women of past and present'.[25]) Whatever is affirmed of her is immediately contradicted or negated. She comes close, but then she hides herself. She is as near as breathing but will not be touched. She pursues but cannot be found. And even when she is found, in stanza four, and the longing for the encounter with divine love is met, the mystery and paradox merely intensify. In her closeness there is wounding as well as healing, deadening as well as quickening, a loving in which terror as well as ecstasy finds a place, in which the speaker finds herself drawn into a darkness which does not admit of comprehension.

I am trying, in such discourse, to find a language which holds in tension positive feminine imagery for the divine – absolutely necessary to counteract the centuries of negative female naming or the yawning absence of women from the tradition – with the insistence that God is beyond any and every name and image, including female ones. There is a danger in feminist theology and liturgy of reinscribing the very stereotypes of the feminine which we are attempting to challenge, of imposing a new and unthinking feminist dogmatism that simply replaces one set of gendered absolutes for another, albeit opposite, set. Naming and praying to God as Mother may be no more – and indeed, might be less – liberating than continuing to pray 'our Father', if the underlying model of motherhood reinforces women's identity, value and social role in terms of biological motherhood. Marjorie Procter-Smith rightly insists that our language to and about God needs to be 'emancipatory'[26] (or what Stephen Burns prefers to term 'expansive'[27]) and not merely 'inclusive', constantly pushing against the caricatures and limitations of each and every metaphor or image. One strategy for coming against the hegemony of patriarchal discourse and protecting against the emergence of a new, feminized dogmatism is to multiply and celebrate diverse and novel images for God, drawing not only on the human realm but on natural and animal imagery: to 'bring many names', as Brian Wren suggests,[28] and as Gail Ramshaw illustrates in her plethora of playful, original metaphors for God (God as Alpha, Advent, babies, bath, cup, David, exultet, feast/food, gaze, health . . . and more[29]). Another and opposite strategy is to refuse all images and metaphors, to cancel out gendered as well as every other socialized form of human discourse as an adequate route towards divine mystery. This is the feminist apophatic.

In the end, neither one of these strategies is sufficient in itself as a means of liturgical discourse. We need both; only by holding the tension between kataphatic and apophatic ways of speaking and knowing will we preserve the elusive character of all God-language and pay proper respect, on the one hand, to divine initiative and mystery, and, on the other, to the affirmation that God does indeed self-reveal, self-surrender Godself to the world. In employing both of these strategies – both within a single work such as 'litany to a dark god' and more broadly across the range of my liturgical and poetic writing – I am trying to find a language that can reflect my own and other women's dual experiences of pleasure and pain, of certitude and unknowing, of light and darkness, of exhilaration and limitation, of self ownership and of self surrender – a way of speaking, praying and writing that proclaims both experiences as capable of reflecting divine grace.

End note

Having written the above piece, I was re-reading Janet Morley's essay, 'I desire her with my whole heart',[30] in which she reflects upon the meaning and value of writing psalms and prayers that name God as 'she'. She speaks of the way in which, in excluding the feminine in its official theological and liturgical discourse for centuries, the Church has also suppressed much else associated with the feminine; conversely, to begin to address God anew as female is to bring into consciousness and into one's relationship with God these repressed aspects of experience. Morley names three main aspects of experience that have been so repressed and are now being reclaimed: weakness, sexuality and the 'dark side' of human nature, 'with its chaotic and mysterious emotions'. These, I discover, are the very elements brought together and expressed in my 'litany to a dark god'.

Notes

1 Originally published in Nicola Slee, *Praying Like A Woman*, London: SPCK, 2004, pp. 140–1. From a personal source, I gather it has been banned from use in one theological college chapel, on the grounds of being heretical and even 'occultist'!

2 For accounts of the Womenchurch movement, see Natalie K. Watson, *Introducing Feminist Ecclesiologies*, Sheffield: Sheffield Academic Press, 2000, chapter 4.

3 Marjorie Procter-Smith, *In Her Own Rite: Constructing Feminist Liturgical Tradition*, Nashville, TN: Abingdon, 1990, pp. 21–5.

4 For an account of these and other feminist theology groups and networks in Britain, see Jenny Daggers, *The British Christian Women's Movement: A Rehabilitation of Eve*, London: Ashgate, 2002.

5 I will not attempt to list all the significant texts by these authors, since many of them are well known, but offer a representative sample: Janet Morley, *All Desires Known*, London: SPCK, 1998; Jim Cotter, *Prayer at Day's Dawning*, Sheffield: Cairns Publications, 2001; Kathy Galloway, *Talking to the Bones*, London: SPCK, 1996; June Boyce-Tillman, *A Rainbow to Heaven: Hymns, Songs and Chants*, London: Stainer & Bell, 2006; Brian Wren, *Bring Many Names*, Carol Stream, IL: Hope Publishing Company, 1989; Doug Constable, see <http://www.hymnsocietygbi.org.uk> where 13 of his hymn collection, 'People Making Peace', can be found, together with commentaries, in an abbreviated version of his MPhil thesis, 'Making Christian Hymns: A Work of the Church'.

6 Again, the liturgical texts of the Iona community are well-known. See <http://www.ionabooks.com>.

7 The work of women poets is perhaps less well known to theologians and liturgists. Again, space precludes a comprehensive bibliography, but most of the poets listed have selected or collected works, viz: Elizabeth Jennings, *New Collected Poems*, Manchester: Carcanet, 2002; Kathleen Raine, *Selected Poems*, Ipswich: Golgonooza Press, 1988; Carol Ann Duffy, *Selected Poems*, London: Penguin, 1994; Eavan Boland, *Collected Poems*, Manchester: Carcanet, 1995; Anne Sexton, *Selected Poems*, London: Virago, 1991; Adrienne Rich, *The Fact of a Doorframe: Selected Poems 1950–2001*, New York: W. W. Norton, 2002; Audre Lorde, *Collected Poems*, New York: W. W. Norton, 2002; Marge Piercy, *Eight Chambers of the Heart: Selected Poems*, London: Penguin, 1995; Denise Levertov, *Selected Poems*, Newcastle: Bloodaxe, 1986; Mary Oliver, *New and Selected Poems*, Boston: Beacon Press, 1992.

8 Procter-Smith, *In Her Own Rite*, pp. 67–84.

9 For an outline of such a silent Eucharist, see The St Hilda Community, *Women Included: A Book of Services and Prayers*, London: SPCK, 1991, pp. 86–8.

10 Procter-Smith, *In Her Own Rite*, p. 88.

11 See, in particular, Slee, *Praying Like A Woman*, chapter 10, 'The edge of God'.

12 For illuminating discussion on the Shulamite woman, see Christopher King, 'Song of Songs' in Deryn Guest, Robert E. Goss, Mona West and Thomas Bohache, eds, *The Queer Bible Commentary*, London: SCM Press, 2006, pp. 356–70.

13 For a discussion of the literary characteristics of the Psalms, see Klaus Seybold, *Introducing the Psalms*, Edinburgh: T&T Clark, 1990.

14 For example, in Psalm 45; Isaiah 54.1–8; Isaiah 62.3–5; Hosea 2—3.

15 Ephesians 5.25–32.

16 This era has been written about extensively, with a particular interest in female mysticism. See, for example, Caroline Walker Bynum, *Jesus as Mother: Studies in the Spirituality of the High Middle Ages*, Berkeley, CA: University of Califormia Press, 1984; Elizabeth A. Petroff, *Body and Soul: Essays on Medieval Women and Mysticism*, New York: Oxford University Press, 1994; Grace Jantzen, *Power, Gender and Christian Mysticism*, Cambridge: Cambridge University Press, 1995.

17 Popular choruses often employ romantic and erotic imagery, whether consciously or not. For example, 'As the deer pants for the water' by Martin J. Nystrom, 'Hold me, Lord, in your arms' and 'I'm in love with you' by Danny Daniels, and many others, in *Songs of Fellowship*, Eastbourne: Kingsway, 1998.

18 See, for example, Elizabeth Stuart's 'queer' reading of Ephesians 5.25–32 in Robert E. Goss and Mona West, eds, *Take Back the Word: A Queer Reading of the Bible*, Cleveland, OH: Pilgrim Press, 2000.

19 For an interesting and nuanced discussion of romantic relationship as a primary image for contemporary working-class women's relationship with God, and its effects both positive and negative, see Ellen Clark-King, *Theology By Heart: Women, the Church and God*, Peterborough: Epworth Press, 2004.

20 See Carter Heyward, *Our Passion for Justice: Images of Power, Sexuality and Liberation*, Cleveland, OH: Pilgrim Press, 1984; *Touching Our Strength: The Erotic as Power and the Love of God*, San Francisco, CA: Harper, 1989.

21 A well-known example is Carol Ann Duffy's much-anthologized 'Warming her pearls', in which a female servant fantasizes about her mistress as she wears her pearls to warm them. In *Selected Poems*, p. 60.

22 For accounts of the apophatic tradition, see H. Egan, 'Christian apophatic and kataphatic mysticisms', *Theological Studies*, 39 (1978), pp. 399–426; Alan Jones, *Soul*

Making: The Desert Way of Spirituality, London: SCM Press, 1985, pp. 25–7; Philip Sheldrake, *Spirituality and History*, London: SPCK, 1995, 2nd ed., pp. 199–206.

23 In *The Mystical Theology*, chapters 4 and 5, in *The Complete Works* translated by Colm Luibheid, London: Paulist Press, 1987.

24 In *Meister Eckhart: The Essential Sermons, Commentaries, Treatises and Defense*, translated and introduced by Edmund Colledge, London: Paulist Press, 1981, p. 49.

25 Procter-Smith, *In Her Own Rite*, p. 115.

26 Procter-Smith, *In Her Own Rite*, ch. 3.

27 See Stephen Burns, *SCM Studyguide to Liturgy*, London: SCM Press, 2006, pp. 110–15.

28 Brian Wren, 'Bring many names' in *Bring Many Names*, no. 9; also in *What Language Shall I Borrow? God-talk in Worship: A Male Response to Feminist Theology*, London: SCM Press, 1990, pp. 137–8.

29 Gail Ramshaw, *A Metaphorical God: An Abecedary of Images for God*, Chicago, IL: Liturgy Training Publications, 1995.

30 In Ann Loades, *Feminist Theology: A Reader*, London: SPCK, 1990, pp. 158–64.

15

Liturgy and Loss:
A Lesbian Perspective on Using Psalms of Lament in Liturgy

DERYN GUEST

Introduction

It has been around 14 years since I put off my Salvation Army uniform and stopped attending regular services. I did not know I was going to walk out midway through that particular morning service. It wasn't a premeditated move, nor a specific 'light bulb' moment; all I can remember is the growing discomfort of preceding months and the feeling of alienation dawning on me with such a weight that a minor irritation with that particular visiting officer prompted me to deposit one of my children on the lap of my bemused partner and, as the monetary offerings were being collected, slip out the door. Having walked home, I folded the uniform and put it away, knowing it was the last time I would wear it. Did it feel liberative? To some extent, though I had not walked home skipping and cheering. The sense as I remember it was more one of relief as I hastily pulled on the comfortable pair of jeans, T-shirt and trainers in exchange for the unlikely heels, skirt, blouse, brooch and bizarre headwear. It was also a relief that I no longer had to perform the Salvationist identity and therefore hide the significance of the relationship I shared with a fellow female Salvationist.

Fourteen years is a long time; time enough perhaps to come to terms with one's decisions. But what I had not anticipated was the sheer enormity of loss that this action entailed: loss of a religious home akin to the loss of a much loved family of would-be aunts, uncles, nieces, nephews, cousins, grandparents; loss of its liturgical environment – particularly its musical and lyrical heritage, which for all its gendered stereotypes and heteronormativity, had always held profound significance for me; and the loss of relationship with God. When one has come to know God through a particular denomination's understanding and interpretation of 'him', then the break with the community led to a rupture of relationship with that particular version of God. 'He' and I stopped speaking. Well, *I* was certainly no longer on speaking terms since this deity could not be envisaged as condoning my walkout or my later open, affirming, embrace of a somewhat genderqueer[1] lesbian identity. The losses were/are substantial and need to be attended to, closely identified, mourned, before the possibility of healing and rebuilding one's spiritual life can take place. But where does one find the liturgical resources to help with such a quest? Becoming a freelance worshipper did not really help, though the experience of speaking through set liturgies was initially new and meaningful. But ultimately, these liturgies were hampered by the same male-dominated and heteronormative framework of worship I had rejected. I soon gave up on institutionalized religion altogether.

My voice is accordingly that of a disenchanted ex-Salvation Army officer whose lesbian choices inexorably put me outside a long-standing confessional home. However, I also come from the perspective of one living (not yet dancing)[2] on the edge and find myself struggling in the liminal zone occupied by those limping between an earnest desire to get back in tune with some form of spirituality and the resentment and anger that drives one ever further afield from religion and God. Tigert's testimony to the love/hate relationship with a church which at once provided 'healing, hope-filled, spiritually connected, profound moments' yet also 'the most painful, alienating, demoralizing, scary and sad moments' has resonance for me, and, I suspect, for many others who find themselves limping, rather than dancing, on the edge.[3]

Liturgical losses

The absence of formal liturgy in communities such as the Salvation Army can allow, theoretically, for greater freedom for congregants of whatever gender, race, ability, age, sexual orientation and so forth to feel included and able to participate; but in reality the language of songs and choruses, the lyrics of the songster music, and the ideology of the officer's homiletics all combine to produce a world of worship that is staunchly heteronormative. Closeted LGBT/Q-identified[4] members inevitably find themselves on the edges of collective worship in so far as their experiences are unrepresented and their lives and loves ignored (at best), or condemned (at worst). Elizabeth Stuart has described the wider scenario well when she speaks of how the liturgy of many churches fails to address the life, experience and needs of the gay community.[5] This leads to the first sense of liturgical loss: the loss of inclusiveness that has deprived those in same-sex relationships from 'full access to God and to the church'.[6]

However, I come from an evangelical community which places utmost emphasis upon Scripture and there are certain texts that have a profound ability to speak to the experience of feeling lost: most particularly, the psalms of lament. Unfortunately, this is precisely where there has been a second liturgical loss, for the ability of these significant liturgical resources to speak with/for those with reason to be angry, resentful, distressed, frustrated with God and/or with God's institutional representatives, has been neglected.

Walter Brueggemann identifies two costly losses that accrue from the failure to take seriously the psalms of lament. First: the 'loss of *genuine covenant interaction*' that results when the worshipper is limited to speaking only in terms of praise. In such cases, the believer constructs a 'false self' that does not resonate with real life experiences'. Second: 'the capacity to raise and legitimate questions of justice'.[7] As Brueggemann says, the lament psalms bitterly complain, shrilly insisting that:

1. Things are not right in the present arrangement.
2. They need not stay this way and can be changed.
3. The speaker will not accept them in this way, for the present arrangement is intolerable.
4. It is God's obligation to change things.[8]

The speeches are not perfunctory religious exercises; in seeking justice the psalmist expects something to happen and the cry of the lament is intended to mobilize God. Accordingly, 'When the lament form is censured, justice questions cannot be asked and eventually become invisible and illegitimate.'[9]

Brueggemann's comments may reverberate strongly with LGBT/Q-identified congregants who may be all too familiar with the construction of 'false selves' (the only way of remaining in a religious community that tacitly operates a 'don't ask, don't tell' policy). They may also be keenly aware of an enforced invisibility that results when their communities will not tolerate the 'justice questions' they might wish to raise with God and with their church.

Consider Kay's story. Kay is an Anglican priest who secretly lives with her lesbian partner, also a priest. The venomous exchanges that followed Jeffrey John's proposed appointment as Bishop of Reading terrified her, since they publicly demonstrated the hatred that she always knew was out there but was now tangible. Seeing that there was no protection even for celibate gay Christians, she feared that there could be no safe havens and testifies to becoming 'a guarded person – and I don't think that is healthy or holy . . . I go to great lengths to leave people wondering, when it would be so much easier for me and every-body else just to be straightforward, honest and truthful'.[10] Kay speaks of this guardedness as a 'deeply unhealthy way of life',[11] and she is but one example of a host of guarded individuals within the Church, despite the substantial evidence that such lifestyles come at great cost.

The raw, wretched howls of the lament psalms provide a legitimate place for rage and protest, and the neglect of these resources is indeed costly. Inclusion of them within liturgy could provide a voice for rage and hurt and may enable LGBT/Q-identified congregants to remain within their confessional homes. Transformation is the goal of the psalmist, as it is for any contemporary liturgist and this paper explores how one particular lament psalm – Psalm 42 – may provide a pro-foundly resonant liturgical resource for lesbians lamenting on the edge.[12]

Applying Psalm 42

As a deer longs for streams of water
Thus my soul longs for you, O God.
My soul thirsts for God, for the living God.
Oh when will I enter and see the face of God?
My tears have been my bread, day and night
And all day long they are saying to me 'where is your God?' (42.1–3)

The psalmist misses profoundly the worshipping community to which he once belonged. While some commentators suppose the historical context of a homesick psalmist living in exile from Jerusalem, others take a more metaphorical approach. The familiar opening image speaks of thirsting for God but with the anxious undertone of not knowing when that thirst will be quenched, when God's face will be seen again. Its hyperbolic image of prolonged and persistent weeping is not to be hurriedly passed over. The psalmist weeps for his inability, for whatever reason, to re-enter the temple, as he ranges like a parched animal over the dried wadies. Loss of religious community is a grievous thing, even when existing within it is difficult. Tigert notes that to leave the church of one's childhood, one must face significant emotional loss. One is walking away from the community in which one grew and was affirmed and confirmed as a child of God . . . the experience of psychological attachment – especially to the church of one's family of origin . . . is very deep, on both conscious and unconscious levels.[13]

Weeping, probably the most natural and important element of processing grief and loss, is given prime place. And it is not just the occasional swept aside tear; 'My tears have been my bread, day and night' writes the psalmist. In the contemporary lives of exiled LGBT/Q-identified congregants I suspect that much of the healing weeping is suppressed, or allowed out only in private, safe environments. But sometimes one sees a glimmer of it in public. In their paper on the 'Gospel Girl's Gospel Hour' Gray and Thumma report on the popularity of standards such as 'When the Roll is Called Up Yonder', 'Because He Lives', 'There is Power in the Blood of the Lamb' and note how they 'have seen men cry during the Gospel Hour, caught up in the music and the emotion of the evening'.[14] Later, they note how the Gospel Hour provided gay men

with an opportunity for *spiritual reconnection and restoration*. As one person said, 'Many (gays) are scared to go back to church because they were turned away. This is their one touch with God.' Another suggested more poignantly, 'Gay anger against God is dealt with here'.[15]

Weeping, in my experience, readily comes to the fore when one is confronted with the familiar religious music of home. It touches the raw nerve, washes over and breaks through stiffened resistance to re-invite connection; provides an opening for God to meet us when we are not expecting to be met.

The tears have an accusatory presence in this psalm; persistently questioning 'where is your God?' But while this is usually posed by oppressing enemies here it is posed by the speaker who struggles within himself rather than with enemies. It is this lingering, painful suspicion and self-doubt that gives the psalm its distinctiveness and pathos. The apparent abandonment by the deity is a source of shame and humiliation.

The mocking question 'where is your God' is another that is probably faced by many LGBT/Q-identified persons who find themselves on the receiving end of clobber-texts and institutional discrimination and oppression.[16] And it is a question that can be readily internalized in the assumption that institutional condemnation is founded on God's prior (justified) condemnation. Tigert has commented on the debilitating effects of shame which derive to some extent from the 'social and religious message that to be gay or lesbian or anything other than heterosexual is something to be ashamed of and hidden as well as scorned'.[17] In her view 'Overcoming shame is part of the core spiritual and psychological work of overcoming homophobia' since it lies 'at the core of numerous psychological and spiritual concerns – depression, anxiety, addictions, isolation, violence, perfectionism, and spiritual alienation'.[18] One also has to deal with the shame that exists about shame itself ('meta-shame') for she believes 'that this combination of religious sexual shaming and meta-shame sends many gay/lesbian/bisexual/transgender persons out of the doors of the church as if they are running for their lives, never to return', while keeping those who remain silent.[19] Speaking of the impact of shame she says

> The level of pain that people carry and cause to others in order to avoid facing their sexual shame is too high a cost to continue unabated. Thus we must create environments in which persons feel safe to take a step away from these poles of withdrawal and avoidance and move toward healthy self-esteem and love of self and others.[20]

It is accordingly important to spend time with the weeping, the shame, the alienation, before skipping too readily to the generally more positive final elements of psalms of lament (that of thanksgiving and praise).

> *These things I keep (sadly) remembering and pour out my soul upon myself –*
> *How I used to pass by among the throng, how I solemnly led them to the House of God*
> *With a ringing cry and thanksgiving (amid) the roaring of those making pilgrimage.*
> *Why are you laid low, O soul, and why do you roar within me?*
> *Wait for God! For I will yet praise him for deliverances before his face.* (42.4–5)

The joyful sounds of temple worship form a contrast with the silence of God. While God seemingly abandons, the psalmist doggedly remembers happier days of worship, its celebrations, its gladness, its vitality – but this exacerbates the pain. The commentarial tradition has tended to sweeten the psalm and redeem it from its despairing qualities. Kraus, for example, suggests that this remembrance of past happiness indicates a move out of sorrow and despair: 'there is really no reason . . . [to] dis-solve and disintegrate amid groaning. Almost in wonder the psalmist asks himself, What are you doing? He encourages himself to wait patiently and focus his thoughts on the song of thanksgiving.'[21] It is true that the imperative to wait/have hope for God appears to offer a ray of light for the future, but Kraus is surely too optimistic in his recovery of the poet's spirits. When the psalmist asks why his soul roars within him, he uses a verb (*hāmâ*) that can be used of the roaring of waves. Given the water imagery to come in verse 7, that later image of raging, turbulent chaos waters could be kept in mind here. His soul is not becoming quieter in readiness for deliverance, rather his soul is in a tumultuous, raging state amid its being 'laid low'. The shame referred to above would fit with this sense of his soul (his life, sense of very being), lying prostrate in humiliation, while, simultaneously within, that same soul rants.

> *[My God] my soul is laid low within me*
> *On account of this, I will remember you*
> *From the land of Jordan and of Hermon, from Mount Mizar* (42.6)

The self-imperative to wait for God and look to future opportunities for praise certainly sinks from view very quickly as the psalmist thus returns again to his humbled state, yet there is still a wilful, desperate holding on to remembrance as the psalmist wrestles, determined to hang on to the neglecting deity.

While lesbians may be exhorted by their secular companions to aban-don the abandoning deity, or be exhorted to leave by their religious leaders, Alison Webster suggests it is not such a simplistic decision. In fact, confronting lesbians with a stay/leave decision is

> certainly deeply unhelpful, both psychologically and philosophically . . . strong ideological pressure to 'leave Christianity behind' can be counter-productive if it encourages us to take short cuts in our assess-ment of what Christianity has meant to us, in both positive and nega-tive senses. If we take the post-Christian option and leave, we tend to adopt a linear model of 'leaving', whereby we think that we can 'close the Christian chapter' of our lives at will if we try hard enough. We hate ourselves if we feel so much as a twinge of longing to sing a Charles Wesley hymn or to watch *Carols from Kings* at Christmas. We imagine that this is proof that we have failed fully to purge Christianity from our hearts and minds. It is my contention that it is

an inadequate model of religious identity that assumes that this kind of straightforward choice can be made. I would like to suggest that there is a sense in which religious identity cannot be dispensed with at will in this way. Religious identity is too complicated for that. . . . What I am seeking, are new models of religious identity that befit this complexity.[22]

Thus although religious communities may tolerate wavering between decisions for a short period, Webster acknowledges that some of us 'have been wavering for so long that we have to begin to think through what it might mean that this condition is probably permanent'.[23] This desire for cognitive restructuring has already been encouraged in secular therapeutic literature. Joan Sophie, for instance, identifies such restructuring as 'probably the major process of coping necessary for acceptance of oneself as lesbian or bisexual' and, furthermore, 'underlies most of the other coping strategies'.[24] Sophie recognizes that this restructuring process will involve one's 'religious beliefs and values' though she does appear to appreciate how resistant those beliefs are to being restructured. The renegotiation advocated by Webster will thus be vital for those who choose to hold on to religious belief despite the contrary circumstances.

Chaos waters summon Chaos waters at the sound of your waterfalls
All your breakers and your billows pass over me (42.7)

English translations of this verse have been rather weak. *Tᵉhôm* is the term used in Genesis 1.2 where we read that 'darkness was upon the face of the *Deep*'. *Tᵉhôm* is the primordial abyss, the waters of Chaos, and while Israel's deity is presented as one who has tamed them, they retain a glimmer of independence and the fear that the waters might break loose is ever-present. The psalmist has accordingly chosen an evocative term to describe the depths of grief and loss and there is no shying away from the sources of these troubles: it is God that permits or indeed sends these torrents. As Broyles wryly notes: 'instead of the living God supplying streams of water for the speaker's thirsting soul (42:1–2), he drowns him'.[25]

Again, there has been a tendency in the commentarial tradition to offset the despair of the psalmist. Weiser criticizes him for not looking at the 'powerful beauty' of the ferocious waterfall at the Jordan described in verses 6–7, but choosing rather to navel gaze at 'his own calamity'.[26] Moving the reader's gaze away from such undesirable self-indulgence, he suggests that the psalmist 'comes to realize that we are not at all helped by weeping and grieving, but only make our cross and our suffering worse by our sadness'[27] and he refers readers to the hymn 'Leave God to order all thy ways'. However, that hymn's twee verses do not do justice to the psalmist's sheer terror of being overwhelmed by the depths. Better then to have a liturgy that embraces fully the tenor of the biblical images and which is prepared to go to the lengths that the psalmist is prepared to lead us to, namely, that the deity is not only seemingly abandoning but also punitive and betraying. Faced with such a prospect, lament psalms are invaluable resources, for they offer speakers the words and images to confess their sense of radical dissonance:

> They are speeches of surprised dismay and disappointment . . . sharp ejaculations by people accustomed either to the smooth songs of equilibrium or to not saying anything at all because things are 'all right'. They are the shrill speeches of those who suddenly discover that they are trapped and the water is rising and the sun may not come up tomorrow in all its benevolence. And we are betrayed![28]

This speaks resonantly to those who find their sexual lives radically at odds with their spiritual lives. In her restorative publication, Tessier speaks of her own experience of unravelling and focuses helpfully on the incongruence experienced by lesbians when pieces of their life situation no longer fit together. When incongruity becomes too much it produces crisis and

> For many women, this is the time when things fall apart. Old assumptions disintegrate in the face of new feelings and experiences, and the whirlwind of chaotic change sweeps away assumed structures and models. Attempting to hold the pieces together may involve denial and projection. We may attempt to suppress all erotic feelings, inadvertently cutting ourselves off from the very power source we need to navigate these turbulent waters.[29]

This is why psalms of lament may be such a vital resource for those who identify as LGBT/Q Jews and Christians. They bewail the way a people have been betrayed; abandoned by their deity to a miserable existence where they are subject to the gloating derision of onlookers, bereft of the one structure that not only gave them pride and stability but a means of access to God – the temple. Our contemporary versions of the temple – be it church or synagogue – may as well be deemed lost in so far as certain branches of those religions have closed their doors to (openly practising) LGBT/Q-identified members. If liturgy is to meet these people at this point in their experience, it needs strong language and imagery, it needs to be open to expressions of dismay and despair, to permit the acknowledgment that God can send weal and woe, light *and* darkness (Isaiah 45.7), and to give voice to protest.

Therapeutic literature that contains chapters on counteracting the effects of one's religious upbringing often points to the urgent need for clients to discharge hurt and anger as part of the healing process. For liturgy to work therapeutically, it needs to provide a safe, sacred space for the expression of deep emotional distress before one can begin to explore, as Webster tries to do, new ways of being lesbian (or queer) and Christian. The psalms of lament provide canonically sanctioned resources for the expression of all the hurt and pain, grief and bitterness, sense of betrayal, anger and recrimination without fear of further retaliation by an offended deity. 'Reflected in these lament expressions is a deity who is not easily shaken or offended and who does not need to be pacified', writes Broyles.[30] Liturgy that does this has, in my view, the potential to be truly transformative.

> *By day the Lord commands his steadfast loyalty*
> *And by night his song is with me, a prayer to the God of my life*
> *I keep saying to God, my crag, 'why have you forgotten me?'*
> *Why must I walk, gloomily, amid the oppression of the enemy?*
> *With a shattering in my bones, those harassing me hem me in,*
> *Saying to me all day long 'where is your God?'* (42.8–10)

Amid the waves and billows, the psalmist latches on to God's *ḥesed* (steadfast love, enduring loyalty) and hangs on, as to a crag. I prefer 'crag' to the more usual translation 'rock' (v. 9a) since the psalmist could have chosen a more common noun for rock (*ṣûr*) and because crag gives the sense of hanging on to an outcrop amid the pouring torrents. The psalmist's trust in God's *ḥesed* seems to be grasped only with the fingertips: the crag is clutched on to for dear life, in the face of the reality of being forgotten.

At night – always the bleakest time – the psalmist has only a remembered song, a prayer to one who has inexplicably abandoned. The night theme is continued in verse 9b, for 'gloomy' derives from *qādar* (to be dark). It can also mean to mourn, but gloomy is more suggestive of the primary sense of darkness signified by this verb. And now the conventional enemies make their oppressive appearance, harassing, hemming in (the verb *ṣārar* signifies being restricted, cramped, in narrow straits, being pressed hard, in addition to being distressed) all the while deriding and mocking 'where is your God?'

Readers who are still coming to terms with their same-sex preferences may quickly pick up on these references. In her paper on 'Psychotherapy with Women who Love Women' Falco writes of the damaging effects wrought by negative cultural attitudes about lesbianism and associated lack of support. When troubles arise in the process of lesbian identity formation (as it is almost bound to happen for those within religious communities) 'they have few people they can turn to who will understand the depth of their tumult. Indeed, many fear that their pain will be mocked by being told that they deserve their turmoil for having "chosen" such a lifestyle'.[31] The psalmist's angst no doubt rings true for such people.

Readers may hear the psalmist's words in different tones. Some might understand the tone to be one of misery and wretchedness, others might detect an emerging tone of protest: Why have I been forgotten? Why must I be oppressed? Why am I left to mourn? Why put up with the suggestion that God wants nothing to do with me? One cannot unequivocally decide which tone is the more appropriate. What is clear, however, is that the enemies only exacerbate his pain, with their question 'where is your God?' reinforcing his own anxious fears.

> *Why are you laid low, my soul? And why roar within me*
> *Wait for God because I will yet praise him my deliverer and my God*
> (42.11)

Psalm 42 thus reaches its climax with only the most tentative resolution. We leave our psalmist clinging desperately to his crag, almost drowned by the depths, enduring the accusations and harassments of those who openly declare God's abandonment of him and his plight. In this predicament he, remarkably, utters words of self-encouragement. They have to come from his inner reserves of strength since there has been no response from the abandoning deity. His urgent 'message to self' insists that there will come a time when he will praise God for deliverance, when God can again be called 'my' God.

Scholars are convinced that Psalm 42 finds its completion in Psalm 43 and commentaries routinely encourage readers to read them together so that they arrive at the final positive conclusion. However, while there are structural reasons to treat both psalms as a unity, the fact that they have been separated is a gift, since it allows the lament to stand alone and speak its terms starkly, giving time to pause and reflect at a critical distance before the transition to praise, listening to the psalmist as he clings to his crag.

Conclusion

Swenson has recently demonstrated how the psalms can be used as a resource for people in pain and/or caring for persons in pain. In her conclusion, she reiterates how the psalms

> dignify the place of complaint and strident cry out of conditions that seem unbearable. They do not model super-human endurance and cheer in terrific suffering. Neither do they tell how a person can be healed through complaint, or through silent suffering, for that matter. However, they do give voice to conditions that may seem inexpressibly terrible, and they articulate the kinds of theologically challenging questions that a suffering person may hesitate to ask out loud.[32]

These challenging questions and voices of protest occur within psalms uttered in faith. Time and time again, one finds in the stories of LGBT/Q-identified people testimonies of extraordinary faith in contrary circumstances. However, it has often been a matter of clinging on to this faith with fingertips, working it through and renegotiating not with the help of one's home church/synagogue, not with the healing properties of transforming liturgy, but in private or in the therapy rooms of secular society.

For liturgy to reach these congregants before they are driven away, it needs to be comfortable with lamenting before God, with complaint and protest, with images of the neglectful and abandoning God, and it needs to provide space for transformation. As noted above, the psalms of lament declare dissatisfaction with the status quo and demand change. For LGBT/Q-identified persons this involves resistance to the heterosexist ethos in worshipping communities, resistance to religious opposition to practising same-sex partnerships, rejection of the idea that we are a 'problem',[33] and throwing to the wind concerns about offending anyone – especially God. Rather the Church (in particular) needs to attune itself once more to this right of complaint and re-accommodate lament into liturgy. Only by so doing will worshippers be able to develop and mature as equal covenant partners with their deity. In therapy, clients are encouraged to set new boundaries, limits, ground rules. Renegotiation is vital. Psalm 42 takes us only partly into that renegotiation period, but it does provide a basis for what J. Michael Clark has called 'a place to start'.[34] For the moment, we operate on the edges; Countryman, however, sees virtue in this. Indeed

> this awkward business of living on the boundary looks very much like vocation – a call from God . . . The boundary where we're living, however inconvenient, is a place rich in spiritual discovery – which means, of course, that it is also largely unchartered territory. No ready-made tradition tells us how to be gay and lesbian Christians. This is a vocation God has created in our own time to bring about a new enrichment of the gospel.[35]

Amen to that.

Notes

1 I borrow the term 'genderqueer' from Joan Nestle, Riki Anne Wilchins and Clare Howell, eds, *Genderqueer: Voices from Beyond the Sexual Binary*, Los Angeles and New York: Alyson Books, 2002, and use it here to designate a female-born person whose more comfortable mode of gender performativity would traditionally be described as masculine. Genderqueer is a term, however, that is deliberately resistant to male/female, masculine/feminine binaries and signifies here a mode of self-expression that exceeds those limiting and all-too-rigid categories.

2 I appreciate the work of those who have expressed the joy of dancing on the edge (see, for example, 'So Here We Are' by Rosie Miles and 'Dancing on the Edge' by Alix Brown in Geoffrey Duncan, ed., *Courage to Love: An Anthology of Inclusive Worship Material*, London: DLT, 2002, pp. 78–9, 122) and I hope that all LGBT/Q-identified people working through the profound losses that occur when coming out in judgemental and rejecting religious communities eventually get to the dancing stage, but this paper addresses the experience of the wilderness period and gives time, space and verbal expression for the spiritual therapeutic work that needs to be undertaken before finding one's liberation on the edge.

3 Leanne McCall Tigert, *Coming Out While Staying In: Struggles and Celebrations of Lesbians, Gays and Bisexuals in the Church*, Cleveland, OH: United Church Press, 1996, p. xv.

4 I separate Q from LGBT with a forward slash in order to indicate that 'queer' is not an identity label. Although it is sometimes used as an umbrella term for non-straight people, queer strategically upsets the homosexual–heterosexual binary and transcends LGBT categories. Similarly, I used LGBT-*identified* to indicate that it is not necessarily a case of 'being' lesbian or gay so much as having been positioned as such or choosing to adopt that label for strategic purposes.

5 Elizabeth Stuart, 'Liturgy and Worship' in Elizabeth Stuart with Andy Braunston, Malcolm Edwards, John McMahon and Tim Morrison, *Religion is a Queer Thing: A Guide to the Christian Faith for Lesbian, Gay, Bisexual and Trans-*

gendered Persons, London: Cassell, 1997, pp. 105–13.

6 Stuart, 'Liturgy', p. 108. This substantial loss, however, is gradually being nourished by the creation of new liturgies written precisely for lesbian, gay, bisexual and, to a lesser extent, transgender-identified Christians.

7 Walter Brueggemann, *The Psalms and the Life of Faith*, Minneapolis, MN: Augsburg Fortress, 1995, pp. 102, 104.

8 Brueggemann, *The Psalms*, p. 105.

9 Brueggemann, *The Psalms*, p. 107.

10 Michael Ford, *Disclosures: Conversations Gay and Spiritual*, London: Darton Longman and Todd, 2005, pp. 62–3.

11 Ford, *Disclosures*, p. 67.

12 In what follows, the translations of Psalm 42 will be my own and the verse numbering will follow that of English translations.

13 Tigert, *Coming Out While Staying In*, p. 118.

14 Edward R. Gray and Scott Lee Thumma, 'Amazing Grace! How Sweet the Sound! Southern Evangelical Religion and Gay Drag in Atlanta' in J. Michael Clark and Robert E. Goss, eds, *A Rainbow of Religious Studies*, Las Colinas, Texas: Monument Press, 1996, pp. 33–53, 39.

15 Gray and Thumma, 'Amazing Grace', pp. 46–7, emphasis in original.

16 The clobber texts include Genesis 19; Leviticus 18.22, 20.13; (Deuteronomy 23.17); Romans 1.26–27; 1 Corinthians 6.9; 1 Timothy 1.10; Jude 7; and 2 Peter 2.10. Examples of discrimination and oppression can be found in LGCM *Christian Homophobia – The Churches' Persecution of Gay and Lesbian People*, London: LGCM, 2000.

17 Leanne McCall Tigert, *Coming Out Through Fire: Surviving the Trauma of Homophobia*, Cleveland, OH: United Church Press, 1999, p. 58.

18 Tigert, *Coming Out Through Fire*, p. 59.

19 Tigert, *Coming Out Through Fire*, p. 60.

20 Tigert, *Coming Out Through Fire*, p. 68.

21 Hans-Joachim Kraus, *Psalms 1 — 59: A Commentary*, Trans. Hilton C. Oswald, Minneapolis, MN: Augsburg, 1988, p. 440.

22 Alison Webster, 'Queer to be Religious: Lesbian Adventures Beyond the Christian/Post-Christian Dichotomy', *Theology and Sexuality*, 8 (1998), pp. 27–39, 30.

23 Webster, 'Queer to be Religious', p. 30.

24 Joan Sophie, 'Internalized Homophobia and Lesbian Identity' in Eli Coleman, ed., *Integrated Identity for Gay Men and Lesbians: Psychotherapeutic Approaches for Emotional Well-Being*, New York and London: Harrington Park Press, 1998, pp. 53–65, 57.

25 Craig C. Broyles, *Psalms*, Peabody, MA: Paternoster Press, 1999, p. 197.

26 Arthur Weiser, *The Psalms: A Commentary*, London: SCM Press, 1962, p. 350.

27 Weiser, *The Psalms*, p. 349.

28 Brueggemann, *The Psalms*, p. 19.

29 L. J. Tessier, *Dancing After the Whirlwind: Feminist Reflections on Sex, Denial, and Spiritual Transformation*, Boston, MA: Beacon Press, 1997, p. 100.

30 Broyles, *Psalms*, p. 33.

31 Kristine L. Falco, 'Psychotherapy with Women who Love Women', in Robert P. Cabaj and Terry S. Stein, eds, *Textbook of Homosexuality and Mental Health*, London and Washington, DC: American Psychiatric Press, pp. 397–412, 401.

32 Kristen M. Swenson, *Living Through Pain: Psalms and the Search for Wholeness*, Waco, TX: Baylor University Press, 2005, p. 218.

33 Discussions at synods and church conventions have focused attention 'over-whelmingly . . . on what others see as the "problem" of gay and lesbian Christians, rather than the problem that heterosexual Christians pose to us. This latter is far more serious a problem, given the damage it inflicts on gay and lesbian lives, or encourages others to inflict' since, in the midst of the debate the 'genuine pastoral and emotional needs of gay and lesbian Christians are simply ignored' (L. W. Countryman and M. R. Ritley, *Gifted by Otherness: Gay and Lesbian in the Church*, Harrisburg, PA: Morehouse Publishing, 2001, pp. 2, 3). For Ritley, 'one of the first steps in healthy gay and lesbian self-definition is the rejection of the role of "problem" and the refusal to be punished for the heterosexual community's failure to deal with its own problem' (p. 3): 'what is needed is not simply and passively asking for the church's acceptance, but creating a gay spiritual understructure powerful enough to reshape the very terms in which the church perceives and understands us. Such a reversal is not easily achieved' (p. 4).

34 J. Michael Clark, *A Place to Start: Toward an Unapologetic Gay Liberation Theology*, Dallas, TX: Monument Press, 1989.

35 Countryman, *Gifted*, p. 6.

16

The Stag and the Doe:
Archetypes of the Spirit

ALISTAIR ROSS

Baptist worship: a Baptist's view

A leading conservative Anglican in the United States once said 'My idea of heaven is an Anglican liturgy and a Baptist sermon; hell is a Baptist liturgy and an Anglican sermon.'[1] In my theological training as a Baptist minister 25 years ago the word 'liturgy' was never used and the predominant focus in worship was on the preaching of the word of God, with some small attention paid to Communion or the Lord's Supper. While other Baptist theological colleges paid more attention to Communion, liturgy was still a relatively alien word in this Baptist world.

In his remarkable book *Gathering: A Theology and Spirituality of Worship in Free Church Tradition*[2] the British Baptist Christopher Ellis provides what has been hailed as the first major liturgical theology from a Free Church perspective. He offers both a history and a perceptive evaluation that encompasses what Baptists did and do do liturgically. The first new Baptist book of liturgy for 20 years, *Praise God*[3] provided a fresh approach differing from its prescriptive predecessor *Orders and Prayers for Church Worship*[4] and responding 'to a new wave of freedom, self-expression and informality'[5] while structuring itself around the Christian year rather than specific worship tasks. I found it refreshing because it provided a structure but left space for creativity. It did have limitations, however, so this was replaced by *Patterns and Prayers for Christian Worship*[6] attempting to meet the needs of a diverse Free Church tradition with no fixed liturgical pattern. What did exist ranged from 'liturgical formality to charismatic exuberance, from reformed traditionalism to ecumenical experiment',[7] though the experience of the majority of Baptist worship was still an evangelical form of preaching allied to informal charismatic worship – predominantly using songs rather than hymns – which had been learnt at large worship gatherings such as Spring Harvest. While I had often written prayers and given space for this in worship preparation, this was essentially the form of worship I participated in. This was to change.

Several events happened in the mid 1990s that radically reshaped my thinking about worship and led me to adopt a fresh approach to liturgy. First, I moved to Birmingham and renewed my friendship with David Bryan, then the New Testament tutor at Queen's College, now the Queen's Foundation for Ecumenical Theological Education. As I became more involved at Queen's as a visiting lecturer in pastoral care and pastoral theology, then later as a pastoral tutor and as Director of the Bridge Pastoral Foundation (formerly the Clinical Theology Association) located at Queen's, I experienced a diversity of worship and liturgical reflection and expression that opened my eyes and my spirit to new ways of encountering God.

Second, I began to participate in creating alternative worship for students doing pastoral counselling at St John's College, Nottingham. As part of a small tutor team we produced liturgy that reflected the traditions of the faith and embraced the spiritual and psychological journey that counselling training evokes. I can still recall the spine-tingling moments when, after the students had left the evening prayers, the four tutors knelt in the candlelight around the four sides of an icon placed on the floor, and in the silence offered thanksgiving for the numinous presence of God. What struck me is how isolating Baptist ministry can be with worship often left just to the minister, and how luxurious it was to share in the creation of liturgy with others bringing their experience of different Christian traditions.

Third, in December 1997 I went to Iona for a week's prayer and reflection joining with the skeleton staff at the community. The ethereal quality of that place, the relative isolation in which one could be alone but not lonely, the crisp December dawns that bathed the stone, land and sea with luminous warmth gave space for new experiences of an embodied worship held by a liturgical frame of being. These days spoke to me of death and resurrection and something indefinable was given birth in my psyche and spirit. I now realize that in part it was the recognition that I could leave the employment of the Church, without leaving the worship and presence of God. Church had become a place where I was restrained both theologically and liturgically, serving up what other people wanted rather than being true to myself – a story I tell in *Evangelicals in Exile: Wrestling with Theology and the Unconscious*.[8]

My journey is not so different from numerous others, as from the late 1990s many more people in the Baptist tradition began to write new liturgy to meet both the needs of old and new generations of worshippers. Chris Ellis produced *Gathering* for the Baptist Union and a wide range of contributors worked to produce *Gathering for Worship* edited by Chris Ellis and Myra Blyth,[9] which has become the most comprehensive resource for Baptist worship and liturgy yet available. At its best, *Gathering for Worship* is ecumenically inclusive and draws from the rich worship and liturgical traditions from other denominations. It remains, however, distinctively Baptist in so far as it focuses on a dynamic of the gathering and sending of God's people in and through worship, that is an essential underpinning of Baptist belief and practice. It has been felt by some to rather neglect a sacramental understanding of worship, though Baptist interest in the sacraments is elsewhere recently strongly signalled in John Colwell's *Promise and Presence* and *The Rhythm of Doctrine*.[10] While *Gathering for Worship* is gender inclusive in terms of its language, it fails to deal with concerns raised by feminist theologians and liturgists about the nature and name of God. Similarly it fails to address the issue of sexual orientation, although perhaps this simply reflects the difficulty the Baptist denomination has in this area as a whole. *Gathering for Worship*, then, represents a rich liturgical resource that shows the huge developments Baptists have made in the last decade, primarily through drawing on the resources of other traditions and liturgies, albeit with its drawbacks, notably its exclusion of the vital concerns of many people who long to worship in a way that embraces and recognizes their whole nature and being. It is still very 'wordy', a common failing of typical Baptist worship with the lack of any suitable focus on the visual, the experiential, the embodied and the symbolic – including the psychological symbol of the archetypes. Yet there is another area that is neglected and this is the psychological, the sphere of human nature dwelling in the psyche. In common with many other liturgical resources little reflection or space is given to the impact or effect that worship can have on a human being. At best worship can be structured in a way that allows space for the spirit and psyche to inhabit the same space, both individually and collectively.

Space for the spirit and psyche

In what follows, I attempt to put words to experiences of the psyche that can happen in worship. While such experiences cannot be orchestrated or manufactured through any amount of liturgical reflection and preparation, there needs to be an acknowledgement that in worship something ontological happens. We can structure worship in a way that allows ontological space for the psyche – and this is one of the reasons that retreats with a focus on silence can be so powerful, renewing and life changing. I recall my brief time on Iona as iconic: freed by the security of a physically boundaried space – an island, when I was set apart from other activities, in the company of others through conversation and common worship. In this space, spirit and psyche came together, which gives me hope that this can be made possible elsewhere in all aspects of worship. Here is a personal narrative of my recollections:

> Deep dark brown eyes stared directly into my soul. Standing at the edge of a dark wood my senses came alive at that moment as eyes locked. In a warm sun-bathed clearing surrounded by dense forest stood a magnificent beast, not some kitsch Victorian image of the 'Monarch of the Glen' but a visceral form of nature and life. My eyes took in this powerful image of a heavy antlered head: scarred, age-worn and proud. The quivering nostrils, the steamy breath, the moisture-laden fur all spoke of aliveness and strength. The air shimmered with expectation. A breeze rustled, and a slight movement shifted my gaze to a still form reclining at the edge of the scene – a doe, partner to this proud stag, gazed contentedly out, oblivious to my presence. Time stood still until, ears quivering, the doe gracefully arose, nudged the stag and retreated to the far side of the wood, the stag following behind. I suddenly remembered to breathe and was left feeling both relief and sadness, with the beguiling question 'what had I witnessed and somehow magically participated in?'

This brief visual recollection is composed of images that emerged variously in dreams, mental pictures and imaginings over a specific time. Some came from my own dreams; others during a time of reflection in the service of worship; from an altered state of consciousness experienced during individual quiet and prayer; and from the dream of a close friend. This kaleidoscope of images struck me with a force that I took to be significant, too powerful to be ignored yet tantalizingly elusive. This chapter is a reflection on this 'dream' using the language of psychology and spirituality. My purpose in writing is to find a way for the therapeutic and the theological to coexist and to enliven the spirit within all of us through the Spirit.

A helpful place to start is with the meaning of the often misunderstood and misused word 'archetype'. While the origins of the word are in early Greek philosophy, Jung introduced it to the twentieth century in a way that has entered into the fabric of modern thought. There are three main uses of the term. It can mean an original model or prototype that has shaped future models – so you could say 'the Beatles were the archetypal pop group'. It can also mean an ideal example – so 'Johnny Wilkinson is the archetypal English rugby player (when fit)'. The main use is to refer to an inherited pattern of thought that connects with symbolic imagery, often derived from past cultures and present individual experience shaped by present culture. It is a much more complex concept than this brief summary can fully convey and is helpfully discussed by, for example, Andrew Samuels.[11] Definitions never fully convey how very powerful an archetypal experience can be. Samuels writes,

> Because archetypal layers of the psyche are in some sense fundamental, they tend to produce images and situations which have a tremendous impact on the individual, gripping him and holding him in a grip, often but not always with an accompanying feeling of mystery and awe; he will be unable to remain unaffected.[12]

Archetypes then arose out of Jung's reflections on the complexity of being human, drawing on psychological language (psyche) and religious and spiritual traditions from East and West (soul). He talks of images that transcend historical periods or specific cultures and carry meaning from generation to generation, and so bear a timeless quality. 'They are the ruling powers, the gods, images of the dominant laws and principles, and of typical, regularly occurring events in the soul's cycle of experience.'[13] To fully understand the power of the archetypal images of the stag and the doe as they speak of the Spirit, it is important to see them in various contexts. Hobson's criteria for an archetype was that it be a specific image that was found in different times and cultures yet with a continuity of meaning. My suggestion is that the stag and the doe are archetypes of the Spirit's activity in a person. Precisely what that activity is will vary from person to person but several themes can be found in the images and experiences that have been recorded. They have a long history to be found in biblical narrative, in religious and pagan traditions, in Celtic mythology, in mystical and contemplative experience, and in contemporary life, experience and worship.

The Bible, in differing translations, refers variously to a stag, deer, doe, hart, gazelle or roebuck. All these references carry metaphorical meaning associated primarily with longing. This is often translated into a spiritual longing for God (Psalm 42.1) yet a more literal reading of this text speaks of a deer longing for water either because of existing in a barren, dry wilderness where water was life itself, or in a grim struggle for survival when pursued by its hunters. Most references are found in the Song of Solomon where the longing is essentially for another human being, expressed in both poetic and erotic terms. The deer/stag/doe as archetypal images found in biblical narratives focus on:

- A desire or longing for God or the Spirit of God that overwhelms everything else (Psalm 42.1);
- A desire or longing for life in a context that overwhelms or threatens everything else (Psalm 42.1);
- An appreciation of beauty and an expression of desire expressed by the symbol of breasts (Song of Solomon 4.5; 7.3)
- Freedom as a source of hope (Psalm 18.33; Song of Solomon 2.8–9);
- Overwhelming satisfaction of being met by another that one becomes committed to, no matter what the cost (Song of Solomon 8.14);
- An expression of love and desire (Song of Solomon 2.7); and
- A complementariness of male and female that does not dominate or oppress (Song of Solomon 2.16).

The power of the words impacting from the biblical narrative in the Song of Solomon does match that of an archetypal experience. The mixture of soul, psyche, embodiment and spirit make a person fully alive to one's self and to the Spirit. Other religious traditions engaged with these aspects of humanness from a different perspective, that of creation. In Celtic mythology, stories and Celtic forms of Christianity, the presence of animals spoke of a new Eden where God could walk with all creation, people as well as animals, in intricate harmony. Traditionally, the Irish monk Kieran (Ciaran) of Clonmacnoise, also known as Kieran the Younger, had disciples that included a bear, a fox, a badger, a wolf and a hind. He told his community that on his death he was to be left on a hilltop 'like a stag' returning to nature, though it is also possible he died from the plague and wished to protect others. A later ninth-century Irish hermit Marban describes 'fall deer and their does' visiting him so that wild beasts become allies in the life of prayer, the struggles of life, and the uniting of God with creation to bring further life and revelation.[14]

In later mystical writings the stag in particular became associated with Christ, the wounded stag on the hill becoming a symbol of a crucified God. Popular children's writers C. S. Lewis and J. K. Rowling also use the image of a white stag. Lewis uses a stag in a wood followed by the children to take them back from Narnia to home. Rowling uses the stag as a patronus, a mystical/spiritual/magical image (shared with his dead father) to rescue Harry from the dementors that suck all life out of you. Part of the appeal of both Lewis and Rowling is their allusions to classical, mythical and archetypal images that connect the past with the present and take the reader into another world where time stands still. This strikes me as a description of the best experiences of worship. Another example of this is found in the work of Thomas Merton written towards the end of his tragically short life while living as a hermit. On 6 September 1965 he recorded these words:

> Last evening, when the moon was rising, I saw the warm burning soft red of a doe in the field. It was still light enough, so I got the field glasses and watched her. Presently a stag came out of the woods and then I saw a second doe and then, briefly, a second stag. They were not afraid. They looked at me from time to time. I watched their beautiful running, their grazing. Every movement was completely lovely, but there is a kind of gaucheness about them sometimes that makes them even lovelier, like adolescent girls.
>
> The thing that struck me most – when you look at them directly and in movement, you see what the primitive cave painters saw. Something you never see in photographs. It is most awe-inspiring. The *muntu* or the 'spirit' is shown in the running of the deer. The 'deerness' that sums up everything and is sacred and marvellous.
>
> A contemplative intuition, yet this is perfectly ordinary, everyday seeing – what everybody ought to see all the time. The deer reveals to me something essential, not only in itself, but also in myself. Something beyond the trivialities of my everyday being, my individual existence. Something profound. The face of that which is both the deer and myself.
>
> The stags are much darker than the does . . . I could sense the softness of their brown coat and longed to touch them.[15]

As I have shared with others my experience of the stag and doe as archetypes of the Spirit, it has been moving when others have shared similar personal experiences with me. Here are the words of someone entering into my space and experience in a way that enhanced all I had thought and written.

> It seems to me that imagery depicting a stag or doe speaks of the way of the heart rather than the mind. There is a beckoning to the still places deep within our (my) soul. Somehow the mind in these moments is too solid, clamouring as it does with a brazen harshness

that jars in their company. Being in the presence of the deer encourages and invites stillness, a calming, an entering into another wilder, freer, gentler place of 'being'.

The stag or the doe has a quality of presence, of stillness (quietness) and of being that is at once both elusive and inviting – almost as if it welcomes searching. It is not immediately to be 'found' but it is 'there' even when we walk past utterly unaware. Only those searching and prepared to pause will really 'see' and discover what others blindly miss.

There is too a quality of mystery that is captivating, ethereal but deeply real – a sense of the 'other'. This otherness is not akin to cold distance – rather I am aware of a sense within myself that, in entering its presence, there is a 'meeting' in which I leave enriched and changed whilst the deer seems to retain a quality of constancy, of 'unchangingness'. Most of all I am aware of a deep sense of peace that embraces and persists long after the encounter has occurred. I am left with a feeling of wonder and respect. In many ways I emerge invigorated and more fully alive for having 'known' a moment in its company.

There is a sense of 'knowing' and 'unknowing' at one and the same time – of being 'known' with an intimacy that sees into the very core of me and entering into the mystery of the place of 'unknowing'. The superficial, practical aspects of life that occupy so much space in the everyday life have a habit of disappearing – they lose significance and, for a while, life is experienced at a deeper more authentic level and I find that possibility overwhelmingly beautiful. Maybe that's why it is moments like these that should be treasured because we could not sustain the intensity over longer periods. There is a sense in which we enter a place unfettered by the restrictions of time – a deeper place that has a quality of eternity about it. To me there are connections in that Jesus waits, He is never forceful though He is powerful. The doe has her own quality of power that is related to her ability to draw others to her and welcome them in.[16]

Christ can be seen as both masculine and feminine, stag and doe. The stag and the doe as archetypes are essentially relational, speaking of vulnerability and strength, aloneness and togetherness, wildness and gentleness, grace and strength paradoxically entwined. Avoiding traditional gender stereotypes, each has their own strength and each invites the person into the life of the divine through the Spirit. The challenge is to enter into worship, prayer and reflection in a way that allows time for the Spirit to arrive, like the archetypes of the stag or the doe. Unconsciously I may have been influenced by the works of Edwin Muir or of another poet Kathleen Jamie who argues 'for an engagement of the whole being through a kind of practical earthly spirituality. These often startling encounters with animals, birds and other humans propose a way of living which recognizes the earth as a home to many different consciousnesses – and a means of authentic engagement.'[17] For me this authentic engagement needs to be part of worship through the use of prayer/poetry/visual art/silence/sound that evokes another place where the Spirit can work with this raw material in us and around us. The poem that emerged from me is offered here as a resource in worship.

> The doe/stag stands and witnesses
> The healing rhythm of the forest
> The rise and fall of the sun
> The shadow and shade of the moon
> The haunting cries of beak and claw
>
> The stag/doe reclines and dreams
> The healing rhythm of the heart
> The rise and fall of emotion
> The shadow and shade of memory
> The haunting cries deep within the psyche
>
> The stag, the doe and the Spirit
> witness and dream
> all that we are
> and all we will yet be

My hope is that by connecting with an archetype, the nature of which will be different for every person, there can be a shared experience in the desire to connect, to touch, to share, to enter into the timelessness, and to allow those moments of awe we all so need. Language strains to convey and communicate, metaphors reach their limits as we come alive through experiences of worship encompassing body, mind, spirit, psyche, sexuality and soul as each aspect intermingles, overlaps and embraces our being whole in the presence of a holy God.

Notes

1 David Moyer, a leader of the American chapter of Forward in Faith, quoted in <http://thewitness.org/article.php?id=535>.

2 Christopher J. Ellis, *Gathering: A Theology and Spirituality in Free Church Tradition*, London: SCM Press, 2004.

3 Alec Gilmore, Edward Smalley and Michael Walker, *Praise God: A Collection of Resource Material for Christian Worship*, London: Baptist Union of Great Britain and Ireland, 1980.

4 Ernst A. Payne and Stephen F. Winyard, *Orders and Prayers for Church Worship*, London: Baptist Union of Great Britain and Ireland, 1960.

5 *Praise God*, p. xi.

6 *Patterns and Prayers for Christian Worship*, Oxford: Oxford University Press, 1991.

7 *Patterns and Prayers for Christian Worship*, p. v.

8 Alistair Ross, *Evangelicals in Exile: Wrestling with Theology and the Unconscious*, London: Darton, Longman and Todd, 1997.

9 Christopher J. Ellis and Myra Blyth, *Gathering for Worship: Patterns and Prayers for the Community of Disciples*, London, SCM Press, 2005.

10 *Promise and Presence: An Exploration of Sacramental Theology*, Milton Keynes: Paternoster Press, 2005; *The Rhythm of Doctrine: A Liturgical Sketch of Christian Faith and Faithfulness*, Milton Keynes: Paternoster Press, 2007.

11 Andrew Samuels, *Jung and the Post-Jungians*, London: Routledge, 1996.

12 Samuels, *Jung and the Post-Jungians*, p. 29.

13 As quoted in David M. Wulff, *The Psychology of Religion: Classic and Contemporary Views*, New York: John Wiley and Sons, 1991, p. 423.

14 Philip Sheldrake, *Living Between the Worlds: Place and Journey in Celtic Sprituality*, London: Darton, Longman and Todd, 1995.

15 N. Stone, ed., *Thomas Merton. A Vow of Conversation: Journals 1964–1965*, New York: Farrar, Straus & Giroux, 1988, p. 207.

16 Personal communication to the author.

17 Kathleen Jamie, *The Tree House*, London: Picador, 2004, back cover.

Part 5

Sound and Silence

Introduction

Worship is more than texts, although of course texts (usually at least Scripture) always have their place in a context of the multiple media of liturgical celebration – including the enacted, sensed and, as the contributors to this section especially remind us, heard and sung.

The three writers who follow here explore different dimensions of song, their alliance with wider forms of music, and indeed those patterns of sound and silence that are the warp and woof of liturgical scenes. They write from different experiences, in different ecclesial traditions (two – Lee Longden and Rupert Jeffcoat – are Anglicans; one – Pink Dandelion – is a Quaker), and from different contexts (two – Dandelion and Longden – from the UK, one – Jeffcoat – from the Antipodes). At times, they scrutinize the sounds of Christian assembly; at other times they lift up its aural and musical dimensions for celebration of their riches.

Rupert Jeffcoat writes from Australia ('the edge of the world?', he asks) and draws on his background and present experience as a cathedral musician. His playful essay reveals the continuing vitality of the cathedral tradition, not least to unsettle possible assumptions about what passes as 'traditional', and in so doing provides us with insights into many imaginative juxtapositions within cathedral music that might inspire its own contemporary engagement with different contexts. Lee Longden offers a powerful analysis of what he calls 'transcultural musical encounter' that links strongly with other material collected in this volume concerned with postcolonial criticism. He articulates incisive postcolonial perspectives that further reveal the potential in dialogue between liturgical and emerging postcolonial theologies. Pink Dandelion complements these different explorations of music in a beautiful reflective piece that invites attention to the intimacy of silence as it might be experienced in Quaker spirituality, and by others in turn.

Together, these essays offer lively and at times evocative guides towards the edges of sound and silence, where words fail and where divine presence is, and may be, found.

17

Bridge and Chopsticks

RUPERT JEFFCOAT

In the game bridge, one is not supposed to declare one's hand – at least not up front! But it may help to say that I am providing my side of this conversation as a cathedral director of music and also as an ordained Anglican minister, so I am doubly vulnerable!

Going together

Music and liturgy are often assumed to be the horse and carriage of worship – but 'cathedral' music is in fact music from the margins – notes from the frontier, jottings from no-man's land. For some there is something of a bygone age about Book of Common Prayer psalms done by robed choir, complete with bombastic canticles and inflated anthems that declare their 'pretensiosity' – a combination of virtuosity and pretentiousness!

But rather than be a defence of 'traditional' music, my reflections here are in fact about methodology. For some, methodology is a skirting round the edge of a subject, a setting up of the terrain, before one engages with the 'subject' itself, but, I contend, *how* we approach a discussion of music might be paradigmatic for our approach to theology and vice versa. We may often assume that 'logical' arguments proceed linearly and follow up thoughts in preceding areas. But what if our experience is multilayered, disparate and involving? Following a line of thought (the quickest way from A to B) does mean missing out on the sideshows and entertainments laid on for us on the byways: and who is to say that they *are* byways until we have experienced them? Perhaps we could allow both linear and lateral methodologies to journey together, complementing and even complimenting each other, allowing for a joyful co-exploration of God's universe in music and worship.

Linear v. lateral

It seems to me that humans are able to take in only one thing at a time, and this tyranny has controlled everything from the way we argue, to systematic theology, to musical analysis. A 'story' or the musical exploration of a theme is time-specific: it matters about the order in which we 'discover' the relatedness of thematic material. In Brahms one sometimes only notices a thematic link after it has returned, such is his skill with motivic elision.[1] How we hear and decode music relates to how it becomes chewed up and modified in its context and experience inside a piece of music.[2] Much 'educational' presentation of musical processes[3] imagines that there are themes and an 'accompaniment' which remain neutral or unaffected by the processes undergone throughout the movement. For years, folk would comment that Mozart wrote out his 'recapitulations' wrongly (they often differ in details from the initial presentation), without realizing that after ten minutes of symphonic development of the theme, if we believe it to be an organic entity, is bound to be affected by its 'life-story'.[4] Music's multivalency means that tackling things logically (a loose colloquial term which usually means merely chronologically) does a disservice to the invention. And just as the universe seems to have no 'centre', music and theology may also have no 'centres': we may perceive that the edges (the branches) that are seen as outposts of the main tree (head office) are more interdependent than first appeared.

It is worth noting our assumption that music has to 'go somewhere', that it should 'travel' – in terms of modulations, drama, purpose or colour. Charles Rosen[5] talks about the modern ear getting impatient if we attempt to listen to, say, a baroque suite (which is mostly in the same key) since the contemporary listener expects rapid change. Similar perhaps to the very small changes that take place in some minimalist music (say in Reich's *Six Pianos*), a Handel keyboard suite does exhibit change (of metre, tempo, dynamics and register as well as more subtle issues of articulation in performance) but often not a great deal to our ears. The typical baroque 'movement' often exemplifies one 'reservoir' of rhythms and a particular constructional device. Yet in a world where one had to create one's own music, the activity of actually making it happen meant that 'passive' music-listening was less prevalent. The 'world' of music was very different and that points us to dealing with the needs of today's world with its rather hectic view of time.

Erik Routley in discussing Friedrich Karlheinz talks of there being no taboos in music: 'strictly speaking nothing in the combination of sound and silence per se is beyond the bounds of possibility'.[6] Such extreme liberality makes it harder to discuss the role of music, for while in liturgy we have certain processes and linguistic analysis (for example, of doctrine), with music this seems rather perverse. For many years, many Roman Catholic churches frowned upon instrumental music (tainted by the 'secular' world) and many Orthodox congregations still use only voices, and at a pinch bells. Theology informs their reasoning, but it is not a theology of music, it is a theology of musical appropriateness. Music and worship then seem to be more than the sum of their parts, and it is likely that in hitch-hiking round different worship routines that we will find music destabilizing not only us but itself. Of course, many Christians might wish to hold a contrary view that worship provides a solidity in their changing lives (with church music often being seen as an 'old' form[7]).

Homeless and happy?

Most people assume (as in the notion of tonal centres in music) that there is a home, a security. Just as people use biology for their theology of sexuality, so musicians have used physics for their appeal to the natural order of things[8] and the supremacy of tonality in the harmonic series. This is where each note sets up vibrations that are mathematically related, and the chief notes (of tonic, dominant, third and so on) appear therefore to be cosmically ordained. The harmonic series does seem to be 'natural': a violin string playing, say, an open G will sound exactly one octave above if stopped exactly halfway (the vibrating length thus being 50 per cent of formerly).[9]

Serialism, by contrast, was a sort of anti-Newtonian 'network' where the notes of works were only related to each other and must follow a sequence. That, for many, music that is serial in construction sounds other-worldly is no proof that it is not right, true, good or beautiful. Indeed, Schoenberg's music of roughly 1907–18 would later come to be described as 'atonal'.[10] *Pierrot Lunaire* is one such work, and yet it is also remarkable that works without a tonal centre often tended to harbour a story, a conceit or a dramatic outline to help the compositional structure. And as late as the mid 1930s, Benjamin Britten's suggestion that the Royal College of Music stock Schoenberg's scores was vetoed![11]

With regard to 'dis-location', the experience of the Jews in the diaspora to, say, Latin America, is illuminating: the very dislocation creates a sense of identity and helps articulate questions. If music too were 'dislocated' it might help us to ask more meaningful questions about its role and purpose in our religious life. So while decentring tonality is or was for many a break too far, we might compare this with our own preconceptions of our own importance. Hundreds of years ago, Galileo concluded that the earth was not quite the centre everyone thought it was, and yet in music we still expect things to revolve around us and our commodification of it.

Darwinian music?

This becomes more noticeable when one looks at music history. When Mozart allegedly said 'Bach was the father; we the children', he was in fact referring to C. P. E. Bach, the son of J. S. Bach. It is Johann Sebastian Bach that the world now considers great (thanks to the nineteenth-century rediscovery and promotion of his work), but in his own time, far from being mainstream, J. S. Bach was stranded up a gully, composing recherché or passé music.[12] To us nowadays the chief stream ('Bach' in German) has been Johann Sebastian, and imagining the world of music without him would be inconceivable. It is as if evolution has come through him – yet amazingly somehow music got where it did without his input, which is at once nonsensical but true! By contrast, Louis Spohr and Giacomo Meyerbeer were lionized in nineteenth-century Europe, but hardly anyone plays their music today; yet their contemporary success gave them a considerable influence over composers, musicians and the public.

So in discussing music (let alone music in worship), we should not confuse what we do with what has been done before, and what we will end up doing. There would seem to be no 'apostolic succession' to our musical heritage, and hunting for one might be to miss the point. The evolutionary principle doesn't quite seem to apply, for we cannot say simply that the fittest survives, for sometimes there seems to be no 'bloodline' to the next generation. And yet Alexander Goehr holds the view that in 'ritual', music's meanings and associations are 'self-evident'.[13] This seems to me almost precisely wrong, for while we may wish such things to be self-evident, this would be to assume that we all share the same background. His analysis of music as communication (written nearly 20 years ago) does not help us today when our Christian experiences are so atomized and pluralized that common ground on many matters is seldom shared.

Pushing the envelope

How can we unpick the context of liturgy? It is possible to hold the view that Anglican cathedrals have opted (or more likely unwittingly collaborated) in a systematic lowering of 'standards' – not perhaps the 'musical standard' achievable (though one can certainly contest the idea that we are 'better' now than we were) – but simply that liturgical expectations of how we encounter boundaries and how we respond have been desensitized. Many who claim to love 'Cathedral' music often wish to hold it in aspic, thereby contributing to its demise.

In the act of worshipping, we get an idea that we encounter God – but so often we don't want that to change us. Dreaming of what music can do in liturgy can be a lonely voyage, and yet knowing the destination before one starts is to miss the point of the journey, which is the journey itself. Some theorists see distinctions between 'functional music' and 'art music'. Edward Cone[14] notes that hymns can do their job, but once they become conscious of a human audience they shift genre. Indeed, the BBC's *Songs of Praise* (and similar programmes) often seems to be more 'entertainment' than 'worship' because it targets people and their enjoyment rather than God.

Playing with and playing for time

Music could be said to be made up of three elements – melody, harmony and rhythm. While this is oversimplistic, we should acknowledge that the three realms are interdependent. For example, notes are vibrations: higher notes are simply faster vibrations, and very low notes are slow vibrations that one often feels as rhythm, so the elements interact with one another. Likewise in most tonal music harmonies are made out of notes that are intimately related to the very melodies they support and some composers play with the ambiguities of this. It is indeed rich to see music as a 'relational' formula which mirrors something of the concept of the Trinity, since there is sense of the interplay in its very operation. And on a wider basis the interplay of context means that a musician could be said to work in a 'Trinitarian' fashion – as himself/herself and with personal inspiration interfacing with various heritages.

Music plays with time, using it to create both content and form. We cannot just box it up to make a simple 'soundbite' message. If listening to, say, a Mahler symphony is a spiritual experience, as many would aver, then we should be wary of those who think this can be made into an elixir-like equation. Allowing music (or, for that matter, Scripture) to be itself and play with us is an important part of our receptivity as human beings: just as the Bible is full of ambiguities and contrasts, so in liturgy one can have the most delightful ironies played out. Indeed, irony and stories need time to unfold, and music's mystery is that we cannot experience it in any other way but in 'time'. Milan Kundera points out (in discussing Janacek operas) that sometimes voices and orchestra 'disagree' and comment in ways that enhance the drama.[15] In general our liturgies have tended not to explore simultaneity (which anyone used to watching TV will cope with) or contrast, and this would seem to be a field ripe for harvesting. Perhaps lessons might be learned from the multifocal celebration of the likes of Orthodox services – while the priest is at the altar, others are happily elsewhere, lighting candles, kissing icons, engaged in devotions in related but different zones.

Music and musicians – perhaps only they – perform prophetic utterances which may disturb as well as affirm the community since their language goes beyond the edge of rational explanation. We often talk of human beings as the only animals that can truly be said to 'speak', so there is something ironic, perhaps, that points to important feelings only being expressible beyond words. Mendelssohn once said that music says it more precisely than words,[16] and we may have all noted that at funerals the most poignant moments come not during the eulogy – which, perhaps focuses on someone's drinking exploits – but in the simple piano piece that captures the simplicity, the wonder and the glory of life. And all of this takes place in an ever-shifting context: somehow the 'truth' is distilled and enfleshed in time and in space, through the action of sounds and its arena.

If there's no bridge – jump!

Take an example of this instantaneous but multivalent approach in language. In Japanese the word *hashi* means 'edge' – as in edge of a table; but it can mean 'chopsticks' and is also the word for a bridge. By design or default (even allowing for the context and pronunciation) all these concepts are 'media': chopsticks mediate food to the mouth, a bridge brings two sides together, and an edge mediates one plane to another. This is notably useful when we consider that religion is about links: we link our experience of the world to the experience of 'heaven'. Some Christians might say that Jesus is the link between God and humanity: is Jesus then a bridge, an edge, or even the chopsticks we use to feed ourselves? I started with the other meaning of the word 'bridge' – referring to the game of smoke and mirrors. Perhaps all these resonances are legitimate if not entirely 'logical'. If we can do this with one word (with many meanings) then we can see how one 'sound' can be reinterpreted or misinterpreted as a carrier of 'meaning' (even where that meaning is indefinable). And there is yet another metaphor for bridge, used informally: a passage in music that connects two more significant chunks of music.

Is cathedral music a bridge in this last sense – a connector between more significant chunks? Putting aside 'nostalgia' it is reasonable to say that church music has uplifted and spoken to many millions over the years. How can cathedral musicians continue to support people's encounter with God and yet break an oppressive cycle that relies on the tyranny of Western art music? The role of a musician is maybe more to express than explain, not to prove but to show. Rather than utilizing a step-by-step pedestrian perambulation, the musician will push synaptic approaches: lively joinings together, akin to electricity jumping, it may be unpredictable but it is still stimulating!

Un-'wording' music

Working in Australia (the edge of the world?) we encounter from time to time a particular propositional type of Christianity. This is notable in the quest for intelligibility: certain parts of the Anglican Church only allow music to be sung in English. (This ignores the stunning diversity of multicultural Australia, and also tells people to learn English or be damned!) But music itself rather resists being proved 'true' or 'false'. There are rules in the cathedral-style incarnation of music (generally it is sophisticated 'art' music performed well by trained people), but one might also add that it can come with a very unchallenging and unchallenged theology. Music expresses more than we can codify in words, which is perhaps what is so scary for some Christians. It would be nice perhaps to suggest a framework about music in worship, yet unless we go for 'wordless' music we are always going to be prey to the vacillations of meaning and imposition of 'political' motives to music. This is to say that while we share the sound of music (that is the physiological matter of vibrations) we often destroy this commonality by ascribing 'meaning' to the words, which then leads to misunderstandings.[17] Contrafacta (in the sixteenth century) are an interesting note to the discussion: in the mid 1500s Latin anthems were banned in England so existing anthems were re-worded (not just translated, since some of the theology around Mary and the sacraments was not acceptable). Do differing sacred words put to an existing 'sacred' piece make it a different piece of music?[18] And what then happens when you then put 'secular' words to it, as also happened? There is an element of music that possesses us beyond our capacity to deal with it – it is a 'Logos', an idea that defies our comprehension yet still somehow beguiles us into encounter.

The aliens are coming!

Could a lack of comforting conclusion be instructive? The Church – who else is going to? – needs to experiment more with what is legitimate as musical Christian expression. Assuming we have the 'basics' right only makes us like a chained dog who, when baited, strains at the leash: we never make it off our patch, let alone hit our target. But rather than confirm our current doings, worship leads us into a perpetual regression of focus: we encounter a never-ending mind-shift, develop what was 'the edge' to become more central, and then we seek the next edge and so on.

In the Bible there is a rather alluring habit of someone 'alien' affecting the story, where somebody or something from the outside effects change. It is often the outsider who brings insight to the main group of people. Welcoming the 'edges' can help us to discover a more central truth (the epithet 'central' tellingly betrays how our language perpetuates the tyranny of 'capital'-ization, the metaphor of head as main part). The journeying nature of faith makes the quest never quite realized, and allows fresh vistas from every new foothill. And with that in mind it is probably right that a 'non-Christian' gives some insight here to the church on music's calling: 'to accept the local, the contemporary, the immediate, and so transform it, or contrast against it, that we obtain glimpses of a visionary, even transcendental reality'.[19]

In Charles Ives's music we notice that worlds collide, that 'genres' break in on each other. The context is New England church music, often conjured up by some Salvationist chorales or the sound of the American organ. Working like a collage, the introduction of marching bands or orchestral music into the serenity of the 'worship-mode' perhaps has lessons for our religious life. Some religious experience is monochrome, being a cocoon away from the world, yet music in this fashion takes us from our ghetto to an edge where we may feel discomfort, confusion and even disorientation. Music can summon up other worlds: in some instances this is very specific (e.g. the off-stage 'army' band in *Cosi fan tutte*, or movements in Berlioz *Symphonie Fantastique*), but music also creates other 'worlds'. For while many talk of music's ability to hint at the 'beyond', music also contains the ability to transport us there too. [20]

Leaving home: travelling light

When I hear talk of Jesus as 'pioneer', I sometimes imagine him with a wagon in the American Midwest forging a new path ahead of us. The image of travelling won't go away. When we travel we make decisions about what comes with us – do we take what is fundamental to our community, or take something more personally meaningful and sentimental? Appreciating that differing perspectives exist (as we can see, say, in an analysis of Brahms's music) means that it is hard to decide what would count as 'peripheral'. And so when we come to worship, how we worship God depends on our perspective. Voices in postmodernism would seem to reclaim the past as one of a number of possible homes, and the future too is also a home. Singing beautiful music (with only a few people in the room, à la choral evensong) is almost certainly a recherché activity – yet it can remain an equally valid witness to God's reality.

English's glorious verbal flexibility allows 'travelling light' to be not just an adjective and noun but also a verb and adverb. We say that beautiful music 'moves' us and 'enlightens' us, but perhaps it is in fact one process – that it is *only* when it is travelling that it can illuminate our lives. If we are called as Christians to go to the edge, then we can't also be back at base camp. In travelling, in leaving home, we may be more ready to meet God if we are not weighed down by baggage. Maybe God is a nomadic God who dares not have a palace in case we settle down at home and forget to worship God in spirit and in truth?

Notes

1 For example, the first 44 bars of Brahms's Second Symphony where the niggling semitone 'works' on several time and pitch levels as an ornament and dissonance. See Walter Frisch, *Brahms and the Principle of Developing Variation*, Berkeley, CA: University of California Press, 1984, for a fuller discussion.

2 For example, compare the openings of the first and fourth movements of Tchaikovsky's Fifth Symphony: the opening minor clarinet melody is 'redeemed' (same instrumentation) in the major version in the fourth movement.

3 For example, *Keys to Music* presentations (ABC Classic FM) where some sort of

analysis takes place. They can, however, tend to resemble more 'anatomy' than 'physiology' (where one learns how things fit together).

4 Mozart should have consulted the first textbooks on sonata form such as A. B. Marx, *Die Lehre von der musikalischen Komposition, praktisch-theoretisch* (*The Art of Composition: In Practice and Theory*), Leipzig, 1837. Very inconsiderately, Mozart died 30–40 years before their publication.

5 Charles M. Rosen, *The Classical Style*, London: Faber, 1971, p. 63, footnote 1.

6 Erik Routley, *Words, Music and the Church*, Nashville: Abingdon Press, 1964, p. 49.

7 From a Mendelssohn letter; cited in R. Larry Todd, *Mendelssohn's Musical Education*, Cambridge: Cambridge University Press, 1983, p. 86.

8 Deryck Cooke, *The Language of Music*, Oxford: Oxford University Press, 1959, p. 41.

9 Cooke, *Language of Music*, p. 42: though the insight that over time we have 'revealed' more of the harmonic series (gradual acceptance of the fifth, then the third) needs to be tempered by the realization that time itself does not breed greater understanding. The twentieth century was bloodier than the nineteenth for example.

10 Arnold Whittall, *Music Since the First World War*, London: Dent, 1977, p. 9.

11 Ronald Duncan, *Working with Britten*, Bideford: Rebel, 1981, p. 16.

12 Scheibe (*Critischer Musikus* of 1745); quoted in Todd, *Musical Education*, p. 5.

13 Alexander Goehr, *Finding the Key*, London: Faber, 1998, p. 222.

14 Edward T. Cone, *The Composer's Voice*, Berkeley, CA: University of California Press, 1974, p. 51.

15 Milan Kundera, *Testaments Betrayed*, London: Faber, 1993, p. 139.

16 'People complain that music has so many meanings; they aren't sure what to think when they are listening to it; and yet, after all, everyone understands words. I am quite the opposite. I feel not only with whole speeches, but even with individual words, that they have so many meanings, they are so imprecise, so easy to misunderstand in comparison with music [. . .] A piece of music that I love expresses thoughts to me that are not too imprecise to be framed in words, but too precise' (Letter To Marc André Souchay, 15 October 1842); cited in Peter Mercer-Taylor, ed., *The Cambridge Companion to Mendelssohn*, Cambridge: Cambridge University Press, 2004, p. 190.

17 Peter le Huray, *Authenticity in Performance*, Cambridge: Cambridge University Press, 1990, Chapter 4 – where we read that a French analysis (1829) of a Mozart quartet gave it words as a way of helping to 'understand it'!

18 The polyphonic 'music' (not meant pejoratively but to indicate the 'notes' as distinct from the combination of notes and words) of Thomas Tallis's *O sacrum convivium* (published in *Cantiones Sacrae* 1575) appears elsewhere as *I call and cry* (both nowadays published by Oxford University Press).

19 Michael Tippett, *Music of the Angels*, London: Eulenburg, 1980, p. 116.

20 Jonathan Harvey, *Music and Inspiration*, London: Faber, 1999, p. 152.

18

'Beyond the Blue Horizon':
Transcultural Musical Encounter in Postcolonial Perspective

LEE LONGDEN

Popular music, and its dynamic relationship with its cultural contexts, has, from the last quarter of the twentieth century, formed a fruitful focus for rigorous postcolonial analysis.[1] As Simon Featherstone notes:

> Musical traditions transcribe the most intimate histories of culture, where sounds, languages and bodies meet. Rhythms and harmonies, songs and dances, and shows and recordings are performances of function and pleasure that encompass, shape and express individual and communal identities, and register cultural encounters of both trauma and delight. For these reasons they provide particularly valuable materials for a study of postcolonialism and its concerns with diasporic experience, hybrid identity and contests of cultural value.[2]

Despite the welcome insights into the complexity of transcultural musical encounter offered by such analyses, and an apparently growing trend towards the use of music from other cultures in the worship of many British churches, church music studies have, in company with other disciplines in the study of Christian worship, largely failed to consider postcolonial challenges to the praxis they discuss.[3]

The first phase of the voyage into transcultural encounter represented by this current musical trend seems to be grounded in two broad aims. The first aim is for the music used by multiethnic and/or multi-cultural faith communities to speak more appropriately of their individual and corporate identities, which express the complex and dialogical nature of cultures in relationship to and encounter with each other. The second aim is to broaden the worship horizons of mono-ethnic and/or monocultural faith communities through facilitating encounter with music and cultures with which they may be unfamiliar. With the ready availability of commercial recordings, an increasingly wide range of music drawn from many parts of the world seems to be being included in worship.

Such transcultural encounters carry great potential for the facilitation of transformative growth, if they generate dialogic engagement, embarked on with humility, honesty and openness[4] in the pursuit of achieving the dual positivity of 'a more tolerant and less judgemental and condemnatory view toward other [cultures]'[5] and the realization that each partner might gain greater insight into their own beliefs and worldview through engagement with and understanding of the 'other'.[6]

But, arguably, the fast pace of this recent trend in church music has, in its rush to fulfil laudable aims, led to somewhat unreflective uses of the available resources. Consequently, much of their potential for the facilitation of genuinely transformative encounter seems to have been subverted in favour of the 'musical tourism' of superficial engagement with culturally sanitized musical texts.

This article embodies some reflections on aspects of over 20 years of musical practice that I have experienced, observed and participated in, as a musician – progressively chorister, organist and music director – and, latterly, as an ordained minister in the Church of England. It encompasses a number of contexts, from cathedral, through collegiate environment and theological college, to local parish church, both in Britain and overseas; and crosses most, if not all, church traditions within my denomination.

In choosing, as a white, Western, man, to view this practice through a postcolonial optic, I am conscious of the danger of colonizing or subverting its discourses through my position of relative privilege. But I write as one who has reflected at length on the difference between superficial engagement and transformative encounter, through my long and tortuous journey as a performer from Western art music into jazz; and benefited greatly from dialogue with different cultures and people of diverse ethnic identities. For this reason, my aim, through raising some of the questions generated by a postcolonial critique, is to speak to, and of, white-majority Anglophile churches. I do this in the hope of raising consciousness of some of the issues implicit in unreflective transcultural use of music, with the motive of encouraging my sisters and brothers to listen carefully to what is *really* being said through music by marginalized voices both in our own churches and in the historic profile of global Christianity, and to act on the challenges they issue to a Eurocentric worldview.

As the experiences of one presbyter-musician can only ever be fragments of the totality of musical practice in such churches, this study aims to offer not so much conclusive answers or authoritative advice as to, in a small way, stimulate further debate and critical reflection in readiness for the next stage of our journey into encounter.

What is this thing called love? What is this thing called, love? What! Is this thing called love? What does it matter?[7]

Much current use of music from other cultures or ethnic identities by Anglophile churches appears to tread one of two roads. First, that of a supposedly representative cultural agent intended to convey the distilled essence of a culture, ethnic identity and/or geographical location. One expression I recently experienced was the use of a number of different genres of African music as a soundscape in a presentation by a local representative of an international charity concerning its work in that continent. The music seemed to be intended to engage our emotions in 'getting a feel' for the continent, but the individual items embraced a large number of countries, traditions, ethnic identities and cultural contexts, and frequently did not match the images, people or contexts pictorially represented in the slides we were viewing.

The second road seems to be that of adding 'spice' to a congregation's worship experiences through encounter with 'something different' that is assumed to form a point of departure from the community's primary musical identity.[8] Commonly, this is expressed through the use of a single musical item, for example an Argentinian *Sanctus*, in the context of an otherwise totally Anglophile liturgy.

On one level, these apparently expansive themes could be viewed as usefully raising awareness of possibilities for dialogic encounter with an increasingly wide range of worship-enhancing musical resources. But, when viewed through a postcolonial optic, each raises a number of questions for reflection.

The first considers the issue of what is encountered by participants in the musical exchange. At its simplest level, the answer is 'a piece of music'; but this truism conceals a musical text's complex web of cultural representation in which many discourses concurrently operate, come into conflict and occasionally find satisfactory resolution.

Numerous authors acknowledge the power of music to engage the emotions[9] in adding 'a deeper dimension of participation to worship'[10] as non-verbal and rational elements are conjoined in what Brian Wren (drawing on Augustine of Hippo) terms 'praying twice'.[11] Consequently, as Martin Luther notes, for good and ill, music has the ability to speak to a wide range of people and conditions:

> Next to the Word of God, music deserves the highest praise. She is a mistress and governess [*sic*] of those human emotions . . . which control men or more often overwhelm them . . . Whether you wish to comfort the sad, to subdue frivolity, to encourage the despairing, to humble the proud, to calm the passionate, or to appease those full of hate . . . what more effective means than music could you find?[12]

But, as Simon Featherstone rightly identifies, musical texts do not exist in a vacuum: they are created and received in concrete contexts, so in one sense they inherently speak to and of particular cultures and peoples.[13] The texts act as bearers of meaning and convention, functioning as symbolic signifiers within particular interpretative systems. But, as Simon Frith evidences, to regard the text – music or lyrics – as the primary mode of conveying meaning is somewhat reductive.[14] A more nuanced and layered construct of meaning seems to be brought to consciousness through the act of performance, arguably causing the text to fully actualize the kind of potential of which Luther writes only when it is linked to an appropriate context.

In turn, this raises the question of what constitutes an 'appropriate context' for its use. If the musical text, when considered in isolation is, as Paul Gilroy suggests, often somewhat cryptic in bearing meaning,[15] is the only appropriate context the cultural setting of the text's initial creation, or are there factors that can facilitate its effective cultural translation? The question is particularly pertinent to this study. Expressed another way, does the broad commonality of a worship setting provide sufficient rooting for the text to make encounter with it authentic and meaningful? When viewed through a postcolonial optic, the issue can be reframed in terms of whether it is possible, or indeed desirable, for such cultural agents to 'escape the effects of those forces that construct them'.[16]

Commentators who favour world music's somewhat optimistic 'affirmation of the potential for the transformability of local music outside the specific historical and geographical circuits of its formations' would claim that, through bringing 'once remote traditions' on to a single plain of discourse, 'free, innovative play and dialogue' is possible.[17] But a less utopian postcolonial critique would raise questions of whether such contextual translation sanitizes the musical text through robbing it of its cultural meaning; about whose plain of discourse the encounter takes place on; and about by whose rules dialogue might proceed.

This is significant, since some of the current use of music from other cultures by white-majority churches juxtaposes individual musical items alongside entirely Anglophile liturgical texts and practices. So returning to my initial question, and adding to it: what is encountered and what is taking place through this transcultural exchange?

On one level, encounter with a musical 'other' could be interpreted as offering challenge to dominant Eurocentric worldviews. But some expressions of this interpretation appear to gloss over its problems. If we return to the two aspects of transcultural music use I identified above, the issues can quickly be realized.

Whenever a single text is presented without reference to its context of creation, in order to representatively 'illustrate' a culture, ethnic identity and/or geographical location, there is an inherent risk of reinforcing stereotypically exoticized Orientalist views of the cultural 'other'.[18] As Featherstone (drawing on Bernth Lindfors) notes: '[it creates] striking spectacles of cultural difference, a display of otherness that recalls, quite alarmingly, the nineteenth-century predilection for living ethnic curiosities that marked the first phases of mass popular culture'.[19]

Those encountering the text arguably have no way of making the encounter meaningful, as they remain unfamiliar with both the original cultural context to which it refers and the systems of meaning within which it functions. And, as John Hull identifies, the resulting bewilderment can act as an effective barrier to learning, as the receiving participant retreats behind defences designed to prevent their looking foolish.[20]

Similarly, reinterpreting the musical text from contextually specific cultural actor to cross-cultural ambassador seems to remove many useful points of departure from which meaningful transcultural dialogue might begin. The text is assumed to speak for itself, but, as the discussion above illustrates, when taken from its cultural bearings, of what it speaks and the language it communicates through become far from clear. Consequentially, the superficial engagement of musical tourism can become the only operative discourse in the encounter.

Using music from other cultures to add an additional dimension to worship through encounter with 'something different' can prove no less problematic, when viewed from a postcolonial standpoint. Recontextualizing the musical text, through juxtaposing it with liturgy and practice of an 'alien' culture, carries the danger of sanitizing it through the processes of cultural appropriation. Mike Johnsont, writing of the appropriation of Native American symbols and religious ceremonies by 'Euro-Americans', claims this to be 'a form of racism' in which 'a dominating [group] or colonizing people take over the cultural and religious ceremonies and articles of a people experiencing domination or colonization'.[21]

The importance of authentic encounter with the cultural bearings of a musical text to transformative dialogic engagement became clear to me through my journey as a musician into jazz. Additionally, it appeared to me that such engagement, when effective, most usefully happens on a plain of discourse that subverts the conventionally dominant participant's normative assumptions and interpretive systems, and so forces them on to the margins.

As a young musician I had been extensively schooled in the traditions, performance conventions, interpretative strategies and techniques of Western art music.[22] I had been immersed in some of its multiplicity of cultures and had internalized its cultural norms.

I encountered popular music as a child, but showed little interest in listening to it. As a teenager I ventured into light music, but never really made the move across to popular music.[23] Later I ventured into Manchester's 'clubland'[24] for the first time, and began to work as a backing musician in social clubs.

Here I encountered some of the texts of jazz, and found myself on the margins of a musical world for which I had few interpretative tools. The conventions of this performance culture were alien to me. Previously, following the practice of Western art music, I had regarded a fully notated musical text as normative, and its accurate performance as my task. Now I faced a page on which the bare minimum of symbols was written, rather than a multiplicity of musical notes; and single-line melodies, with seemingly cryptic instructions like 'Count Basie swing style' were my guides. Gradually, by a process of trial and error, I began to chart a course through this unfamiliar musical landscape.

Through these encounters, the repertoire I performed was considerably broadened, but my playing was never transformed. Despite my degree of technical competence, I was never able to adequately master many of the styles of popular music, particularly jazz, and improvisation remained a painful experience. My approach to the texts I encountered, and interpretative strategies, remained those of a Western art musician who chose to play popular music.

Just over a decade later I found myself once again on the musical margins. I began to work aboard American cruise liners, and encountered musicians from a number of countries working on the same ship, and indeed in the same band. A major part of the repertoire we performed was music for dancing, and, for the first time, I became part of the rhythm section[25] of a dance band. Again, there were conventions of which I was unaware, and styles that I was not initially able to adequately reflect in my playing. But these years of encounter proved to be significantly different from my experiences in 'clubland'. Through them my playing was transformed, so that, while I am by no means an expert jazz performer, I am now able to express myself fluently and more convincingly.

Reflecting on these two experiences of transcultural musical encounter in the light of the discussion above reveals an interesting point of connection in terms of how what I actually encountered in each context affected its transformative potential.

While I engaged with some of the same musical texts in both reception contexts, there were significant differences between them in terms of what was transmitted. The majority of the performers I worked with in the social clubs were semi-professionals,[26] many of whom, like me, had constructed their musical identities from unreflective listening to each other and to commercial recordings, without engagement with the cultures of the texts. Their musical choices tended to be governed more by what was 'popular' at the time than by a passion for a particular musical style or genre.[27] The repertoire performed in one 45 minute set would juxtapose a number of musical styles. Consequently, while I encountered 'authentic' texts, and was challenged by unfamiliar performance conventions, I only engaged superficially with the cultures they potentially represented. It was a somewhat ersatz encounter in which enough of the authentic was present to unsettle my normative interpretive strategies, but insufficiently present to dislodge them by offering a critical cultural dialogue partner. As a result, I continued to remain at my art-music starting point, despite the straining of its boundaries.

In contrast, while the performance context aboard opulent cruise liners cannot reasonably be claimed as an 'authentic' one for the cultural bearings of jazz, many of the performers with whom I worked on-board had been so immersed in that culture that I found genuine dialogue partners with whom to engage, both musically and personally. Significantly, as one schooled in art music, I was on the margins of that culture, knowing few of the performers to whom they referred, little of the performance conventions and lacking the interpretative strategies to make sense of what I heard around me.

But in this second experience, the culture of jazz was authentically represented to me through the texts and performers in a way that brought me into dialogue with it, and the reception context was sufficiently sensitive to those of the texts' creation to prevent my unreflectively applying my normative interpretative systems to the dialogue process.

Carrying these thoughts back to the transcultural use of music in white-majority churches, I do not subscribe to the view that texts can only be used in their context of creation by the people by whom and for whom they were created. But arguably, for transformative encounter to happen through them, contexts of reception need to be sufficiently sensitive to those of creation to ensure that what is transmitted through the encounter is an authentic cultural voice, rather than a sanitized, appropriated, ersatz.

In addition to these issues of representation, agency and authenticity, viewing our transcultural musical practice through a postcolonial lens encourages white Christians to question our motives and, particularly, whether our use of music from other cultures in our worship causes us to listen attentively to marginalized voices, in pursuit of inclusivity – something Wren (drawing on Paul Westermeyer) describes as 'a theological value, a corollary of unity'.[28]

Or does it act to reinforce the arguably colonizing trends of commercial world music, in which something that is essentially functional is aestheticized for the benefit of Western consumers, with the consequence that difference is sanitized rather than celebrated?[29] Why we might be using such music in our worship forms the focus for the remainder of this study.

It ain't what you do; it's the way that you do it . . . [30]

Dialogue means we sit and talk with each other, especially those with whom we may think we have the greatest differences. However, talking together all too often means debating, discussing with a view to convince the other, arguing for our point of view, examining pros and cons. In dialogue, the intention is not to advocate but to inquire; not to argue but to explore; not to convince but to discover.[31]

Reflection on the first phase of the Anglophile churches' voyage into musical discovery seems to betray the issue that, in some circumstances, the challenges inherent to transcultural encounters have been issued before the dominant cultural discourses of the receiving community have been identified and owned. In other words, if what is to be challenged through dialogue with the agencies of other cultures is not explicitly named, the challenge itself carries the risk of becoming sanitized through a lack of directed focus. Perhaps this accounts for some of the bewilderment I have noted in my research among the members of receiving communities – commonly expressed in terms of having enjoyed the experience of hearing music from other cultures but not really understanding why they were listening to it.

Numerous agendas potentially come into play in addressing the question of why white-majority churches use music of other cultures, but arguably, the crucial first task is to make them explicit, and so open to challenge and transformation in the process of dialogue. As Bob Marley is thought to have said 'don't look at the tool and whether it works: look at the [person] behind it'.

There are numerous possible perspectives ranging from providing challenge to Eurocentric prejudice, through making the musical choices of a community more appropriately reflect the complex corporate web of hybridized identities commonly found in twenty-first-century churches;[32] or keeping people interested in the worship through variety in its music;[33] to just because they like the sound of it. These are only a few fragments of the whole, but, arguably, from any point of initial engagement, setting out a flexible roadmap that accurately charts the starting point and initial steps for the journey is more likely to facilitate rewarding travel than standing at the crossroads remaining perplexed by the multiplicity of potential routes, even if the journey eventually leads down somewhat unexpected paths.

When viewed through a postcolonial optic, the question takes on a more layered form. Issues of power arise in terms of who is directing the path of the journey and for what purpose. Do the church members want to tread this road? Or is the firm hand of the powerful – those who choose the music for worship – subjugating dissent, thus turning a well-intentioned desire for inclusion of a greater number of voices into a tool of oppression?

Conversely, there is consideration of what forms an appropriate concrete action[34] for the prophetic voice of liberation to be raised on behalf of the oppressed beyond empty verbalizing of concepts, where a congregation's worldview seems exclusively Eurocentric. There are no easy answers, but perhaps reaching fixed answers is not as important as being increasingly open to possibilities for growth through critically reflecting on our motives.[35]

But the questions of clarity about motive and starting point require careful consideration, if those white, Western, Christians such as myself are sincerely to act in solidarity with our marginalized sisters and brothers, by using our music choices to facilitate challenge within the framework of 'a new mode of imagining, a new cultural logic, posited over against the . . . colonial manner of thinking and visioning reality'[36] offered by the postcolonial optic.

Returning to reflection on my journey into jazz, these two issues have proved to be important to my growth. My awareness of and approach to my motives and starting point formed crucial differences between my two experiences of encounter.

In my social club years, I was well aware of my training as an art musician, and had a sense that it was not serving me well in jazz performance, but I was not conscious of how far I had internalized its norms of performance practice. My musical identity remained subconsciously grounded in art music, despite my temporary cultural translation into the popular music world, and I was bringing these technical and interpretative strategies to bear on texts and practices that were not part of that tradition. In effect, I was trying, without realizing, to assimilate the jazz texts and techniques into my art music world – an act of attempted cultural appropriation.

When I lived and worked alongside musicians whose musical identity had been formed by jazz cultures, the differences in our respective approaches to the music we were performing were made explicit, and I came to acknowledge and subsequently own my newly explicit cultural starting point, with its strengths, weaknesses, assumptions and prejudices. Consequently, it became clear where other approaches, worldviews, cultures and individuals might issue challenge and help me to see things differently.

This gradually became coupled with a fundamentally different approach to the encounter. Now it was not so much that I wanted to learn how to 'master' jazz, an aim that betrayed a somewhat colonial worldview, as I hoped to be drawn into that world to experience it and learn from it. Through the dialogue with jazz culture, I discovered, as classical pianist David Sudnow found before me, that I had to reconnect with my hands in a very different way as I began to work my way in from the margins and find musical 'place[s] to go' as a jazz pianist.[37]

At the time of writing I still hesitate to self-identify as a jazz performer, and the dialogue continues; I remain partially an art musician. The result of my years of dialogue, in the language of postcolonialism, has been that my musical identity has now become hybridized. Jazz has, along with art music, and other fragments from diverse musical worlds, partially shaped who I am as a musician and as a person. As I continue to reflect, I see that the dialogue of encounter has been transformative, but that it will always remain incomplete.[38]

Carrying this back to Anglophile churches' transcultural use of music, it could reasonably be said that in addition to being sensitive to the accurate hearing of cultural voices through music, communities of reception need to spend time critically making explicit their motives for the encounter and acknowledging their cultural starting points, with all that they embrace, if dialogue is to have the potential to be transformative.

Is that what gets results?[39]

Given the number of issues considered in this study, the question arises of how congregations might evaluate the effectiveness of their current journeys into encounter in order to prepare for their next stage. In some ways, it seems too early to judge adequately, as the first welcome wave of journeying is still underway. But Mary Oyer offers a model through which the task might begin to proceed.

She suggests, reframing the work of Thomas Troeger and Carol Doran,[40] that the music of a church community can be represented by a series of concentric circles around a central axis. The inner circle forms a 'structural' core that narrates the music 'central to its worship life'. The outer 'ephemeral' circle bears testimony to its 'brief and rapidly expiring' transient music choices. Between the two lies a 'conjunctural' circle that embraces music that was once 'ephemeral' but that has stood the test of time, albeit not yet to the point of being essential to a worshipping community. Oyer sees movement between the three dimensions as two-way, in which core items can lose their significance and, over time, migrate to the periphery or indeed cease to be chosen; and new choices assume greater significance.[41]

Consideration of the 'core' in Oyer's model over time could offer some valuable insights into the congregation of whom it speaks and the worldview it represents. For example, a growing presence of music from a number of cultures among structural choices could illustrate an increasingly hybridized musical identity in which a white-majority congregation has been challenged to subvert its Eurocentricity and has begun to listen afresh to historically marginalized voices. The continuing lack of such music in the core, despite its constant ephemeral presence, could be said to point towards musical tourism, and consequently identify the need for a fresh approach to encounter. These examples are deliberately polarized, but Oyer's model appears to offer considerable potential for critical reflection on whether encounter with music of other cultures has proved transformative or touristic.

Maybe this time [we'll] be lucky . . . [42]

Undertaking dialogic encounter with a cultural signifier as complex as music is inherently a journey of risk. But this transcultural journey looks to be too compelling to abandon in favour of the familiar. To explore is not necessarily to colonize. But as this study suggests, in order for such journeying to be more than touristic tokenism or cultural appropriation, white Christians need to be sensitive to a musical text's context of creation and the voices it carries; and be clear and honest about our motives and cultural starting point, including the prejudices they implicitly bear. How we best approach that, both for ourselves, and to help others to move off the ersatz hinterland of superficial engagement with culturally sanitized texts, would benefit from further reflection, study and debate. But that we must do it seems clear. As Mukti Barton writes:

> If White Christians have the humility to hear what Black people in the congregations, Black theologians and Black biblical scholars are saying then perhaps once again both Black and White people will begin to rediscover who they really are, created in God's own image.[43]

Notes

1 See particularly Paul Gilroy, *'There Ain't No Black in the Union Jack': The Cultural Politics of Race and Nation*, London: Routledge, 1987; Paul Gilroy, *The Black Atlantic: Modernity and Double Consciousness*, London and New York: Verso, 1993; Paul Gilroy, *Between Camps: Race, Identity and Nationalism at the End of the Colour Line*, London: Allen Lane, 2000.

2 Simon Featherstone, *Postcolonial Cultures*, Edinburgh: Edinburgh University Press, 2005, p. 33.

3 See Michael N. Jagessar and Stephen Burns, 'Liturgical Studies and Christian Worship: The Postcolonial Challenge', *Black Theology: An International Journal*, 5 (2007), pp. 39–62.

4 Stanley Samartha, *Courage for Dialogue*, Geneva: World Council of Churches, 1981, p. 100.

5 Jon Saliba, 'Dialogue with the New Religious Movements: Issues and Prospects', *Journal of Ecumenical Studies*, 30 (1993), pp. 53–4.

6 Israel Selvanayagam, *A Dialogue on Dialogue*, Madras: Christian Literature Society, 1995, pp. 2–3, Leonard Swidler and others, *Death or Dialogue? From the Age of Monologue to the Age of Dialogue*, London: SCM Press, 1990, pp. 70–1.

7 This section's header, a word play on the title of the 1929 Cole Porter song 'What is this thing called love?', has long been a standing joke for the jazz fraternity, illustrating the multiplicity of meanings potentially conveyed through a single phrase of a single song depending on the inflection used in its performance.

8 See Juan Oliver, 'Just Praise Prayer Book Revision and Hispanic/Latino

Anglicanism', in Ruth A. Meyers, ed., *A Prayer Book for the 21st Century*, New York: Church Publishing, 1996, pp. 256–85, for a fuller discussion of this issue.

9 There has been a long history of such writing, but among recent writers see Andrew Wilson Dickson, *The Story of Christian Music*, Oxford: Lion, 2003, ch. 14, Malcolm Budd, *Music and the Emotions*, London: Routledge and Kegan Paul, 1985; Jeremy Begbie, *Theology, Music and Time*, Cambridge: Cambridge University Press, 2000.

10 James White, *Introduction to Christian Worship*, Nashville: Abingdon Press, 3rd ed., 2000, p. 112.

11 Brian Wren, *Praying Twice: The Music and Words of Congregational Song*, Louisville: Westminster John Knox Press, 2000, pp. 349 ff.

12 Wilson Dickson, *Story of Christian Music*, p. 60.

13 Featherstone, *Postcolonial Cultures*, pp. 33–4.

14 Cited in Featherstone, *Postcolonial Cultures*, p. 36.

15 Gilroy, *The Black Atlantic*, p. 76.

16 Bill Ashcroft, Gareth Griffiths and Helen Tiffin, *Post-Colonial Studies: The Key Concepts*, London: Routledge, 2000, p. 9.

17 Featherstone, *Postcolonial Cultures*, pp. 40–1.

18 See Edward Said, *Orientalism: Western Conceptions of the Orient*, London: Penguin, 1978.

19 Featherstone, *Postcolonial Cultures*, p. 42.

20 John Hull, *What Prevents Christian Adults from Learning?*, London: SCM Press, 1985.

21 Myke Johnsont, 'Wanting to Be Indian: When Spiritual Seeking Turns into Cultural Theft', in Joanne Pearson, ed., *Belief Beyond Boundaries: Wicca, Celtic Spirituality and the New Age*, Aldershot: Ashgate, 2002, pp. 277–94, 281.

22 Art music is often referred to as classical music.

23 'Light music' is considered to form a bridge over the chasm between 'art music' and 'popular music'. Its forms, instrumentation and performance conventions owed more to art-music genres than those of popular music, although through the twentieth century there was an increasing level of cross-over.

24 In the late 1950s and through the 1960s 'clubland' formed a generic term signifying a complex hierarchical structure of clubs that presented live entertainment. In its 1960s heyday, 'clubland' consisted of a bottom tier of working men's clubs; a middle tier of service clubs and smaller cabaret clubs; and a top tier of late-night cabaret clubs, which commonly seated up to 2,000 people and presented revue-style entertainment in which many well-known recording stars participated. The top tier clubs were also gambling and supper venues. By the late 1980s, the time at which I began to work in 'clubland', it comprised only a common tier of working men's, service and social clubs.

25 Usually comprised of piano, bass and drums, and possibly including a guitar.

26 A term signifying one who is paid for performing but whose primary income comes from outside the entertainment business.

27 The issue of cultural identity among social club performers forms an interesting subject for further study in terms of the hybridity of musical identity formed through engagement with a large number of texts drawn from different cultures and musical traditions within a governing discourse of popular taste among audiences.

28 Wren, *Praying Twice*, p. 89.

29 Featherstone, *Postcolonial Cultures*, p. 42.

30 This title is drawn from that of a 1939 song written by jazz composer Sy Oliver.

31 Louise Diamond, quoted in Beresford Lewis, 'The Letter Kills But the Spirit

Gives Life', in Michael N. Jagessar and Anthony G. Reddie, eds, *Postcolonial Black British Theology: New Textures and Themes*, Peterborough: Epworth Press, 2007, pp. 30–50, 47.

32 See Helen Cameron, Philip Richter, Douglas Davies and Frances Ward, eds, *Studying Local Churches: A Handbook*, London: SCM Press, 2005, pp. 44ff; Nancy Ammerman, Jackson W. Carroll, Carl S. Dudley and William McKinney, eds, *Studying Congregations*, Nashville: Abingdon Press, 1998, p. 102; Paul Bayes and Tim Sledge, eds, *Mission-Shaped Parish*, London: Church House Publishing, 2006; Archbishops Council, *Mission-Shaped Church*, London: Church House Publishing, 2004.

33 Richard Giles rightly points out that an inclusive approach to music forms a priority for any congregation 'embracing liturgical renewal'. See Richard Giles, *Creating Uncommon Worship: Transforming the Liturgy of the Eucharist*, Norwich: Canterbury Press, 2004, pp. 70–1.

34 See Gustavo Gutierrez, *A Theology of Liberation*, London: SCM Press, 1974.

35 See in part Israel Selvanayagam, *A Second Call*, Madras: Christian Literature Society, 2000, p. 59.

36 Christopher Duraisingh, 'Towards a Postcolonial Re-Visioning of the Church's Faith, Witness and Communion', in Ian Douglas and Kwok Pui-lan, eds, *Beyond Colonial Anglicanism: The Anglican Communion in the Twenty-First Century*, New York: Church Publishing, 2001, p. 337.

37 Quoted in Begbie, *Theology, Music and Time*, p. 224.

38 Theologians such as Israel Selvanayagam and Kenneth Cracknell contend that a permanent expansive state of dynamic flux characterizes genuine dialogue.

39 A misquote of the second line ('That's what gets results') of the 1939 song 'It Ain't What You Do, It's the Way That You Do It'.

40 Carol Doran and Thomas Troeger, *Trouble at the Table: Gathering the Tribes for Worship*, Nashville: Abingdon Press, 1992, pp. 119–23.

41 Mary Oyer, 'Using Music from Other Cultures', in Charlotte Kroeker, ed., *Music in Christian Worship*, Collegeville: Liturgical Press, 2005, pp. 172–3.

42 Title of the 1963 song from the musical *Cabaret* by John Kander and Fred Ebb.

43 Mukti Barton, *Rejection, Resistance and Resurrection: Speaking out on Racism in the Church*, London: DLT, 2005, p. 97.

19

The Liturgy of Silence:
Quaker Spiritual Intimacy

PINK DANDELION

Early Quakers or Friends placed themselves on the edge of Christianity and of the society they lived in with their radical understanding of their place in biblical history and their consequent understanding of liturgy.[1] For these believers, Christ's second coming was unfolding in the world, experienced inwardly as part of a new covenant with God. This was a participational relationship which paradoxically led Quakers out of worldly action and worldly talk into a *liturgy of silence*, after Revelation 8.1. Worship was based in silence, only broken when participants felt led by God to speak. There was no single minister, no 'front', no outward symbols at all; indeed worship could take place anywhere and at any time. Everywhere and all times had become sacred. This silence was not about absence but about living in intimate relationship with God and experiencing baptism and communion inwardly, after Revelation 3.20. The text was of silence but also of the body. Silent 'unprogrammed' worship was not just equivalent and sufficient but was more authentic than other forms of worship. It placed these Quakers out of the world and out of time, as the future which all Christians waited for collided with the Quaker present.

Quakers in Britain today maintain the same form of radical liturgy: the use of absence to engage with and explore presence. Over time, Quaker theology has changed five or six times but the form of worship remains one of the ways modern 'Liberal' Friends find unity and create identity. They operate a 'behavioural' rather than a belief creed. Indeed, theology is marginal to the identity of the group and treated with caution. In a group based in seeking religious truth, all theology is 'towards' or 'perhaps'. So now the original theological basis of the liturgical form is itself at the edge of the life of the group, radical in its certainty and its relationship with just one faith. New innovative understandings of what is going on infuse the Quaker silence and the liturgies of intimacy with God and not with God are experienced in parallel. New contexts have subverted and reinvented the content of old forms. The 'language of silence', the liturgy of silence, ultimately protects itself and the group unity by still refraining from saying too much and by letting words be few (Ecclesiastes 5.2). Ultimately, the radical nature of Quaker silent liturgy is its ability to continually reinvent its meaning and its intimacies. It remains on the edge.

Early Friends

Christianity is a religion built on waiting. It has been constructed to help humanity remain faithful while waiting for the second coming of Christ, and the culmination of the prophecy of Paul and of the Book of Revelation. In Paul's letters, we find an increasing sense of needing to wait for a little longer before Christ comes again for all. This delay, this meantime, required the formation of a whole series of outward means to help humanity remember what they are about, in the interim. Thus, typically, Christian communities have separated people (ministers and priests), buildings (churches), and a liturgical calendar to help people remember and anticipate. Church liturgy performs the same functions of remembrance and anticipation. They are of 'this present age' and carry the 'mark of this world which will pass', being temporary and essentially meantime, no longer required when the end-time is realized. Church history has been about varying interpretations about how best to wait and about predictions that the time of waiting is now over.

The Quakers of the 1650s fit this pattern perfectly. The first Friends believed they had received a new dispensation in which the second coming of Christ was unfolding, a realizing eschatology. 'Christ is come and is coming' they claimed.[2] 'Is come' to the saints, the Quakers, and 'is coming' to the whole world. Atypically however, their second coming was experienced inwardly, affirmed by their reading of Jeremiah 31.31–34 and Revelation 3.20. At the heart of the Quaker faith lies the experience of direct encounter with God, and the vital and transforming experience that accompanied this for the first Quakers was described by the leaders of the movement in apocalyptic terms. George Fox, the founding leader of the movement, claimed he was taken up into a state beyond Adam, beyond falling.[3] The early Quakers claimed, wholly in line with Pauline prophecy,[4] to be guided directly by God, to be living by faith rather than by the law, to be set free from sin and to have moved into the spiritual adulthood Paul describes. They were the true Church but, significantly and optimistically, all – men, women and children – could be an equal part of the true Church. People simply needed to join the movement and leave behind the priests and ministers whose very authority was now anachronistic.

Essentially, these early Quakers were claiming that there was now a new covenant,[5] a new dispensation, a new sense of time, of God acting in and against the world, a spiritual reality further along the biblical timeline than where other Christians felt themselves to be. Quakers felt they were living in the fulfilment of the prophecy of Paul and of Revelation. This sense of second coming made all the temporary and strategic institutions of the Church redundant and indeed harmful as they continued to hold the people back from the new imperative. In 1 Corinthians 11.26, it talks of breaking the bread until the Lord comes again. For Fox and the other early Quakers, it was thus clear that this was no longer required. Their Communion was complete, after Revelation 3.20. As Fox claimed, the Church had the wrong supper and should now be celebrating the marriage supper of the lamb. The time of remembrance and anticipation was over. It was instead a time of being taken up to a new spiritual place. Quakers often signed their tracts in terms of 'known by the world as [e.g.] Edward Burrough, but truly only known by a few' (that is, the saints and God).[6] It was as if they had a worldly self but were now living outside of themselves in an intimate relationship with God who guided and gathered the movement.

Early Friends typically underwent a six-stage 'convincement' or conviction experience. God would break powerfully into their lives, in God's time, and the sins and shortcomings of their life to date would be revealed. This was a painful and often overwhelming experience. However, the same power or 'Light' which illuminated also offered the possibility of a regenerated life. Friends who repented and chose this new life talked of being transformed and of being able to resist sin. Their lives were changed (Quakers were very visible for their tendency to plain dress, plain speech and the refusal to swear oaths after Matthew 5.34, and to use 'thee' and 'thou') and their mission was to bring everyone into the true Church and work with God to realize the kingdom of heaven on earth. Importantly, this transformation was felt continually. The Christian calendar or particular liturgical observances all became redundant and no place was any more sacred than any other. When the Quaker John Luffe met Pope Alexander VII, he was asked 'But is there nothing to be done for the remembrance sake of our blessed saviour?' to which Luffe replied 'No, no, I have Christ about me and in me and cannot choose but remember Him continually'.[7]

In terms of worship, Quakers adopted a silent form which emphasized the inward nature of true spirituality and its non-worldliness in
extreme terms, and which could facilitate the expectant waiting shared
by all who were part of the priesthood. There was no need for anyone or
anything to be further separated and Quaker meeting houses were only
built as homes became too small to hold burgeoning numbers. Fox
quoted Revelation 8.1, that there was half an hour of silence in heaven
after the breaking of the seventh seal, to justify this liturgy of silence[8]
and to locate it within an end-time theology. It was the end of the old life
and the opening up to the new, the personal prefiguring the global.

As Richard Bauman shows, these early Friends eschewed text and
even outward language except that given them by God.[9] Silence was the
text, the space in which the living Word of Christ could be experienced
and embodied. Michele Tarter's study of the celestial inhabitation of
these early Friends, particularly women Quakers, shows how the body
also became a liturgical site.[10] The enacting of signs, moaning, groaning,
violent shaking, and of course quaking itself, were all part of the witness
which convincement could lead to: 'Ridding religious worship of all
icons and sacraments, including the rite of communion, the Friends perceived themselves as living texts of Christianity, the celestial flesh of a
millennial world'.[11] This open and free(d) form of worship, Tarter
argues, subverted patriarchal modes of liturgical performance.

Absence, leading to distinct sense of Presence, is a radical liturgy
which mirrored the radical claims of the early movement. In this new
time, all that had been necessary before was no longer needed. The
direct connection with God required no mediation and humanity
required nothing to help them remember what was about them all the
time. Anticipation was over as the end-times were realized and being
realized.

Meantime Quakerism

Quakers never named a date when the second coming would happen, as
it was inward and unfolding and were spared the particular disappoint-
ment of watching the calendar pass the expected hour. However, it was
obviously difficult to sustain these kinds of claims even given the huge
success of the movement in the 1650s. By 1666, when even that auspi-
ciously dated year, the plague and the fire of London, and destruction of
the English navy by the Dutch fleet, had still failed to dramatically
change the world around them, we find fewer explicit references to this

eschatological vision. In 1676, when second-generation convert Robert Barclay wrote his *Apology*, a systematic defence of Quaker theology,[12] he does not mention the second coming at all. The last section of the *Apology*, where you might expect to find such references, is devoted entirely to how to live in the world without becoming ensnared by it. This second generation was gathering itself for further delay, and needed to work out its own meantime strategy. Barclay, tellingly, argues over the meaning of 1 Corinthians 11.26 rather than claiming it redundant, pulling Quakers back along the biblical timeline.

It would have been perfectly legitimate and consistent to adopt a more formal liturgy to help remembrance and anticipation but direct encounter with God still lay at the heart of the Quaker experience, even without its end-time urgency. Quakers maintained their inward and silent liturgical form. Paradoxically, remembrance was facilitated by the increasing institutionalization of outward 'peculiarity' (after Titus 2.11). Plain dress (Quaker grey) and plain speech (the use of 'thee' and 'thou'), the numbering of days and months to avoid using the pagan names so that Sunday was the first day of the week, the refusal to pay church tithes or swear oaths, were all carried over from the earliest period but became both the mark of Quakerism and its membership criteria. Quakers were only allowed to marry other Quakers – the pejorative sense of the 'world' still included everyone not Quaker – and transgression of this or other practices often led to disownment. This was the 'gathered remnant' and falling numbers only affirmed the sense of being the true Church in a corrupt and corrupting world.

In the nineteenth century, British Quakerism became more evangelical and eventually abandoned these peculiarities for a more world-affirming and ecumenical sensibility. However, the liturgical form remained constant, that of worship based in silence in which anyone present may minister. Nothing else was needed but a place to sit. And wait. Wait for God's guidance as before but also wait in God's time for the culmination of scriptural prophecy. Quaker liturgy reinvented itself to meet the challenges of the meantime without changing its outward form. This ability to be creative and dynamic is all the more evident in the present day.

Liberal Quaker liturgies

At the start of the twentieth century, a younger generation of Quakers started to question the evangelical Quakerism in which they had been brought up. Fuelled by the fruits of biblical criticism and the optimism of liberal religion and a whig view of history, they chose to reinvent Quakerism away from both world-rejecting and self-denying mysticism and the authority of Scripture. They combined the emphasis the first Friends had placed on experience, with a sense of mission within the world's structures. They wanted their faith to be relevant to the age and open to new ideas and thinking so it would move with the exciting times. They adopted a theology of continuing revelation based on progressivism, the idea that God and God's will was increasingly revealed in each age, giving a chronological authority to the direct encounter which still lay at the heart of Quakerism. The liturgical form, so minimalist in anything explicitly religious, required no rethinking.

Probably unforeseen by these liberal Christians, the emphasis on experience, being open to new ideas, and progressivism, meant this new version of Quakerism need not be anchored to any text or any part of Quaker tradition. In terms of belief, this combination of characteristics led to a diversification of theology within 50 years, accelerated by the increasing number of those joining as adults instead of having been brought up as Quakers. Today, of the 85 per cent who convert into Quakerism,[13] half come from other churches, half from no previous religious affiliation. As early as the 1930s, the question of whether you have to be a Christian to be a Quaker was being asked and today there are Muslim, Hindu, Buddhist and non-theist Quakers amongst the group. In many ways the group is post-Christian simply in terms of how many use an alternative way of describing and making sense of their experience.

Quakers have historically opposed creeds, and in the twentieth century this position affirmed a general disinclination against theology per se as a rational approach, increasingly suggested that words could never get close to the experience, and that theology was trying to be over-exact and was possibly demeaning of what it was talking of. It could also give rise to a false sense of surety or complacency undermining the continuing search which progressivism made normative. Thus theology became privatized and, under the silence of Quaker worship with its lack of vocal confession, often invisible. Theology became a personal story, a way of making sense of the experience of silence, but not something true, at least not true beyond the personal, provisional or partial. This 'perhapsness' about theology characterizes the present-day liberal tradition of Quakerism and has come to be held, paradoxically, with great certainty. It is what I have called the 'absolute perhaps',[14] that out of a rational place, Quakers have become very certain that within the religious enterprise and spiritual quest, they can only ever be uncertain. It is a very different position from other religious groups who generally are sometimes uncertain of their certainties. It makes Quakers suspicious of groups who claim to have the truth, and those who find rather than perpetually seek within the Quaker movement sometimes leave the group.[15]

Theology is thus marginalized and relatively unimportant for the group (while still significant as an explanation system for the individual). Asked what Quakers believe, members typically respond in terms of their liturgical form: 'we have no separated priesthood, no outward sacraments, no hymns'.[16] It may look like an evasion but these kinds of responses are locating identity in the liturgical form, not in any one specific theology. What we can see from this is that the Quaker liturgical form is absolutely central to how liberal Quakers define their Quakerism (unlike other kinds of Quakers in the world), but also how Quaker liturgical form transcends specific theological descriptions.

The centrality of Quaker liturgical form and its highly developed tradition of absence leading to presence is its own form of credal system. But rather than a belief creed, these Quakers operate a 'behavioural creed', a creed of form. While belief is marginal and plural, the form of Quakerism is held to with conservatism and conformity. All kinds of codes and rules 'wrap' and protect the open form and help manage the unmediated.[17] Those having a crisis of faith need not leave a group which places so much emphasis now on the search, but those who dislike the silent worship form find themselves in tension with other Quakers. It is form that defines liberal Quakerism.

As such, this liturgical form transcends any particular theological description. Its radicality now lies not in its end-time authenticity but in its ability to shape and be shaped by the theologies of those who use it. Obviously, those Quakers who are not Christian are not waiting for the second coming of Christ. Indeed, they may not even believe in the first coming. In these terms, post-Christian Quakerism is not operating an end-time or even a meantime liturgical form, even if its roots as such are so clear. Rather, the radical liturgy of silence has been co-opted by new theologies, in which absence can lead to a whole manner of description of presences, or not. Indeed, within the single liturgical form, largely unchanged for 350 years, liberal Quakers are now operating a series of liturgies. In common with other liberal churches, definition is individualized and only outward form is held in common. However, even in this pluralistic form, the silent liturgical forms subvert normative preconceptions of the liturgical, and of the liturgical year. While some Quakers celebrate Christmas now, still no one day is any more special than any other.

Fragmentation is avoided through a 'culture of silence',[18] a critique of the spoken word and the extreme value and multiple use given to silence. In other words, the emphasis on silence precludes sharing disparate theologies in detail or as a matter of course. Ignorance, but also the marginalization of belief, helps maintain unity. Silence is still the means to that beyond the material and the natural place for Quakers to dwell. A postcard reads 'I am a Quaker – in case of emergency, please be silent.' The humour is true. Quakers still critique the outward, still emphasize the authenticity and sufficiency of an inward encounter. And while some Quakers mourn the loss of a Quaker Christian orthodoxy, this orthopraxis maintains the space in which anything may happen. Pluralism today can shift to something else tomorrow. As individual members change their theology without difficulty within the framework of worship, so the group can. Only where theological diversity undermines the theological basis of silence itself might the power of this radical liturgy start to diminish.

Remaining on the edge

The beginning of the Quaker movement was based in an understanding and experience of the unfolding second coming of Christ. As a result, liturgical forms which had merely anticipated these end-times were now redundant, and the Quaker liturgy of silence was a direct consequence of this eschatological interpretation. It did away with all the meantime practices of the other churches and created a shared priesthood with unmediated access to God. Theirs was an inward and embodied spirituality, enhanced by silence in collective worship and by faithful witness outside. In the twenty-first century, Quakers in Britain hold a very different theological outlook. Gone is the certainty of being the true Church and the group theological ethos is based upon seeking.[19] In this open space, where theology is usually held personally and privately, and provisionally, the liturgical form, as minimalist as it is, has become definitional of the group. This group is not theocentric or Christocentric but praxis-centric. Here, the radicality of the liturgical form takes on a new hue, that of the ability to transcend any single system of belief, but also to create the space in which the seeking Quakers can turn in any direction. There is even the possibility that they could return to their end-time roots. Quaker liturgy remains on the edge.

Notes

1 For liturgy, I am using Rahner's definition of 'the worship conferred to God by the church'. Karl Rahner, ed., *Theological Investigations*, Volume 7, London: Burns & Oates, 1975, p. 854.

2 D. Gwyn, *Apocalypse of the Word: The Life and Message of George Fox, 1624–1691*, Richmond: Friends United Press, 1986, p. 206.

3 J. Nickalls, *The Journal of George Fox*, Cambridge: Cambridge University Press, 1952, p. 27.

4 See T. Ashworth, *Paul's Necessary Sin: The Experience of Liberation*, Aldershot: Ashgate, 2006.

5 See D. Gwyn, *Covenant Crucified: Quakers and the Rise of Capitalism*, London: Quaker Books, 2006.

6 P. Dandelion, *The Liturgies of Quakerism*, Aldershot: Ashgate, 2005, p. 35.

7 W. C. Braithwaite, *The Beginnings of Quakerism*, London: Macmillian, 1912, p. 424.

8 Although worship would often last many hours, vocal 'ministry' could be given by anyone present as and when they felt led by God.

9 See R. Bauman, *Let Your Words Be Few: Symbolism of Speaking and Silence Among Seventeenth-Century Quakers*, Cambridge: Cambridge University Press, 1983.

10 See M. L. Tarter, 'Sites of Permanence: Theorizing the History of Sexuality in the Lives and Writings of Quaker Women, 1650–1800', Unpublished PhD thesis, University of Colorado, 1993.

11 M. L. Tarter, 'Quaking in the Light: The Politics of Quaker Women's Corporeal Prophecy in the Seventeenth-Century Transatlantic World', in J. M. Lindman and M. L. Tarter, eds, *A Centre of Wonders: The Body in Early America*, Ithaca, NY: Cornell University Press, 2001, pp. 145–62.

12 See R. Barclay, *Apology for the True Christian Divinity*, Glenside: Quaker Heritage Press, 2002 [1678].

13 P. Dandelion, *A Sociological Analysis of the Theology of the Quakers: The Silent Revolution*, Lampeter: Edwin Mellen Press, 1996, p. xxv.

14 See P. Dandelion, 'Implicit Conservatism in Liberal Religion: British Quakers as an "Uncerain Sect"', *Journal of Contemporary Religion*, 19 (2004), pp. 219–29.

15 See P. Dandelion, 'Those Who Leave and Those Who Feel Left: The Complexity of Quaker Disafiliation', *Journal of Contemporary Religion*, 17 (2002), pp. 213–28.

16 Dandelion, *Liturgies*, p. 69.

17 See P. J. Collins and P. Dandelion, 'Wrapped Attention: Revelation and Concealment in Non-Conformism', in Elisabeth Arweck and William Keenan, eds, *Materializing Religion: Expression, Performance and Ritual*, Aldershot: Ashgate, 2006, pp. 45–61.

18 Dandelion, *Sociological Analysis*, ch. 6.

19 See P. Dandelion, 'From Religion to Ethics: Quaker Amillenialism', in K. Flanagan and P. Jupp, eds, *Virtue Ethics and Sociology: Issues of Modernity and Religion*, Basingstoke: Palgrave, 2001, pp. 170–85.

Part 6

Mediating Liturgy

Introduction

How is liturgy – the work of the people – communicated and mediated through images, technology and global communication? Is worship dependent on media? What is the relationship? These are only some of the questions raised in these essays. The eclectic nature of this section is not only indicative of the breadth of topics that can be covered in this category; it also underscores the evolving shape of this area of focus in our postmodern and post-technological age. The continuing global trends and our world of YouTube, virtual reality and MTV further suggest that liturgical shape, space, practice and theology must continue to engage critically with media.

'Water into Wine: Transforming Worship' by Paul Collins heads up this section and is located in a specific context – one of relative comfort yet with people on the margins. The essay traces one congregation's effort to employ multimedia technology in seeking to connect with a variety of people from across a city. The author locates and discusses the creation and impact of the process and ways in which liturgy can work to transcend and challenge conventional notions of space and time.

The essay by Peter Privett entitled 'The Garments of Gethsemane as Models of Ministry' is a personal reflection on some of his textile work. Discussing the story behind these pieces of liturgical art, Privett, a priest, textile artist and theologian, not only explores the potential of the garments to unfold both focal and unfamiliar themes in the liturgical calendar; he also explores the message they communicate in the specific context of models of ministry.

Creative and critical would be words to describe the final essay in this section. Gary Hall's '"I Dreamed about Ray Charles Last Night": Reflections on Liturgy and the Machine' is a timely exploration and scrutiny of some key insights related to the use of the electronic media in Christian worship. Hall asks that if worship is formational and implicitly political how then will community be nurtured in the electronic age to live a liberated and liberating life in society? Mindful that communication is key in liturgy and that learning/cultivating/nurturing the habits of liturgical participation is crucial in creating space to encounter transcendence, Hall rightly observes that media as a medium in this process is merely preliminary and perhaps provisional. Yet electronic gadgets can assist in the formation of disciples and in relatedness to the divine, one's neighbour and the world. In spite of the danger of recolonizing minds and bodies, Hall argues that the multimedia architecture can give agency to memory and engagement.

Among other things, the essays in this part raise different questions about the very nature and understanding of 'edges', the focus of this volume. How, for instance, will one position oneself in relation to the diversity within edges? What of this complexity of 'edges' given that communication media and globalization have punctured our proclivity towards rigid understanding of location and relatedness? Fluidity, ambiguity and liminality may be operative words here. But they do challenge any attempt to bring closure on edges.

20

Water into Wine:
Transforming Worship

PAUL M. COLLINS

Context and the origins of the idea

St Paul's Church lies to the north of the city centre of Chichester and relates to people across the city alongside the cathedral and three other Anglican parish churches as well as Roman Catholic, Free Church and House Church congregations. Church attendance remains relatively high in Chichester as it does across much of Sussex. In the city of Chichester, there is a broad cross-section of worship traditions and styles from which to choose. The main Sunday morning congregation at St Paul's is made up of a spectrum of ages and social backgrounds. The worship style might be positioned as central churchmanship, with eucharistic worship being central to the life of the congregation, expressed in a generally traditional ethos and style. However, the congregation is open to and used to experimentation with drama and dance particularly at the monthly all-age or all-together worship. Prior to the event in January 2006, there had on occasion been the use of multimedia technology such as data or overhead projectors at the main Sunday morning Eucharist. This had generally been used to project worship songs, but on one occasion there had been a PowerPoint presentation on the shape and contents of the eucharistic liturgy. The congregation has been served by the ministry of a youth worker for several years. The current youth worker has been using multimedia technology in a variety of contexts including a monthly evening worship event, for more than a year. The congregation at the main Sunday morning Eucharist is usually in the region of 175 adults, with approximately 50 children of school age.

The idea of using the church space with a multimedia style of worship arose, it might be said, accidentally. In the autumn of 2005, as a result of requests from the congregation, a monthly short teaching session following worship on Sunday morning had been held on 'liturgy'. One of the sessions was devoted to understandings of liturgical furniture and artefacts. During this session, it was highlighted that seating in churches was unknown in the 'Early Church' apart from the stone bench around the walls of the nave. Mention was also made of Augustine of Hippo's sermons where he describes the use of this open space by the congregation: assembling first to hear the proclamation of the word around the ambo and then celebrating the sacrament around the altar. It was reflection on the possibility that the space of St Paul's could be similarly used, since the fixed pews were replaced some years ago by movable chairs, that led to the event on 22 January. There is some precedent for using the space of the church differently in that over the last few years the arrangement of the church has been changed for Maundy Thursday. On this occasion, the altar has been moved into the body of the nave and the chairs arranged in a semicircle around it, to facilitate the washing of feet and a more intimate atmosphere to celebrate the Eucharist of the Last Supper.

'Brainstorming' and planning

The process whereby the initial idea was taken forward was through an informal, ad hoc set of meetings and conversations. The rector of St Paul's and I met initially to clarify what we thought might be possible/appropriate and to settle on a date on which to hold the event. January was chosen in particular in the hope that the day might not to be too bright with sunshine! St Paul's is a very light and open building and there are issues about using the projection of images and texts because of this. The result of this meeting led to a series of meetings, which included five of us in all: the rector, myself, the curate, the youth worker and the director of music. We held three planning meetings plus a 'rehearsal' on the Saturday morning prior to the event. The rector also consulted with churchwardens during this planning process to dialogue with them and to keep them in the loop of what was being considered and planned. The congregation were also given some (tantalizing) indications of what was being planned on the weekly pew sheet for several weeks prior to the event.

The basic concepts of the worship event with which we worked were first: that the worship would be a Eucharist, second that we would seek to free up as much space in the church building as might be appropriate, and finally we would use multimedia technology to project images and texts to complement the open space; thus facilitating worship without the use of worship books or leaflets. The experiment was undertaken to encourage more thought about all-age worship, and to have the opportunity to consider some of the usual elements of worship in a different style of worship which would include celebrating different aspects of the liturgy concurrently, thus providing a synchronic dimension to the liturgy which would express 'gathering' in a different way from usual.

The theme of the event was taken from the Gospel passage set for the day: the narrative of the wedding at Cana in John chapter 2. Celebration and transformation were identified as the focus of what would be communicated during the worship. The event was planned as a one-off experiment and we sought to be simple/obvious/user-friendly. As part of this strategy we decided to use the device of a 'disembodied' voice to introduce and explain the different parts of the event and its rituals as it proceeded. So a female member of the congregation was asked to be 'animateuse' in order to complement the currently all-male clergy of the benefice.

In planning the event we sought to remain clearly aware of the context of the space of the building, the expectations of the congregation, and the technological hardware to which we had access and our skills in using it. We also remained aware of the limitations that the time available to prepare for the event placed upon us. As a result of holding these opportunities and constraints in mind we settled on the following format of the liturgy for 22 January. The event would include a dramatization of the gospel, and three concurrent activities following it, in which penitence and intercession could be expressed as well as sacramental anointing be made available. Following the concurrent activities the congregation would be asked to reassemble for the eucharistic part of the celebration. Thus gathering would be expressed by the congregation in synchronic events as well as the usual collective style. With a majority of the chairs removed we planned to share the Peace, the Eucharistic Prayer and the distribution of Holy Communion in a large circle around the nave and sanctuary spaces of the church.

As an expression of the wedding theme of celebration two decisions were made; first to extend the eucharistic feast by having more refreshments on hand than the usual tea, coffee and biscuits at the conclusion of worship and also to use home-baked bread for both Holy Communion and a distribution of blessed bread to everyone present, reflecting traditions in the early Church as well as contemporary Eastern Orthodox practice. So as well as asking a member of the congregation to bake a special loaf we also arranged for wine and soft drinks and finger food to be brought into the assembly at the conclusion of worship. The sense of gathering was thus given further dimensions, particularly by attempting to extend the eucharistic fellowship within the worship space itself.

To enhance the sense of celebration we decided to use a digital video camera as a means of projecting images of the congregation, particularly as members arrived and assembled in the nave. Also projected was a prepared looped sequence of images and text as a direct expression of the wedding party theme, as well as a PowerPoint presentation of all the liturgical texts and song texts used throughout the event. This was governed by the availability of three data projectors, at least two notebook computers and a digital camera (none of which belong to St Paul's).

We also gave considerable consideration to the music to be used during the event. We decided to use a combination of very well-known items and some less well-known and even some new items. St Paul's has a strong musical tradition, with a large choir of adults and children. We felt that incorporating and using these resources in the event would be crucial. We chose a simple song of African origin ('Come all you people') as the gathering song, and an Iona chant ('Take O take me') as a communion song; with traditional hymns for the Offertory and Post-Communion ('Alleluia, sing to Jesus' and 'Dear Lord and Father'). St Paul's usual setting for the Eucharist, the Thorne St Thomas setting would be used for the Sanctus, Benedictus and Agnus Dei; while the Coventry Gloria by Peter Jones would be used for the first time. Alongside these pieces it was planned that choir and other musicians would sing and play during the three concurrent events; including responsorial psalms, and plainsong accompanied by flute improvisations in the style of *Officium* by Jan Garbarek and the Hilliard Ensemble.

Practical preparations

Various practical preparations had to be made, which included the making of a screen for the projection of images. A screen had been made and used prior to this at various youth events; on this occasion a larger screen was constructed to facilitate back projection from the chancel to the screen suspended in the chancel archway. The data projectors needed to be sourced and hired, and these tasks were allocated at our preparatory meetings. As well as arranging for the basic hardware to be available, it was also important to check that we had the requisite leads to connect DVD player, notebook computer and digital video camera to the projectors. Other crucial tasks were the looped images, which needed to be sourced and recorded to DVD, and the PowerPoint presentation of texts, which needed to be prepared. Also an outline script for the anima-teuse was drawn up in conversation between myself as the presiding minister and the volunteer from the congregation undertaking this task.

Finally it was important to have a rehearsal time on the Saturday morning when we sought to eliminate any technological problems and to situate the various elements needed for the concurrent events as well as setting out such chairs as were to be left in the body of the nave in a 'U' shape including the font situated towards the centre of the rear of the nave where the rites of penitence would be taking place. Cards with rubrics, prayers and scripture texts were prepared for the various stations in the church and attached church hall, baskets for bread, prayer cards and a bowl in which to burn incense were all identified and made ready on the Saturday.

The shape of the liturgy

- Gathering – pre-recorded music.
- 'Come all you people' – unannounced.
- Animateuse welcomes the congregation and introduces the celebration.
- The presiding minister greets the people.
- All pray the collect for purity.
- The Coventry Gloria.
- Collect of the Day.
- Enacted reading of the Gospel, John 2.1–11.
- Animateuse explains the next stage of the liturgy in its three concurrent parts.
- The three synchronic activities of penitence, intercession and anointing.
- Animateuse recalls the congregation together and explains the eucharistic part of the worship.
- All gather in two concentric circles for the Peace and the Offertory: offertory song.
- The Eucharistic Prayer.
- Holy Communion is distributed to the congregation.
- The bread for general distribution is blessed.
- Post-Communion prayers, concluding song and blessing and dismissal.

- Drinks and light refreshments are brought into church.
- The blessed bread is taken to the west of the nave together with the prayer cards for distribution.

The texts of the liturgy[1]

Come all you people, come praise your maker,
Come now and worship the Lord.[2]

In the name of the Father, and of the Son, and of the Holy Spirit.
Amen.

The Lord be with you
and also with you.

Almighty God,
to whom all hearts are open,
all desires known,
and from whom no secrets are hidden:
cleanse the thoughts of our hearts
by the inspiration of your Holy Spirit,
that we may perfectly love you,
and worthily magnify your holy name;
through Christ our Lord.
Amen.

The Coventry Gloria
Glory to God, glory in the highest,
peace to his people, peace on earth.
We worship you,
glory in the highest,
give you thanks
glory in the highest,
praise you for your glory.
Glory to God, glory in the highest,
peace to his people, peace on earth.
have mercy on us,
have mercy on us,
receive our prayer
receive our prayer
Glory to God, glory in the highest,
peace to his people, peace on earth.

The Collect of the Day

Dramatized Gospel (John 2.1–11)

Three concurrent events

Offertory Song (Alleluia, sing to Jesus)

The peace of the Lord be always with you
And also with you.

Eucharistic Prayer D (Common Worship) and other texts in the Communion rite

The Lord be with you
and also with you.

Lift up your hearts.
We lift them to the Lord.

Let us give thanks to the Lord our God.
It is right to give thanks and praise.

. . .

Holy, holy, holy Lord,
God of power and might,
heaven and earth are full of your glory.
Hosanna in the highest.
Blessed is he who comes in the name of the Lord.
Hosanna in the highest.

. . .

This is his/our story.
This is our song:
Hosanna in the highest.

. . .

Blessing and honour and glory and power
be yours for ever and ever.
Amen.

Our Father, who art in heaven,
hallowed be thy name;
thy kingdom come;
thy will be done;
on earth as it is in heaven.
Give us this day our daily bread.
And forgive us our trespasses,
as we forgive those who trespass against us.
And lead us not into temptation;
but deliver us from evil.
For thine is the kingdom,
the power and the glory,
for ever and ever.
Amen.

We break this bread
to share in the body of Christ.
Though we are many, we are one body,
because we all share in one bread.

Lamb of God,
you take away the sin of the world,
have mercy on us.

Lamb of God,
you take away the sin of the world,
have mercy on us.

Lamb of God,
you take away the sin of the world,
grant us peace.

God's holy gifts
for God's holy people.
Jesus Christ is holy,
Jesus Christ is Lord,
to the glory of God the Father.

Take, O take me as I am,
Summon out what I shall be,
Set your seal upon my heart;
And live in me.[3]

Almighty God,
we thank you for feeding us
with the body and blood of your Son Jesus Christ.
Through him we offer you our souls and bodies
to be a living sacrifice.
Send us out
in the power of your Spirit
to live and work
to your praise and glory.
Amen.

Concluding Song (Dear Lord and Father)

Blessing and Dismissal

Texts for the three concurrent events

Texts for penitence

[a] As we come to meet God in the company of
each other:
choose one of the stones . . .
consider the hurtful things you may have said
and done
during last week;
and the things that have hurt us . . .
hold the stone
over the Font . . .
and as you let it gently drop into the water
let go of your hurts . . .
feel that your hurts are healed and forgiven.

[b] Hear our Lord Jesus as he says to us:

You are forgiven . . .

You are loved . . .

Amen.

[c] And when Jesus saw their faith, he said, 'My child, your sins are
forgiven.'
Mark 2.5

Texts for intercession

[a] As we stand in God's presence today consider those places in the
world and those people you know for whom you wish to pray . . .
Take a few grains of incense . . .
and gently sprinkle them over the charcoal in the bowl . . .
as the fragrance rises in the air . . .
know that God receives them in love . . .

[b] Choose a card and write on it the name of someone for whom you
would like prayer.
You may if you wish just write the person's first name and perhaps
the reason for holding them up to God this week.

[c] When he had taken the scroll, the four living creatures and the
twenty-four elders fell down before the Lamb, each holding a harp
and golden bowls full of incense, which are the prayers of the
saints.

Revelation 5.8

Texts for anointing

[a] God in Christ offers each person forgiveness, healing and wholeness;
as a sign of these great gifts is the Church's ministry of anointing
and prayer . . .

If you wish, a priest will anoint you as a sign that God bestows
upon you these wonderful gifts . . . .

[b] Are any among you sick? Call for the elders of the church and have
them pray over them, anointing them with oil in the name of the
Lord. The prayer of faith will save the sick, and the Lord will raise
them up; and anyone who has committed sins will be forgiven.

James 5.14, 15

[c] You love righteousness and hate wickedness. Therefore God, your
God, has anointed you with the oil of gladness beyond your companions; your robes are all fragrant with myrrh and aloes and
cassia.

Psalm 45.7, 8

Some feedback and reflections

In the weeks before the experimental celebration the weekly pew sheet had encouraged people to bring large cushions so that they might sit on the floor of the nave; a substantial number of people responded to this idea and when worship began there was the sense of something like a large-scale picnic in the midst of the nave.

The synchronic celebration of penitence, intercession and anointing allowed the congregation to enter into these components of the liturgy with fresh insights. This synchronic activity also allowed people to experience the sense of gathering together in a totally different way, enabling them to choose in which elements to participate, and indeed to some extent how they would participate in each component. This also prepared for the different format of collective gathering for the Eucharistic Prayer.

Given the relatively large number in the congregation there were inevitably queues for the three concurrent events, particularly in the nave space for the font and the two stations for the intercession prayers. However, this did not seem to trouble people; indeed even the children seemed taken up in consideration of the particular features of the rite in which they were about to participate. Thus on the whole although there was conversation during the period of the events, the overall ambience was one of recollection and purposefulness.

The suggestion of using incense to express prayer was taken up by many in the congregation; so much so that a dense cloud of incense appeared in the nave. This was certainly troubling for some members of the congregation; however, when the liturgy moved into the offertory for the eucharistic stage of the rite the bowl of incense was removed.

The ministry of healing (the laying on of hands with prayer) is offered at St Paul's on a regular basis after each main Sunday morning Eucharist. Anointing is less frequently celebrated; however, there was a steady number of people seeking this ministry and for them it proved an important element of the celebration and its emphasis on transformation.

Members of the congregation easily formed themselves into a couple of concentric circles around the nave and sanctuary space for the Peace, Eucharistic Prayer and distribution of Holy Communion. It was this element in particular which for myself was transformatory, in the sense that this large congregation was able to instantiate its gathered-ness and fellowship in a way which normally is simply not possible, when the church is arranged in its usual layout of an 'auditorium'.

At the conclusion of the liturgy the sharing of food and drinks, the blessed bread and the distribution of the prayer cards from the intercessions all helped to reinforce the overall ethos of the experiment of transformation and celebration. Also, the rector appealed for feedback from the congregation and many people did provide feedback. Some said that they had come along with some trepidation, feeling rather nervous or sceptical, but had found the experience reassuring and prayerful; indeed some commented that doing the liturgy in this way had made them think much more about what they were doing and why they were doing it, than they usually did week by week. Certainly for some people there was a much greater sense of being together and being involved in the different parts of the liturgy. This leaves us with the sense that there is the will and potential to do something like this again.

Notes

1 The texts of the liturgy are largely drawn from *Common Worship: Services and Prayers for the Church of England*, London: Church House Publishing, 2000, Order One, pp. 166ff.

2 In John L. Bell, *Come All You People: Shorter Songs for Worship*, Glasgow: Wild Goose Publications, 1994, p. 14.

3 In Bell, *Come All You People*, p. 88.

21

The Garments of Gethsemane as Models of Ministry

PETER PRIVETT

Introductory note

This piece is based on a sermon delivered for All Souls Day, 2003, in the Chapel of the Queen's Foundation, Birmingham, where my art installation, the Garments of Gethsemane, had been on display for several weeks. As appropriate for All Souls Day, I used each of the four Garments as a starting point for reflecting on various contemporary 'saints' – 'saints' being understood in a broadly inclusive way as the company of those, both within and beyond the confines of Christian faith, whose writings and lives have touched, inspired, stimulated or moved me with some kind of insight into the call of the gospel.

In the first part of this reflection, I introduce the Garments themselves, offering general descriptions and reflections on the four Garments, the art materials from which they are made and some of the kinds of ways in which I invite participants to engage with them. In the second part of the reflection, I offer a meditation on the Garments exploring different facets of ministry, suggesting how each of them might represent four diverse yet complementary models of ministry.

Given that this piece was originally delivered as a spoken address, meditative in nature, I have attempted to retain something of the original 'feel' of the piece, at the same time as adding in explanatory notes – since the reader is not in the presence of the art installation as the original hearers were.

The Garments of Gethsemane

They are called the Garments of Gethsemane: an art installation consisting of four pieces of clothing about six feet high in red, purple, green and white (the four main liturgical colours reflecting the cycle of the liturgical year), arranged on large A frames so that each one stands upright. On each Garment – variously designed in contrasting colours and fabrics, made with a mixture of machine and hand sewing, using dye, paint and printing techniques, and adorned with beads, bones, leaves and other items – numerous scriptural texts are embroidered, sewn and written.

Originally, I had planned to include images and quotes from contemporary issues, events, newspapers and so on, sewn into the Garments, but the more I searched the more difficult it became. Then, suddenly, the idea came to use words from the Bible. The more I searched for these the more I became aware that they spoke to the present time. The words of the biblical writers still have a power that speaks to our world today. Why was I surprised? The verse: 'because they sell the righteous for silver and the needy for a pair of sandals' (Amos 2.6), for example, is still relevant as big corporate companies constantly search for cheap labour in the poor world.

The four Garments explore the suffering and hope of the world. Each explores one particular aspect. A small instruction beside them says:

> You are invited to touch and handle the garments to discover the texts . . . You may want to use the beads, bones, leaves etc. as a tactile stimulus for prayer and meditation . . . You may want to engage in conversation with others or be quiet with the garments . . . You may even want to imagine what it might be like to inhabit them or wear them . . .

These are key phrases, which break the conventional established barriers between works of art and those who view them, between the artist and those who look at the artist's work. For me as the artist, the invitation involves risking grubby fingers and careless hands as I invite people to explore through the senses.

The Garments were commissioned for a conference for the diocese of Hereford in 2002, which had as its theme 'Gethsemane – Making a Heaven out of Hell'. The process of making them was, in itself, an extraordinary journey of self-discovery, prayer, lament, mourning and discovery of new life, at a time in my own ministry of major change and loss. Having been made and put on display for others to touch, look at, ponder and respond to, the Garments continued on their own journey, eliciting different responses from those who knew nothing or little of my own context and exploration.

The Garments have been used by many different groups: as a focus for a healing service with the Garments acting as starting points for intercession; as stations or foci for meditation – people have been known to sit inside them, and the different texts have been written on small pieces of paper for people to take away; as a focus for preaching in Lent and Holy Week; as a focus for continuing discussion (people have written their own thoughts in a book that accompanies them).[1]

The Red Garment

[Made of cotton, silk, synthetic fabrics: dyed, painted, and printed, gold paint, metal and cotton threads and beads]

The Red Garment describes the pain of the world. Different fabrics pull against each other revealing splits, gashes, and wounds. The pain of hunger, exile and exploitation has dire consequences for all of us. The fabric of society disintegrates under the weight and tension. But it is not only human society which is pulled apart; the earth itself feels the weight of our actions. Indeed the whole of the created order is affected.

While looking for texts I began to read the Lamentations of Jeremiah. Whether this is a historical description of the ten-year siege of Jerusalem or whether it is a poetic piece of ritual didn't seem to matter. The starkness of the words struck chords; texts such as those in Lamentations 4.10 – 'the hands of compassionate women have boiled their own children' – seemed to speak of the possibility in each of us. Note, these are not wicked or inhuman women. The description is 'compassionate'. When we are pressed in on every side, desperate, pushed to the edge – this is what we might all do.

Each Garment is accompanied by a set of meditational questions inviting exploration. The Red Garment asks:

- What are the most important texts for you?
- Do you have any experience that is similar to these?

There are also blank squares and spaces sewn into the Garment.

- What texts or comments would you write here?
- Which texts would you wish to have removed from this Garment?
- What contemporary situations and events would you bring to this Garment?

The Sackcloth Garment

[Ripped linen, cotton, muslin; dyed and painted; beads, bones, shells, cotton and wool threads]

The Sackcloth Garment reveals the feelings and emotions as suffering is experienced. The Garment is made from ripped strips of material – life is shredded.

Many of the quotes are from the Psalms and the prophets. There are numerous references in the Bible to people ripping their garments as a sign of their sorrow, repentance, shame and despair. Was this a spontaneous act or a piece of ritual? There is the obvious question of: 'Why has this happened?' The experience is not only emotional, or of an inward spiritual suffering, since the body is definitively affected: 'my bones are out of joint' (Psalm 22.14). There are also feelings of fury, anger and a desire for retribution: 'take your little ones and dash them against the rock' (Psalm 137.9).

The questions accompanying this Garment are:

- Which texts do you respond to?
- Have you ever felt the same?
- How do you express your anger, despair, pain, frustration?
- What situations, feelings, emotions, would you like to add to this Garment?

The Green Garment

[Recycled clothes, curtains, string, dyed muslin with hand printed leaf prints, silk, painted by Yarpole Youth Club[2]]

The Green Garment explores promises and hope for renewal. It is more fragile, delicate and sheer than the others, speaking of the fragility of hope. The texts are sometimes hidden and you have to search for them. It is significant that each of the Garments is linked by a golden chord. Hope does not stand apart from the others. In no way does this Garment deny the pain and anger of the previous two. Hope comes because of the two other stages, not in spite of them.

The Green Garment asks the following questions:

- Which text do you think is the most important?

- Where do you find signs of hope and encouragement in the world?
- What would you add to the blank spaces on the leaves?
- What might have to change to enable hope to flourish?

The White Garment

[Linen strips, metallic threads, nails, white muslin lining]

The White Garment is made from strips of white linen. It is a coat that is not all sewn up, a coat accompanied by a scarf of nails – a reminder that there is no cheap resurrection. Resurrection is not in spite of crucifixion. It is because of it. Here is a coat that waits to contain the others.

When I had finished making this Garment and placed it on the stand with its white muslin lining, I was struck by the space created inside. It looked like a tomb and a womb – was it waiting to receive or an empty-ing out?

While searching the concordance, I came across numerous references to linen. It is the material for priests set out in the Mosaic law. It is the clothing associated with renewal and promise in the books of Ezekiel and Daniel. It is 'the righteous deeds of the saints' in Revelation (Revelation 19.8).

References to clothing and garments in Scripture are also numerous. They often suggest more than just outward apparel. The robe wrapped around the body of the prodigal son signifies restitution, forgiveness, restoration. Even the hem of a garment swishing through a crowd becomes a source of healing for a woman who has been marginalized by her bleeding. Marginalized, she touches the margins of his clothes.

The White Garment asks these questions:

- Where and when are there times of restoration today?
- What other texts would you add to this coat?
- What are your dreams for the world?
- What contemporary situations can you add to this coat?
- When and where do situations become transfigured and transformed?
- Who would you wish to remember here, and what might be their 'righteous deeds'?

The Garments and glimpses of models for ministry

The Red Garment: a ministry of intercession

The Red Garment was the first to be made. It was originally to be a banner with images depicting the pain of the world. But my amateur skills and inadequacies were to the fore. It didn't occur to me that the different weights of material would pull against one another. So gashes and holes started to appear – initially to my dismay. I began fighting with the material, imposing my will on it, and finally threw it in a corner with cursing and annoyance. A few hours later I returned and, ever the exhibitionist, draped it over my body; suddenly I saw the possibility of it becoming a garment. The rips and the tears were exaggerated and became wounds. They also became the garment's mouths and orifices. Let it speak for itself. Let it give birth to new possibilities . . .

Intercession, according to the *Oxford Dictionary*, is to plead the cause of the other. It implies standing alongside them to enable them to speak. Intercession is the naming of stuff. To remain unnamed is not to exist. To be unvoiced is to be oppressed. Silence, in this negative sense, is to be ignored. Naming brings power, recognition and insight. As Paulo Freire has said, 'To exist humanly, is to name the world, to change it'.[3] The word brings order into the chaos, offering alternatives to the status quo, new possibilities. Naming articulates deep needs, desires and hopes.

The world dominions, powers and empires want the opposite. They desire silence, behaving oneself, keeping quiet and not rocking the boat. This is the manifesto at the heart of all oppression.

Nor is naming only an affair of language or words, at least as narrowly understood. Articulation gives form and body, gives substance. Intercession therefore is about incarnation, that is, it is about being immersed into a situation. This Garment calls us to a ministry of pleading the cause of another, to stand alongside another, to be incarnate, to challenge those who wish silence to be the norm. It is not just a liturgical activity. It is a pedagogical, educative, political and a pastoral venture. This ministry of intercession has at its heart a desire and hope that people will be able to name their own stuff to plead their own cause. It is, ultimately, not a lone, individual, spiritual task, although at times it will be done alone. But it is a community task which challenges our modern preoccupation with individualistic self-concern.

The Purple Garment: a ministry to help articulate the unspeakable

The Purple Garment (the Sackcloth Garment) was intended to be an emotional response to the Red Garment. It shows the other side of suffering. It is about lament as well as joy. This Garment expresses a ministry of the articulation of emotions. It represents the power of the non-verbal which, as we saw above, is part of the work of intercession.

A growing body of evidence proclaims that much of human trans-action is not what you say but *how* you say it and the body language that accompanies this. So perhaps a key aspect of ministry is enabling people not only to find and give words, but also to give expression to the powerful, non-verbal side of their lives and experience.

When confronted with the torn, broken, bleeding pain of the Red Garment, the response may well be to look into the abyss and scream a primal 'No!' There is a need to provide a space where this may happen; where grieving is allowed and despair is recognized. Reconciliation is a ministry that acknowledges the ancient tradition of the Tragic, inherent in the works of the ancient Greek myths which tell us that in facing the abyss, we face the ultimate truths of our humanness.[4] Richard Holloway speaks of such an experience of the abyss in which he is 'invaded by a terrible sense of ultimate meaninglessness . . . engulfed by the void, made to look into the abyss of emptiness that life seems to be stretched upon'.[5]

There is a real challenge which confronts all ministers and pastors: to resist the false messianic desire to fix it. As pastors faced with the abyss, with the primal 'No' of others, deep fear of the abyss can be stirred within ourselves. The experience of the other awakens the rawness in our own souls and psyches. The Purple Garment calls us to the essential and powerful ministry of being able to sit alongside the other in their pain and anguish – a ministry of presence, of not offering advice. Carol Shields gives an example of just such presence in her novel *Unless*, in which she tells the story of Norah, the daughter of professional parents who drops out of university and sits begging outside a large department store in Toronto. Her parents desperately want her to come home, for things to be as they were, for it all to be made better. Her sisters, how-ever, offer an alternative response, and give up their school games sessions on Saturdays to go and sit alongside their sister on the street.[6] Unless we have stared into the face of the abyss ourselves how on earth can we face that in others?

The status quo, the powers and dominions want us to behave, to keep everything under control, to kiss and make up, to deny the raw truth of our existence, to cover everything with a wonderful sugary coating of love and to deny that there are differences. But we are called as pastors to do otherwise.

The Green Garment: *a ministry of finding, storytelling, remembering and celebrating shoots*

This Garment is made from recycled clothing: old curtains, scraps and discards, remnants and my old trousers! The texture of this Garment is really slippery, making it difficult to arrange. It is a looser and more fragile robe. You have to search for the texts here. It tangles sometimes and never sits how you want it to! It is free and uncontrollable.

I would like to suggest that this Garment calls us to a ministry in search of story – story which sometimes lies hidden, ambiguous, not yet named or formed within a person, a community or an object; story which is sometimes non-verbal, yet needing to be spoken. Walter Brueggemann suggests that the task of second Isaiah was to awaken the memory of Israel: to get them to tell and remember their deep stories. The task of Isaiah in exile was to help people remember their stories, to fight the giants of amnesia which resulted in them thinking that the Babylonian empire was permanent, enduring, absolute and perpetual. The powers and dominions want people to forget, to be homogeneous, to sing from the same hymn sheet and to ignore their roots, their differences. [7]

Therefore this Garment also calls us to a celebration of difference and diversity – and this is, again, a community task rather than something that can be achieved by any one person. It is a task that will need co-operation with others and with those of goodwill, whatever their name, identity or conviction. It calls us to a ministry of surprise – surprises that come from unexpected quarters. It is also a ministry of creative imagination, the ministry of 'what could be'. Such a ministry calls us to take seriously not only the tradition of the Tragic associated with the Purple Garment, but also to wear its sister garment and embrace the tradition of the Comic. Sally Vickers speaks of this tradition in the notes to her novel *Mr Golightly's Holiday*, drawing on the work of the literary critic Northrop Frye, who suggested that

temperamentally, we tend to favour either the tragic or the comic outlook. It was his contention that Dante, Shakespeare and the authors behind the New Testament were, in essence, finally comedians –

hence *The Divine Comedy* – by which he meant not that they were a fund of belly laughs but that ultimately they saw life as more powerful than the forces which conspire against it.[8]

The White Garment: a ministry of the hospitable space, of enfolding

Two powerful images have been associated with this idea of offering hospitable space and enfolding. The first is the popular medieval image of Piero della Francesca's Madonna of Mercy, which depicts the Madonna holding out her cloak and gathering people beneath it.[9] The other is Hildegard of Bingen's extraordinary vision of Mother Sophia in which she sees Lady Wisdom as a momumental regal figure bearing, in the centre of her bosom, a woman in red surrounded by a great tumult of persons brighter than the sun, all decorated wonderfully with gold and jewels. These are the daughters of Sion and with them are the lyres and musicians who play them and every type of music and the voice of perfect merriment and the joy of joys.[10]

The White Garment was completed on the Eve of Easter (Holy Saturday) and forms a meditation on John's Gospel. It is made of strips of white linen: white, which I have since discovered, is ambiguous in biblical imagery, since this was the colour of the clothing of priests and Levites but also the colour of leprosy – hence, the colour of both decay and glory. Perhaps this ambiguity is also suggested in the stole of nails which adorns this Garment. John will not let us see resurrection without the crucifixion. In fact it may be for John that the death *is* the resurrection. Yet even though I was well aware of this theology, I did not expect the power of the finished effect when I put the completed Garment on to the stand and was struck by the space created inside the Garment – a space that looked like both a tomb and a womb.

Associated with this garment is the enigmatic reference to the spices at the burial of Jesus, which John tells us weighed 100 *pounds* (John 19.39). This is a vast amount, something like 150 bags of sugar. If we consider our usual way of buying spices in small 16 gram jars, then try imagining 3,200 such small pots! How did Nicodemus and Joseph get this amount of spices there? It would have almost doubled the weight of the body. How did they carry this weight?

We are suddenly transported out of the world of reality, I suggest, and into the mysterious realm of symbol. Suddenly we are taken from the end of the Gospel to the beginning and that extraordinary story of the wedding at Cana which is, similarly, marked by enormous quantities – this time of wine: some 180 gallons, nearly 1,000 bottles (John 2.6) – more than enough for any wedding. The generosity of wine and the generosity of spice suggest that we are called to a ministry of utter abundant generosity: to a ministry of generous hospitality and of generous space.

Other texts also hint at this ministry of generous hospitality: the father's embrace of the returning prodigal son and his provision of a new 'garment' for a huge celebration (Luke 15.20–23); Jesus' commands to the disciples to love one another (John 15.12–17) mirrored by his own example of washing their feet (John 13.3–5) – these and other such texts speak of the radical nature of the hospitality Christians are called to exercise. There is no place here for meanness of spirit or nitpicking. There must be space for everybody. Hans-Ruedi Weber, in his seminal study of the biblical view of children, argues that the story of the blessing of the children (Mark 10.13–16) indicates far more than a mere pat on the head from Jesus. Rather, Jesus' touching of the children was a messianic gesture of immense significance. Weber refers to a rabbinic treatise which speaks of the resurrection of the people of Israel when God embraces, then presses them to his heart and kisses them, thus bringing them into the life of the world to come: just so does Jesus embrace the children.[11] And a key aspect of this is that the children have no merit; it is a totally gratuitous act. Hence, this welcoming space is intended not for those who have earned it or who say the right things or who proclaim the right doctrine. Christ's act of utter generosity is totally counter to our human desire to control or place conditions.

This Garment therefore calls us to the folly of gratuity, to the ministry of the prophetic alternative, to a ministry of grace, to a ministry of blessing whose purpose is to call out the good in the other.

Notes

1 Some of the comments include the following: 'The first impressions were of the artistic use of shades of one colour for each garment'. 'The texts are so moving, hard hitting, thought provoking.' 'It's a unique experience; I would wear this garment to remind me of what life is all about and Easter at this time where conflicts in the world need our prayers.' 'I have come to the conclusion that the nails on the White Garment are trophies.' 'Wow – made me think, ponder, consider and worship a God who dares to get messy with us.' 'They are the best aid to prayer I have ever seen.' 'A sense of flow within the stillness of life, solidity and the spaces in between . . . as I believe in all expressions of faith, not purely Christian. The messages are relevant beyond that.' 'I'm immediately drawn to the Green Robe. . . . Jack O the Green, Herne the Hunter, the

cycle of life with this being rebirth after the white of buried promise.' 'A beautifully moving expression of ideas through pain to the peace.' 'This is disturbing and enlightening.' 'I would remove the words from the Red Garment, "The hands of compassionate women" because the ending is so grievous and contradictory or retain the words in order to learn the meaning of compassion in 2006.' 'All we have to do to decide what to do with the time given to us.'

'May everyone be happy/May everyone never be separated from their happiness/May everyone be free from hatred and attachment/From the hearts of all the holy beings, streams of light and nectar flow down/Granting blessings and purifying.' [*Comments from a Buddhist nun*]

2 Yarpole is a small Herefordshire village three miles north of Leominster. A small group of 9–13-year-olds from the parish youth group were involved in an all-age silk painting project that created new vestments for the parish church and were so productive that a surplus green painted vestment was used in the Garments project.

3 Paulo Freire, *Pedagogy of the Oppressed*, New York: Continuum, 1970, p. 88.

4 See Denys Turner, *The Darkness of God*, Cambridge: Cambridge University Press, 1995 and Melvyn Matthews, *Both Alike To Thee*, London: SPCK, 2000.

5 Richard Holloway, *Looking Into The Distance*, Edinburgh: Canongate, 2004, p. 10.

6 Carol Shields, *Unless*, London: HarperCollins, 2002.

7 Walter Brueggemann, *Hopeful Imagination*, London: SCM Press, 1986, pp. 109–30.

8 Salley Vickers, *Mr Golightly's Holiday*, London: Fourth Estate/HarperCollins, 2003, p. 354.

9 Birgit Laskowski, *Piero della Francesca*, London: Konemann, 1998.

10 Matthew Fox, ed., *Illuminations of Hildegard of Bingen*, San Francisco, CA: Bear and Company Inc., 1985, p. 70.

11 Hans-Ruedi Weber, *Jesus and the Children: Biblical Resources for Study and Preaching*, Geneva: World Council of Churches, 1979, p. 19.

22

'I Dreamed about Ray Charles Last Night':

Reflections on Liturgy and the Machine

GARY HALL

In Joan Osborne's dream about Ray Charles, the great man regains his sight and loses his creativity; because he is mesmerized by MTV. There is a final warning from Ray to 'be careful what you're wishing for, 'cause when you gain you just might lose'.[1] New ways of seeing can be exciting and mesmerizing; access to new technologies brings both potential and risk.

What we have gained or lost with the burgeoning of digitized culture is a matter of comparison, of relativity and of opinion: too many variables, too much subjectivity. We might, however, begin to identify pertinent questions about the meaning and effect of electronic media – meaning digitized music, sound samples, video and other projected images, computer-generated ambience – in the construction of liturgical space for Christian worship. What the following remarks are *not* about is the phenomenon of online pseudo-worship (and online virtual life in general) – though it may be interesting to speculate whether, in the face of media saturation and relentless distraction, computer-mediated communication will eventually eclipse regular gatherings of Christian people.[2] There is much to be said about developments in Christian web presence which, however well-meaning, clothe what is essentially a serious and demanding faith tradition in the weightless garb of parody.[3] But I will leave that virtual conversation aside for now, along with pragmatic discussion of, for example, images projected to illustrate talks in church (which seems to be more about the confluence of worship and pedagogy) or about autocue to replace hymn books.[4]

These things matter, but I am trying instead to identify whether more fundamental issues are at stake when electronic media are used to fashion or complement the liturgical landscape of Christian worship, ritual which (just to be clear) involves congregated bodily presence and collective intention. The issues highlighted will undoubtedly reveal my particular preoccupations, ideological convictions and perspectives on society, functioning 'as a kind of religious and cultural Rorschach test, where what the researcher sees is often a projection of their own values, hopes and concerns'.[5] I acknowledge from the outset, and from a position of easy access, the remarkable and exciting phenomena of recording and communications technologies; I frequently enjoy cinema, television, multilayered music events; computers, internet and mobiles have become almost indispensable at work and home. Yet, I want to take seriously, for example, Jean Baudrillard's (melancholic and pessimistic) assessment of media-saturated late-capitalist culture – the culture in which many of us live, worship and have our being.[6] Baudrillard's themes – of 'mediatization' and loss of contact with 'the real', of pastiche and hyper-reality, of simulation and the colonization of consciousness, of complicity with a culture of consumption – need to be picked up in a conversation about worship. Worship is not detached from the facts of its particular sociocultural context. If worship is formational (of persons, community, worldview) and implicitly political, then how is community nurtured, how are prophetic and liberating words heard and imbibed, and how are participants equipped to live a liberated and intentionally liberating life in the world?

Idealization, receptivity and the blurring of edges

We can idealize the worship event as formative and transformative, dispelling delusions, dragging us from our dull preoccupations and self-concern in order to continually relocate us in the heart of the particular reality where we seek to live well as disciples. This has not necessarily been our regular experience of worship events. Personally, matters were not greatly improved when in due course I became responsible for the preparation and leading of worship. Ventures into multimedia liturgical events were prompted in part by a desire to animate Christian narrative for an absent people, and in part by our frustration with the way in which routinized patterns of worship were simply not connecting – with our hearts and minds, our ordinary yet complex lives, a postmodernist mindset or our God in the world. The problem seemed to lie not simply in the inherited language and styles of liturgy and hymnody, but rather in the way those things were being adopted and performed – or not. As though the words and gestures, the ritual and story were somehow not being *occupied* in any full-bodied sense. Something else seemed to have taken possession of our hearts and minds, even (dare I say) of our souls.

This book is about edges – borderlands, liminal spaces, margins. Edges can be uncomfortable places to be, but may equally be romantic and non-committal. From a life of relative privilege and security it would probably be fatuous to imagine myself being 'marginal' in any meaningful sense.[7] If I have sometimes dallied along a precipice or wandered in borderlands, I have usually done so by choice, with the option of returning to familiar securities. Cosseted by and large against the relentless anxieties and random dangers experienced by much of humanity, the only edges which some of us need to contend with are the blurred, evaporating edges of our disarmingly fluid identities and the sense of a world experienced simultaneously as immediate and global, tangible and virtual. We may want to push against boundaries, which have become suffocating, while all the time witnessing televisual episodes from distant lives, some of which we aspire to, others which alarm us as they teeter on the edge of survival. Their *distance* is part of our present reality, a reality which overall can be either disorienting or exciting, oppressive or expansive. I certainly do not wish to dismiss the potentially paralysing or destructive sense of struggle within people who can appear to be comfortable and secure; neither can I underestimate the potentially alienating experience of a guilty bystander's perspective in a media-saturated world. But I do want to raise the question of where each of us is located and where we *feel* we are located, for communications media have modified our sense of location and relatedness to other lives, and determine the nature of our interaction. The very notion of 'edges' has become radically complex. The perspective assumed in the idea of 'being on the edge' is continually open to change.

Image-driven and computer-dependent media effectively shape our perspective on the world (and our place in the world), not least when more threatened lives and threatening worlds encroach on our consciousness, occasionally creeping under our skin and across the barricades erected around our fragile yet desensitized psyche. Other people's edited realities are regularly piped into our routine existence – persisting, insisting, intermingling with crass or inconsequential entertainment which is also piped through the same channels and received in the same way. Images of conflict, struggle and climate chaos linger amid our other experiences of stability, contentment and 'fun', occasionally building to a crescendo and eclipsing playfulness with foreboding. 'And yet the catastrophe remains mostly an awareness "in the mind", not in the heart. It generates depression but not grief, apathy but not resistance. People seem to be becoming more and more the voyeurs of their own downfall.'[8] Which experiences are most real? Which call for full-bodied response? Are we filling our lives with distraction from realities too intense, too frightening to bear? Or, on the other hand, 'what if our cultural environment increasingly expects, imagines, provides for and nourishes panic? And has no sure means of affirming or restoring the actual "time of the self", the wider mental world?'[9] Discerning priorities for intentional faith-based action is as complicated as working out how to act effectively *at all* in the midst of distant lives which merge with online social networking and experiences of our immediate environment and interactions. These and other dilemmas of the 'postmodern condition' are present with us in a worship gathering.

Worship is not just for me or about you

So we might best assess the use of multimedia technologies in worship not as a distinct question, but in relation to the sociocultural meanings with which they are laden, the physiological and psychological effects they can catalyse, and the particular theological/ideological moods which undergird each liturgical event. Those 'moods' can be established by the person leading or preparing worship. They may equally be determined by the collective personality of a congregation. When we started developing multimedia worship events as a small group in Leicester, one aspiration was to counter the excessive focus on and influence of particular personality – an established trait in some Protestant worship traditions and a core element in contemporary celebrity culture. Personality can impose itself just as effectively, even amplified, through a multimedia event, whether or not the worship leader appears as a disembodied voice.[10] Nevertheless our conviction was that video, ambient music, electronic art installations and chant could be useful ingredients for establishing (effectively anonymous) liturgical forms which work against the anti-participatory and potentially distracting reliance on the particular personality of a worship leader or director. We imagined the inherited liturgical forms of monastic traditions as functioning in a similar way, 'holding' and drawing in the worshipper to a ritual more expansive than the immediate needs and mores of a particular gathered people. Not that we wanted to lose ourselves in any but a gospel sense,[11] nor to overwhelm or disregard the particularity of each unique congregation, each unique worshipper, but simply to improve the chances for each participant to be held within a worshipping community, released enough to process some of the media-intensified flux of life experience, and thereby shed excessive self-concern in contemplation of our fragile and glorious interdependence. The intention was not to make worship more 'popular' (it didn't) or 'entertaining' (sometimes it was), but rather to safeguard liturgical spaces and practices where the gospel story might be re-presented, entered into, contemplated in full-bodied fashion, where Scripture narrative might more easily be heard in relation to wider global concerns. Clive Marsh describes a simple way in which film can be used liturgically towards this end:

> The interplay of the three voices – biblical text, filmic text, preacher as interpreter – then invites the hearer (worshipper) into the interpretative act. The presence of three voices itself counters the view that preaching is simply a matter of an authoritative interpreter *telling* the congregation what a text *means*. The use of film thus contributes to the notion of God 'speaking' in between and through the multiple voices seeking to interpret the Word of God (in Scripture and world) today.[12]

Liturgies shaped and tested over generations carry the remnant of witness to divine encounter stripped of distracting personality, in order to hold and engage the glorious, global variety of personalities who continue to reanimate those liturgies. To that extent, liturgy is not designed to address our individuality: its significance is precisely in the fact that it does not, and thereby has the potential to release us from the current plague of hyper-consciousness and the flattery intrinsic to a mediated, simulated culture. To take off our shoes and enter into Yahweh's 'I am that I am' rather than watching ourselves in a mirror singing Gloria Gaynor's 'I am what I am'.

The immediate difficulties and counter-cultural implications are evident to anyone living with media-saturated adolescents, or to those familiar with local worship consultations where the conversation is regularly about personal preferences, boredom or what might appeal to absentees. Anxiety about the lost sociocultural habit of meeting for worship is voiced in bitter or nostalgic terms, but rarely do we acknowledge that mass media saturation is intrinsic to a highly organized, domesticated society used to living in a world designed to meet needs and desires (while continually generating more) and where we expect to be endlessly and individually *addressed*. When worship or preaching deviates from this cultural expectation, there can be disquiet, irritation, disorientation. Those living in an environment where a high premium is placed upon stimulation, gratification and choice are liable to bring those cultural values and habits into the sanctuary. Electronic media in worship can unintentionally reflect those values and habits, simulating a virtual environment which further distances a worshipper from a world we cannot choose to control. Yet the liturgical event *could* contradict cultural habits, by allowing complex and uncomfortable feelings which arise to be held, faced, chanted, offered up, accepted as source of insight and connection with reality, rather than being overlaid by recordings of pan pipes and videos of blue whales. This same tendency to avoid difficulty and to generate falsely peaceful (or 'happy') emotion in worship precedes the use of electronic media; the point being made here is that those media can perpetuate the same problem. But they don't have to: liturgical landscape which opens the participant to the God who simply *is* and which contributes to the formation of disciples preparing to engage with others-as-other and with a world which (in one sense) simply *is* will be experienced quite differently:

> In a mediated world, the opposite of real isn't phony or illusional or fictional – it's optional. Idiomatically, we recognize this when we say, 'The reality is . . . ,' meaning something that has to be dealt with, something that isn't an option. We are most free of mediation, we are most real, when we are at the disposal of accident and necessity. That's when we are not being addressed. That's when we go without the flattery intrinsic to representation.[13]

Sound-and-light machines can be enchanting in the best sense, or can be hypnotic.[14] They can assist our formation as disciples, our dialogue with and relatedness to God, to the natural world and to other lives close at hand and far away – or they can mesmerize as effectively in church as they do in the home or dance club. Worship leaders can feel pressed to grab and hold the attention of a people – and particularly of children – socialized into the role of passive-yet-demanding audience rather than that of collaborator. The resulting loss can be interpreted as a surrender of vital spaces, of the expansive 'indifference' of inherited liturgy which welcomes without indulging or diminishing us. It is quite possible, on the other hand, to rediscover and reclaim vital breathing space, 'metaphorical space',[15] through thoughtful use of expansive and restorative electronic imagery and sound. Images can be metaphoric and conducive to worship, as long as we attend to what the likes of Neil Postman had to teach us about the effect of television culture on our thinking, knowing and learning.[16]

'If you don't eat your meat you can't have any pudding'

For liturgy is learned. Actors need to know their scripts, particularly if they are to improvise well. Those of us schooled in the days before electronic cut-and-paste, for whom Christian worship has been part of the fabric of ordinary life, carry a legacy of language and habit which is now, here, rare. We absorbed and repeated sung or spoken words which did not always carry immediate or self-evident meaning for us; the meanings gradually came to birth as the words and ideas – heard, learned, digested even unintentionally – took root. In the ordinariness – which could admittedly be dull, odd, disengaged, distracting, irritating – ritual and language somehow formed and connected us. The legacy was ours, yet did not belong to us; it required effort while supporting that effort and making it fruitful and satisfying. Worship at its best tended to carry us into a reality deeper, richer and infinitely more vast than our local gathering and current fashions, thereby liberating us.

Effort, slowly absorbing language and meaning, learning ritual . . .

I'm conscious of how strangely alien the ordinariness of our particular past lives now seems. I'm not sure how it matters that my children's generation cannot experience the same as *ordinary*. Perhaps it does matter if theological realities only gradually dawn on us as we live with and savour them, as we wrestle with epiphanies and poetics in a communal, ritual setting.

> My kids laugh at me when I tell them about life when I was 14. They say, 'Go on Dad, tell us again'. There were no Walkmans, videos, Nintendo or Xboxes, no internet, no mobiles. No computers. No DVDs. There were only three TV channels. They cry laughing. But it made us hungry and thoughtful. And we had great things like the Sex Pistols. We're breeding a generation who won't invent anything. They've got everything. They're stimulated all day and they're never bored. I think there should be an hour of boredom every day for all kids.[17]

A media-saturated culture, a culture where cursory reading and rapid response to streams of undifferentiated information, images and noise and jolts is almost necessary, may be inhospitable to the very notion of a critical mass of worshippers willingly awaiting some chemistry between faith-story, emotions and perceptions. That kind of attention became retro half a century ago when the hypnotic power and social engineering of television easily stole hearts and minds away from worship ritual, from a gathering designed not so much for entertainment as for creative commitment.[18] In practice, the potential chemistry between Spirit and spirits had long been at risk of being smothered beneath a blanket of banality or the burden of unrealistic expectation (or of none at all). Indeed, routinized worship events implicitly run the risk of becoming detached from any evident experience of the numinous, past or present, and of becoming self-referential, ineffectual or desolate.

It is at this juncture, in certain contemporary contexts, that electronic, image-driven media were introduced in an attempt to reconnect with a more expansive consciousness. Learning from the aesthetics and methodologies of rock events, club culture, blues bars and cinema, worship architects have attempted to re-create a liturgical setting within which heart, mind, body and soul are freer to encounter, discern and respond to God in a way that revivifies and realigns daily living. But the experience of a rock concert, nightclub or blues bar – however uplifting, unifying, inspiring, cathartic – is *not* equivalent to the experience or intention of liturgical worship: the power of Christian liturgy lies in its capacity to evoke, align, order and integrate the collective experience of Christian people.[19] And it requires work. The art of mutual, continuing commitment implicit in liturgy is not required in the other events, and may be simply bewildering to an over-stimulated existence prone to 'the flattery intrinsic to representation'. The 'vicarious religion' described by Grace Davie as characteristic of modern European Christianity only works when *someone* performs and sustains the ritual, when *someone* remembers.[20] We may be entering a period where those who carry the memory of Christian worship are as vital and rare as the book people of Ray Bradbury's dystopian *Fahrenheit 451*.[21] Gutenberg's transforming technologies during a previous pivotal epoch brought all the advantages of a printed Bible, and arguably ushered in a new era of forgetfulness (*'It's written down; why bother to remember it?'*). Forgetfulness reaches another level when learning by heart is replaced by the crude cut-and-paste transfer of information from one virtual space to another. Life and its representation become pastiche. At which point we are ripe for colonization by whatever charms or deceives us. Recorded, amplified and projected media are less malleable than written text and therefore prone to turn participation into observation of a performance; and these newish media are, in their very nature, illusory and potentially hypnotic.

Redeeming the dreamtime

Multimedia architecture may, nevertheless, function as an aid to restoring habit and memory rather than further eroding memory and engagement. Ambient recorded plainsong may awaken yearning to chant a collective response to God; the projected video of wilderness or universe may – with their implicit 'I am that I am' – move us from self-preoccupation to self-occupation; vast light images of Christ Pantocrator may evoke the actual question, 'Who do people say that I am?', and prompt a recovery of desire for life in all its fullness. Gospel kerygma may be reanimated, and representation may lead to full-bodied engagement. What is lost may be found.

On a more or less monthly basis for a few years in the centre of Leicester, we co-created a small venture in what was then called multimedia worship. 'Multimedia' did not always imply *electronic* media, though in practice that was usually what we meant. One of those *eden* events was reported as follows:

> Descending to the basement at Bishop Street, you can sit and chill on sofas, surrounded by images projected onto gauzy screens in the dimly lit room – Celtic icons, video media/art and intricate patterns. Your senses are then presented with food for contemplation and worship which stimulates the brain and stirs the soul . . . . Palm Sunday. Big-screen images of Jesus entering Jerusalem, from the animated film *The Miracle Maker*, fuse with slow-motion footage of JFK riding towards assassination and Nazi parades cheered by adoring crowds. David Bowie's 'Heroes' provides the soundtrack, complemented by monastic chant and rip-hop from Bristol group *Massive Attack*.
>
> There is poetry, spoken not from the front but from the back, where the team have set up an impressive bank of computers, amps, video projectors and mixing equipment. There is intentionally no visible preacher to distract from the full-sensory, absorbing environment.
>
> The congregation is invited to create a trail of scarves, paper and candles, which provide a focal point for reflecting on Palm Sunday and all it preceded. Chanted prayers, images and music fill the basement. At the end, people just sit and continue to reflect, or talk over coffee . . . We imagine a friend, into clubbing and dance culture but definitely not church, feeling at home here.[22]

The chanting, the prayers, the people sitting and continuing to reflect and talk together, these were unremarkable – except in the context of a cultural aversion to stillness and attention, laced with the risk of being confronted by vivid reality which refuses to be contained or ignored. Such unbidden confrontation is unnerving at the best of times, yet there seems to be an indispensable element of fear in approaching the sacred. This threshold fear we have learned to avoid, having collectively forgotten where it might lead. Stillness itself is systematically avoided or shattered in the battle for commercial attention. When contemplative fear mingles with the anxiety which stillness itself can now give rise to (these two things are sometimes indistinguishable), then an instinctive response might understandably be to quell the anxiety by flooding the stillness. Another song, frenzied prayers, entertainment of one kind or another . . . There are myriad ways of doing this in a worship context, and electronic media multiply the options. A certain skill and awareness are required if this game is to be avoided.

The anxiety aroused by stillness may be experienced more acutely by (typically younger) electronic-dependent people, which only increases the temptation to make use of those media. Kalle Lasn describes a scenario where young people are taken camping and thereby deprived of their familiar stimulants:

> If you have read Elisabeth Kubler-Ross, you will recognize that the stages your kids are going through – denial, anger, depression, bargaining – closely mimic the stages of grief, as if they are adjusting to a loss. Which in a real way they are: the loss of their selves. Or rather, the loss of the selves that feel most authentic to them. Their mediated selves. Those selves that, when disconnected from the urban data stream, cease to function.[23]

What happens to a people who spend ever-greater proportions of life in fabricated virtual experiences is gradually being understood and documented.[24] More immediately, we can watch a child, rarely still or relaxed without electronic accessories, sitting motionless and silent for hours before a screen. The prospect of passing a day without electronic stimulation causes visible anxiety and symptoms not unlike chemical withdrawal. Having escaped the tyrannies of one form of enslaving religion[25] and shunned obligation to social expectation or 'duty to God', later generations willingly place themselves with lowered resistance before the suggestive power of media grooming, where new fears are both created ('*Am I keeping up? Do I look good? Am I noticed?*') in order to be abolished, with the simple purchase of the right product.[26] It takes little imagination to recognize the emergence of a new spirituality of indulgences whose relentless stream of *muzak* evaporates essential, unsponsored space. When, at the same time, the very notion of what is real is continuously besieged, then much is at stake when we bring video and ambient music into a worship environment amongst people conditioned by other experiences of mediated culture.

Yet we continue to do it. Because there are instances when sound-and-light machines can serve an effective liturgical purpose in providing a threshold to a point of attention and functionality which might otherwise be a step too far. And there is another reason: namely that these media technologies and styles are inextricably woven into the fabric of many lives.

> No individual, if he wishes to influence others, is totally free to choose his own style of action and persuasion: he is subject to constraints imposed by the culture in which he finds himself. If communication is to take place, there must be constraints which are recognized by both the speaker and his listeners, the artist and his public, the leader and his followers. Utterances that are interminable or spasmodic; artistic works or performances without recognizable form; leadership which appears random or impractical – all these fail to communicate because they do not work within the constraints imposed by the rhythm of human activity and the conventions of culture and civilization.[27]

Accepting and dispelling fear

Communication is part of the equation; learning the habits of liturgical participation is another part. Electronic media might beckon people towards the edge of a less guarded encounter with transcendence. 'I am afraid to be alone with great music because I am afraid to be alone with my inner self, with my potential self, with (if you will pardon the expression . . .) the self of the world' writes Evan Eisenberg. He continues: 'the fear of music and the fear of silence are the same. Both can be allayed by talking, reading or moving about.' But there can be spaces, occasions, where the fear is more bearable, where it need not be allayed so readily, where the instinct to guard against the chaos of our dispersed identities can be resisted, because there is trust in the possibility of being loved.

Comparing the experiences of music and of silence, Eisenberg describes how great music can more easily be listened to in a concert hall than at home, on the one hand because not much else can be done in a concert hall, and on the other because 'the burden of the music is shared and so easier to bear, as a pulpit sermon is less onerous than a personal rebuke'.[28] We can create an event where shared attention is strongly encouraged (because it's difficult to do something else) while being made more bearable than it would be in isolation. Film, ambient or evocative music, well-chosen projections can serve that purpose if great musicians, vocalists or classic architecture are unavailable (and even where they are). But these media are *preliminary* because they are representations, time-space shifted impressions, evocations of memory, a transition towards a threshold less constructed:

> Music and silence are both supposed to be golden, but most are hedged with ritual, or else trivialized – music to Muzak, silence to 'peace and quiet', meaning a comfortable background hum. Otherwise they may gild everything, big and little, and that we don't want. We want to keep sex dirty, friendship efficient, work detached or crooked. We don't want to be so noble. Music or silence, either one heard clearly, would ennoble every thing or else explode it. By playing background music we kill both birds with one stone.[29]

Though we live with background noise and continuous stimulation, we are not yet lost in Huxley's *Brave New World*. But Huxley, like Bradbury, has something vital to say to a people seduced by outsized wall-screens, where rapid living, complexity and over-stimulation have effectively diminished stillness, concentration and liberty; where alert attention – like restful sleep – becomes increasingly rare, and where it is often taken for granted that the world is described and ordered primarily by the architects of media output. We heed their warnings, and place our trust elsewhere: because we can still worship in spirit and truth without an electricity supply.

Notes

1 Joan Osborne, 'Spider Web' on the album *Relish* (1995).

2 Futures are anticipated in, for example, Helen Cameron, 'The Decline of the Church in England as a Local Member Organization: Predicting the Nature of Civil Society in 2050', in Grace Davie, Paul Heelas and Linda Woodhead, eds, *Predicting Religion: Christian, Secular and Alternative Futures*, Aldershot: Ashgate, 2003, pp. 109–19. For discussion of some of the broader questions about religion in relation to information and communication technologies, see Moreten T. Hojsgaard and Margit Warburg, eds, *Religion and Cyberspace*, Oxford: Routledge, 2005.

3 See, for example, the project reported in *The Times*, 21 September 2007 under 'Church island offers sceptics a second chance to become virtually good', online at <http://www.timesonline.co.uk/tol/comment/faith/article2500485.ece>. Accessed 21 September 2007.

4 Nathan D. Mitchell, 'Ritual and New Media', in Erik Borgman, Stephan van Erp and Hille Haker, eds, *Concilium* 2005/1: 'Cyberspace – Cyberethics – Cybertheology', London: SCM Press, pp. 90–8, suggests interesting perspectives on this phenomenon: 'Recall that originally the Bible was not a mere "text", but a kind of "tablature", a musical "score" intended for performance . . . . a culture driven by computer technology reacts to pages quite differently from the way traditional Christian *ritual* reacts to them.' (p. 93).

5 Gordon Lynch, *The New Spirituality: An Introduction to Progressive Belief in the Twenty-first Century*, London: I.B. Tauris, 2007, p. 7. Lynch is describing writings about 'the new spirituality'.

6 For an overview of Baudrillard's theory of culture, see Jean Baudrillard's *Simulacra and Simulation*, Michigan: University of Michigan Press, 1994.

7 'I want to cast a sceptical eye at one of the most common forms of discourse which abounds in religious circles and indeed in circles which would probably be horrified to be thought of as religious. This is a way of talking about, and from, the experience of alienation and marginalisation in which these experiences are taken to be something particularly sacred or holy . . .' (James Alison, *On Being Liked*, London: Darton, Longman and Todd, 2003, p.65).

8 J. B. Metz, *The Emergent Church: The Future of Christianity in a Postbourgeois World*, New York: Crossroad, 1981, p. 9.

9 Rowan Williams, *Lost Icons: Reflections on Cultural Bereavement*, Edinburgh: T&T Clark, 2000, p. 143.

10 One high-profile example of creative worship was undermined to some extent by deference to a charismatic personality: The Planetary Mass at Sheffield Ponds Forge is described in Roland Howard, *The Rise and Fall of the Nine O'clock Service: A Cult within the Church?* London: Mowbray, 1996, pp. 93–5. That particular story re-inforces the conviction that creativity, if it is to be authentically liberating, needs to be woven into established liturgical tradition and the wider Christian community.

11 'It is altogether insufficient to treat the liturgy merely as the corporate expression of "subjection" which man as a social being owes to God as his Creator. Although correct, this is far too abstract an expression of the liturgical mystery. It . . . leads to the misconception that liturgy is worship carried out by "society," by "the group" *as opposed to* the individuals who compose the group. Hence the confusing deduction that the individual's chief function is to lose himself, to submerge himself, to divest himself of every trace of individuality and personality in order to vanish into the group . . .' Thomas Merton, *Seasons of Celebration: Meditations on the Cycle of Liturgical Feasts*, New York: Farrar, Strauss and Giroux, 1965, p. 9.

12 Clive Marsh, *Cinema and Sentiment: Film's Challenge to Theology*, Milton Keynes: Paternoster Press, 2004, pp. 24f.

13 Thomas de Zengotita, *Mediated: How the Media Shape Your World*, London: Bloomsbury, 2005, p. 14.

14 'Cybergnosis' is a playful neologism which evokes Aldous Huxley's *Brave New World*, blurring notions of knowing and of hypnotism.

15 'Everywhere we imagined ourselves standing turned into a cliché beneath our feet . . . Crowded by the ideas and styles of the past, we felt there was no open space anywhere . . . What haunts me is not exactly the absence of literal space so much as a

deep craving for metaphorical space: release, escape, some kind of open-ended freedom.' Naomi Klein, *No Logo*, London: Flamingo, 2000, p. 63.

16 Neil Postman, *Amusing Ourselves to Death*, London: Methuen, 1985, is a classic work on the effect of electronic media on our symbolic environment and our very idea of knowing.

17 Ian Brown, former lead singer of The Stone Roses, quoted in Michael Odell, 'Would You Vote for This Man?' *The Guardian*, 15 September 2007, <http://www.guardian.co.uk/theguide/music/story/0,,2168249,00.html>, accessed 20 September 2007.

18 I agree with Clive Marsh when he writes that 'Whatever the intent of those leading it, or those interpreting it with hindsight, worship was often being received, and thus functioning, in a very similar fashion to entertainment.' *Cinema and Sentiment*, p. 18. In the same passage, and more pertinent perhaps, Marsh goes on to recall the impact on church participation of the launch of ITV in 1955 and the broadcasting of *The Forsyte Saga* in 1967 as examples of developments which 'interweave with the general pattern of increasing secularisation in British society throughout the 1960s'. My dad says the same. For a more detailed social history of post-war British Christianity, see Callum G. Brown, *The Death of Christian Britain*, London: Routledge, 2001.

19 'Ecstatic religious experience, the phenomenon of group cohesion, of being buoyed and supported by others, by forces larger than oneself, is both an essential component of sustained work for justice and fundamentally amoral. That is, the experience of transcendence is not foundational. It is an experience of creativity, connection, and energy that is as likely to be evoked by the Religious Right and by the Klan, as by politically progressive religious groups . . . The fact that a group feels a tremendous surge of vitality says nothing about either the truth of its claims about reality or the legitimacy of its projects for cultural and community formation . . .' Sharon Welch, *Sweet Dreams in America: Making Ethics and Spirituality Work*, London: Routledge 1999, p. xxii.

20 'For particular historical reasons (notably the historic connections between Church and State), significant numbers of Europeans are content to let both churches and churchgoers enact a memory on their behalf (the essential meaning of vicarious), more than half aware that they might need to draw on the capital at crucial times in their individual or their collective lives.' Grace Davie, *Europe: The Exceptional Case. Parameters of Faith in the Modern World*, London: Darton, Longman and Todd, 2002, p. 19.

21 Ray Bradbury, *Fahrenheit 451*, Woodstock, IL: Dramatic Publications, 1986.

22 'God in the Basement . . . And Other Places' by Mandy Stevens and Sian Street, in *Flame: The Methodist Magazine*, Issue 15, November–December 2002.

23 Kalle Lasn, *Culture Jam: How to Reverse America's Suicidal Consumer Binge – And Why We Must*, New York: Quill (HarperCollins), 2000.

24 'We are the first two or three generations in history to grow up in a predominantly electronic environment. . . . We still haven't answered the most basic questions . . . Let alone the big-picture issues, such as what happens to a whole culture when its citizens start spending half their waking lives in virtual environments . . . Ten years ago we didn't think twice about the chemicals in our food or the toxins generated by industry . . . . Our mental environment is a common-property resource like the air or the water. We need to protect ourselves from unwanted incursions into it.' Lasn, *Culture Jam*, pp. 12f.

25 'At a stroke, the Reformation abolished all safeguards against fear, in the hope of abolishing fear . . . This was one of the world's most important revolutions, a revo-

lution against fear, which lasted several centuries . . . However, when religion stopped frightening people, people invented new fears to frighten themselves, as though they valued fear as a necessary part of the sensation of being alive . . . Since the eighteenth century, security has become, almost universally, the official goal for this life, but an unobtainable goal, a paradise, ever harder to locate, invisible in a cloud of doubt . . . Insecurity has become the commonest complaint of our time.' Theodore Zeldin, *An Intimate History of Humanity*, London: Minerva, 1995, pp. 174f.

26 Rachel Stevens, 'By 12, girls have seen 77,500 ads. And does it make them happy?', in *The Independent* Media, 7 October 2007, online at <http://news.independent.co.uk/media/article3036006.ece>. Accessed 10 October 2007.

27 A. E. Harvey, *Jesus and the Constraints of History*, London: Duckworth, 1982, pp. 6–7.

28 Evan Eisenberg, *The Recording Angel: Music, Records and Culture from Aristotle to Zappa*, New Haven and London: Yale University Press, 2nd ed., 2005, p. 167.

29 Eisenberg, *The Recording Angel*, p. 168.

Part 7

Inconclusions

Introduction

The Edge of God might have ended in any number of ways – a summary in conclusion, indicators of unfinished business, or perhaps even a manifesto of some kind. However, following our conversations in post-colonial theology, gendered theology and body theology, and on sound and silence, and mixed media, in worship, we have chosen to give that last word in the collection to a piece by Pam Lunn – to what she calls a 'Postcard from the Edge'.

In her 'postcard', Lunn conveys her engagement with various Christian traditions over time, describing moves and shifts along the way, to eventually now locate herself in a place 'on the margins of a religious body that is itself on the margins of the Christian Church' (that is, the Quakers). Yet, perhaps crucially, her narrative retains its provisionality throughout, and so contains the sense – perhaps the expectation – that the future will involve 'moving on again'.

It is the attitude of ongoing exploration that we as editors particularly wish to lift up at this point, at the close of this book. For some readers, moving into conversation with at least some of the perspectives represented in *The Edge of God* may (have) require(d) new openness. And it is certainly the case that much of the conversation in the book is yet to be heard at the level of denominational liturgical resources for the churches. So we hope for more conversation, and, with Pam Lunn, for more movement to the edges, in the spirit of Lunn's ending for her piece, pointing as she does to permacultures intended to maximize edges within systems, which assist the flourishing of 'enhanced diversity, productivity and growth'.

23

Edge to Edge:
A Postcard from the Edge to Others Living at the Margins

PAM LUNN

I was raised Christian: middle-of-the-road Church of England, and school religious education – which in the 1950s and 1960s was confessionally Christian and not, as now, taking a 'comparative religion' approach. So I learnt the Bible stories, drew maps of the missionary journeys of the Apostle Paul, imbibed the language of the Book of Common Prayer and the Authorized Version of the Bible, and partook of the rhythms of the liturgical year – although in that particularly unlovely form that must have been common in 'low church' parish churches in the 1950s.

I recall little aesthetic pleasure from those childhood church services. We were taught in Sunday School the significance of the colours of the altar cloths used at different seasons in the Church's year – but I recall none of that. I remember palm crosses, followed by little posies of flowers at Easter. I remember mostly dreary hymns, badly accompanied on a Hammond organ. I remember a rather ugly self-consciously modern church building (this was on a new post-war housing estate) that was multifunctional, with folding partitions that could screen off the chancel and leave the nave as a blandly empty church hall, to be used for jumble sales, Cubs, Brownies, Scouts and Guides, Mothers' Union meetings; and anything else that needed a meeting space.

But I was introduced to the Book of Common Prayer, and the rhythms of its language remain with me, most of it learnt by heart – not through deliberate effort but through endless repetition. My later brief encounter with the Alternative Service Book has left no trace at all. And I learnt to chant the psalms and canticles and to read the strange notation that showed how to fit the words to the notes. Some of those words and some of those chants have also remained with me.

But adolescence came, and I questioned all of this. The naively pious teaching we received – whether in church or school – had no means of responding to even the most simple of questions. I recall asking, at about age 12, in a school religious education (RE) lesson which had focused on God's bounty and goodness, 'If God gives us everything we need, why is there drought and famine in other parts of the world?' It was clear that the teachers were merely embarrassed and had no resources to acknowledge its legitimacy as a question, let alone to open up a discussion that might have responded to it.

I stopped going to church, except for the monthly church parade when the Scouts and Guides paraded their flags down the nave aisle and up the steps into the chancel. I became uncomfortable with that as well – the word *militaristic* was not then in my vocabulary, but the feeling to accompany it certainly was. My family moving house when I was 13 saved me from having to negotiate a withdrawal from something I had been so much part of – it was easy, in the new place, merely to omit rejoining the Girl Guides, the church, or anything else connected with organized religion. I rejected doctrinal Christianity as intellectually untenable and the Church of my upbringing as hopelessly compromised with the dominant oppressive structures of society – but I never lost a deep engagement with the questions to which the Church purported to have the answers.

Becoming an undergraduate in 1968 opened up a new world in many ways. Not only was there the pervasive student unrest and political questioning, but there was also a politicized and engaged Christianity. The Student Christian Movement in Cambridge at that time was a questioning and stimulating place to be, and I found there kindred spirits who had also rejected the simplistic religious teaching of their childhoods. I recall that, when a Billy Graham crusade came to the university, many of us in SCM organized to picket it, with leaflets about a socially engaged gospel.

This period also offered new liturgical experiences. There were the obvious ones, such as sung evensong in any number of the college chapels, which showed that liturgy could be aesthetically attractive, and that could in turn be a gateway to something more. There was St Francis House, a small group of Franciscans who had a ministry to the university, and offered liturgical experiences I had never previously even heard of – such as the imposition of ashes on Ash Wednesday. There was the experience of singing in the University Choir – a completely secular musical society, except that to sing Bach's *St Matthew Passion* in King's College Chapel on four consecutive nights was a significant spiritual experience that was, of course, deeply liturgical in character.

But alongside these more traditionally styled experiences, the churches, college chapels and student societies also reflected the wider societal upheavals and offered ways of prayer and worship unheard of in my childhood parish. There were the Gelineau Psalms, so different in both words and music from anything previously encountered; there were hymns by Sidney Carter and Brian Wren, with 'singable' tunes and words that spoke to that generation, blurring the boundary between hymns and protest songs; there were the Galliard collections of songs with relevant words and accessible music;[1] and there were books of prayers by Michel Quoist,[2] newly available in English.

And there was the shockingly breathtaking *Liberation Prayer Book*,[3] produced by the Free Church of Berkeley, which changed the whole idea of what liturgy could be. The book starts with an alternative liturgical calendar, noting such dates as the birthday of Martin Luther King, Jan Palach in flames in Prague, the birthday of Harriet Tubman or the ending of the Selma march (no page numbers). It has prayers (in the form of Collects) for 'justice in the economic system' (p. 40), for 'national liberation movements' (p. 41), for 'the planet' (p. 42) [this was in 1971!], for 'travelers, hitch-hikers and drivers' (p. 45) and so on. It has a section entitled 'Guerrilla Liturgies' (pp. 141–202) which includes: 'A lament for victims and executioners' (pp. 141–56); an 'act of disaffiliation' to separate from the institutions of society that had become 'demonic' (pp. 157–65); a 'decontamination' liturgy which was a 'form or words to accompany some action at a place which does not expect it' (pp. 166–80); a liturgy to mark out a sanctuary for refugees (pp. 181–90); and one to consecrate a public park (pp. 191–202). The book also has a liturgy for visiting prisoners (pp. 101–9), with a preamble that begins, 'This form is not suitable for a prison-appointed chaplain, making official visits. It assumes a fellowship between prisoner and visitor; that is, it is intended primarily for *political* prisoners, in the broad sense' (p. 101). In the decades since, we have become more accustomed to socially concerned liturgies, but this book was new and groundbreaking. Interestingly, the *form* of its liturgies is very traditional, seizing the structure and pattern of familiar church worship (the shape of the liturgical year, use of biblical texts, collects, litanies, eucharistic forms, liturgies for births, marriages and deaths, etc.) and turning it to new and radical ends by the choice of content.[4]

So, for a while, there were exciting and innovative explorations into liturgy and church life which drew me back towards Christianity, without ever convincing me again of its core Christological doctrines. But the 1960s faded, student life gave way to earning a living and I drifted into an agnosticism impatient with all institutional or ritual forms. But life in such a wasteland is difficult to sustain with any joy, and in my thirties I found my way to the Religious Society of Friends (Quakers). This, too, grew from a seed sown during my student days, when one of my closest friends in college was the daughter of a lifelong 'weighty' Quaker. Weekends spent visiting at her home always included being taken to Quaker Meeting for Worship on Sunday morning. For my friend's mother, there was *never* any question of her 'not being able' to get to Meeting because she had visitors; nor was there even the remotest possibility of suggesting that you, as visitor, might just have a lie-in on Sunday morning while others went to the Meeting. No matter who you were, if you were visiting that household at a weekend, you went to the Meeting on Sunday – that's just how it was, and there was no space to dissent! But I am grateful for it, because it introduced me to Quaker worship, at a time in my life when I had no inkling that it might later be significant for me.

In my thirties, seeking out Quakers in my own locality, the Society of Friends felt like the last possible place to be – the edge of any church life, beyond which I would truly fall off the edge; there was nowhere else to go. The basically silent Quaker Meeting for Worship is not without its rituals (see the chapter by my colleague Pink Dandelion elsewhere in this volume) but it is free of the requirement to stand up, sit down, do this, say that, sing this, think that, feel this – all of which aspects of traditional liturgical worship I had, by that time, come to find painfully intrusive, inappropriate and faintly ridiculous – certainly not anything I wanted to spend my time engaged in. Ironically, I could still enter into worship during an eastwards facing mass in a foreign language (as I discovered one year on holiday), or sitting in King's College Chapel listening to the Byrd Mass for Five Voices being sung – these were as good as a Quaker Meeting for Worship, I felt. I could sit in contemplation and let the music and the words, not in English, just wash over me, with no insistence that I engage actively with them.

For over 20 years this form of shared silent 'waiting' was a nourishing and upholding form for my spirituality. I rarely gave spoken ministry during Meeting for Worship, finding rather that the hour's silence took me to a very deep, quiet place from which words were largely absent. I would 'surface' at the end of the hour and take some moments to move again, after the stillness, or to speak again, after the silence. There is space among Quakers for this way of being, and no pressure to be otherwise; there is also a deep sense that words, in the end, miss the point of our encounter with Spirit, and so a refreshing absence of creeds, forms of words, or discussions of belief.

Within the spectrum of liberal religion, the Britain Yearly Meeting of the Religious Society of Friends is a broad church even though a numerically small denomination. Some British Quakers, though not the majority, are traditionally Christian, though with a distinctively Quaker understanding of what that means. Some have backgrounds in other faiths – Jewish, Buddhist, Sufi, Hindu, for instance. Some are non-theists, and some of these are also members of the Sea of Faith network. Many are what might be termed 'cultural christians' (lower case 'c' intended). I use this term in the sense implied by a report in the *Guardian* newspaper on 13 February 2003: 'This is a Christian country simply in the sense that most of its citizens think of themselves as Christians . . . in a report on the 2001 census, it was revealed that 42 million people in Britain – some 72% of the entire population – stated their religion as Christian.'[5] Of these 42 million self-styled Christians in the census, only 4.5 million regularly attend church.

Some years ago I was in a seminar on gender, ethnicity and identity, in which a Jewish woman was giving a paper. During questions afterwards she made reference to 'you Christians', to which the woman who had asked the question objected, saying that she had no objection to be called a 'gentile' but objected deeply to being called a 'Christian' as she had spent her whole adult life trying to overcome what she perceived to be the wholly negative effects of her 'Christian upbringing'. The Jewish woman replied that personal beliefs were not the issue: 'You have to come to terms with being Christian just the same way as you have to come to terms with being white. From where I'm standing, you're a Christian.' This was greeted with blank incomprehension from the majority of 'white Christian' women in the room; and with vigorous nods of agreement and affirmation from the several British Muslim women present. I have been pondering ever since the implications of being 'culturally Christian' but not 'doctrinally christian'. Not only was I raised Christian, in wider cultural terms, my education and social milieu meant that I also soaked up the influences and patterns of Christianity in literature, art and music. Christianity has shaped my religious imagination and my spiritual formation; it seems almost 'hard-wired' into my brain. Clare Short has said of herself: 'I speak as a fully signed-up ethnic Catholic, as I learned to call myself in Bosnia'.[6] In the way that, in Bosnia, Clare Short met 'ethnic Muslims' and began to understand herself as an 'ethnic Catholic', there are many of us, born before, say, the mid 1950s who had the kind of religious upbringing and education that renders us 'ethnic Christians'.

So I had an early Christian formation, I rejected it, I re-found some of it, and seemed to have settled comfortably into Quaker ways of worship. But then, as I passed through midlife into the somewhat liminal space of the mid to late fifties, things started to shift again in my inner world. I call this a liminal time of life because it is, it seems to me, between two more clearly defined stages. The particular work of the 'mid-life passage', as Gail Sheehy[7] calls it, is largely negotiated, but the transition to 'third age' has not yet been reached. In terms of paid work, 'retirement' is now visible on the horizon, in a way that it was not a few years ago, but it is not here yet and work still claims a large amount of time, commitment and energy. But, but . . . there are other things stirring.

Even the minimal formalities of Quaker meeting began to feel constricting and somehow, for me, often inauthentic. The Quaker understanding that all times, all actions, all places, are sacred – there are no times or places that are special and somehow more sacred than others – had always appealed to me and I began to feel at odds with the fixed hour on Sunday morning, the fixed place of the Meeting House, the fixed action of sitting still. I gradually found that I would rather be working in my garden, or walking across fields or through woods. Solitary and physically active contemplation outdoors was better for centredness and mindfulness than sitting in Meeting for Worship. Solo walking holidays, out on the hills or the cliffs, brought a refreshment of spirit that was not available elsewhere. And gradually the experience grew, that any daily activity was contemplation, and not only the more obvious triggers to mindfulness.

I wondered sometimes if this was just idleness, mere complacency – perhaps falling away from a spiritual path rather than expanding it. And then, by chance I came across a small book on the Enneagram types in spiritual direction. The author says, of my type, that as it finds balance and wholeness: 'prayer becomes simply living and breathing . . . translation into spiritual – let alone religious – terms is unimportant'.[8] This was both reassuring and amusing; it made me laugh at my anxieties – I was merely coming true to type! As with many writings on aspects of the life cycle, or characteristics of various life stages, they often prick the bubble of anxious self-scrutiny and reveal this latest stage in one's own personal spiritual struggle to be merely another aspect of growing up.

So perhaps my journey has brought me 'home' – or at least to a place that can be home until I find myself moving on again – and home is on the margins of a religious body that is itself on the margins of the Christian Church. This is not a trivial matter – if the wider Christian Church did not exist, the Society of Friends would almost certainly not survive; if the Society of Friends did not exist, I and many others would find ourselves in a less hospitable wilderness. Institutions are needed, not only for those who form their core, but also for those who need something to be on the edge of. A marginal place is not nowhere, neither is it just anywhere – it is on the margins of a particular *something*. And this is not a one-way effect: in creating productive biological systems, Permaculture designers seek to maximize the amount of 'edge' in a system[9] – places of enhanced diversity, productivity and growth. Welcome to the edge!

Notes

1 Peter Smith, ed., *Faith Folk and Clarity*, Great Yarmouth: Galliard, 1967; *Faith Folk and Nativity*, Great Yarmouth: Galliard, 1968; *Faith Folk and Festivity*, Great Yarmouth: Galliard, 1969.

2 See, for example, *Prayers of Life*, Dublin: Gill and Macmillan, 1965; *The Meaning of Success*, Notre Dame: Fides, 1968.

3 John Daiman Brown and Richard L. York, *The Covenant of Peace: A Liberation Prayer Book*, New York: Morehouse-Barlow Co., 1971.

4 Seventeen years later, and in Britain rather than the USA, Janet Morley's book of prayers and poems, *All Desires Known* (London: MOW/WIT, 1988), did something similar, taking the traditional Prayer Book form of the Collect and making it speak – among other themes – of gender inclusiveness, rather than patriarchy.

5 Staff and agencies, 'Census shows large rise in UK ethnic population', in *The Guardian*, 13 February 2003, <http://society.guardian.co.uk/news/story/0,7838,894757,00.html>.

6 Sara Boseley, 'Deadly Serious', *Guardian*, June 1999, <http://www.guardian.co.uk/guardiansociety/story/0,,291240,00.html>.

7 Gail Sheehy, *Passages: Predictable Crises of Adult Life*, New York: Bantam Books, 1976.

8 Suzanne Zuercher OSB, *Enneagram Companions: Growing Relationships and Spiritual Direction*, Notre Dame: Ave Maria Press, 2000, p. 74.

9 See, for instance, Patrick Whitefield, *The Earth Care Manual: A Permaculture Handbook for Britain and Other Temperate Climates*, East Meon: Permanent Publications, 2004, especially chapters 2, 11, 12.

Acknowledgements, Copyright and Sources

The editors gratefully acknowledge Linda Crosby, Mary Matthews, Lawrence Osborn and Natalie Watson for advice and assistance in the copyediting and production of *The Edge of God*.

The editors and publisher are grateful to the following for permission to include extracts from published sources. Every effort has been made to trace copyright ownership, and apologies are made to those who have not been traced or given formal reply at the time of going to press. Information will be gratefully received on any omissions or inaccuracies in this respect.

The Archbishops' Council, London, for numerous quotations from *Common Worship*.

Canterbury Press, for short quotations from *Common Praise*.

'Make Way' by Graham Kendrick © 1986 Thankyou Music.*
'I Will Give You Praise' by Tommy Walker © 1985 Thankyou Music.*
'I Will Sing of the Lamb' by Stuart Townend © 1997 Thankyou Music.*
'From Your Throne, O Lord' by Chris Cartwright © 1991 Thankyou Music.*
'We Stand Together' by Lex Loizides © 1996 Thankyou Music.*

* Adm. by worshiptogether.com songs excl. UK & Europe, adm. by kingswaysongs.com www.kingsway.co.uk. Used by permission.

Adrienne Rich, for the phrase 'dive into the wreck' adapted from 'Diving into the Wreck', in *The Fact of a Doorframe: Selected Poems 1950–2001*, New York: Norton, 2002, pp. 101–3.

ACKNOWLEDGEMENTS, COPYRIGHT AND SOURCES

SPCK, London, for short quotations from Janet Morley, *All Desires Known*.

The Presbyterian Church in New Zealand for a quotation from *A Litany of Light and Darkness*.

Detailed references to the use of these materials can be found in the footnotes of this book.